Singing in French

Singing in French

A MANUAL OF FRENCH DICTION AND FRENCH VOCAL REPERTOIRE

Thomas Grubb

WITH A FOREWORD BY PIERRE BERNAC

SCHIRMER
CENGAGE Learning

Australia • Brazil • Japan • Korea • Mexico • Singapore • Spain • United Kingdom • United States

Singing in French A Manual of French Diction and French Vocal Repertoire
Thomas Grubb

For product information and technology assistance, contact us at
Cengage Learning Customer & Sales Support, 1-800-354-9706
For permission to use material from this text or product,
submit all requests online at **www.cengage.com/permissions**
Further permissions questions can be emailed to
permissionrequest@cengage.com

Library of Congress Control Number: 77-18473

ISBN-13: 978-0-02-870790-7

ISBN-10: 0-02-870790-7

Schirmer
10 Davis Drive
Belmont CA 94002-3098
USA

Cengage Learning is a leading provider of customized learning solutions with office locations around the globe, including Singapore, the United Kingdom, Australia, Mexico, Brazil, and Japan. Locate your local office at **international.cengage.com/region**

Cengage Learning products are represented in Canada by Nelson Education, Ltd.

To learn more about Schirmer, visit **www.cengage.com/schirmer**

Purchase any of our products at your local college store or at our preferred online store **www.ichapters.com**

Printed in the United States of America
9 10 11 12 13   21 20 19 18 17

To El, Rie, and Mel

Contents

Musical Examples

Foreword
by Pierre Bernac

In vocal music, the sonority and the rhythm of the words are an integral part of the music itself. They inspired it no less, and at times even more, than the idea they express. A literary text has its own and proper music. If the singer ought to make an effort to sing each work of music in its original language, the reason is that the music *of* the poem is as important as the music set *to* the poem. The music of the words and the music itself are one and the same; they should not be disassociated.

The artist who attempts to sing all his repertoire in the original language realizes that a careful study is required to enable him to render justice to the literary texts as well as to the music. Not only has he to make himself understood to those who know the foreign language, without any faults in his pronunciation and especially without spoiling it with the typical accent of his own language, but also, and this is very important, he has to acquire the same quality of sound, of voice production, that he has in his own language, or in the languages most favorable to his voice.

My long experience as a performer and as a teacher makes me believe firmly that one does not have to speak a foreign language fluently in order to sing it not only correctly but also expressively. But if it is by overcoming technical problems that the singer succeeds in performing the musical line, it is also by overcoming technical problems that he will succeed in performing the literary text in a language that is foreign to him.

The French vocal repertoire contains some of the most genuine masterpieces ever written in music. But English-speaking singers are sometimes reluctant to attempt their interpretation because of ideas they may have about the difficulties of singing the French language. Again, I can take advantage of my long experience in teaching it to English and American singers to assure them that they can sing in French as well and as comfortably as in any other language, if they are taught the *proper basis*.

This is why I am proud and happy to present this book, which to my knowledge has no equivalent. It is remarkably conceived and cleverly realized. Its author is not only an excellent linguist, but first of all an excellent musician as well. He has a thorough knowledge of his subject and great experience in applying this knowledge.

Singing in French is the perfect basis for anyone who has to teach this repertoire and a most precious book of reference for any singer who has to interpret it. In my opinion this is an invaluable contribution to the study of French vocal literature.

Pierre Bernac

Paris, France

Preface

This book, written and revised five times over the past nine years, was a product of sheer necessity for my coaching both at the conservatory and at home. Following the French dictum *On n'est jamais si bien servi que par soi-même,* "He who helps himself is best helped," this manual of French singing diction and vocal repertoire was compiled to be used both as a text for the classroom and as a source of reference in the private studio.

It was my class schedule at the Manhattan School of Music that initially determined the outline and scope of this manual: two weekly classes, one hour apiece, for two semesters, with no more than fifteen students per class. This is ideal, I admit, and happily, the Manhattan School realized the importance and intricacy of such a course. I dedicate the first semester to a mastery of all the sounds and of the legato (through chapter 2). The second term is then spent in the application of the skills learned in the first to the singing and performing of the French vocal repertoire. Not all of my colleagues, I know, have been so fortunate—budget problems, outdated "priorities" (*who* said singers need theory and music history *more* than diction?), administrative or departmental confusion. Nor will the situation be rectified overnight. But this manual can be easily adapted to a course of almost any length if the instructor is willing to organize it effectively and efficiently. In only one class hour per week in a fifteen-week semester, the most and best that can be accomplished is a mastery of the sounds, of the legato, and their application to one or two songs.

Work in depth is always better than skimming, when a skill is involved; the singer can later transfer what has been thoroughly learned to other materials. Above all, a course in diction for singers must *not* be "academic.'' Instead of endless tests on the memorization of the rules, reading the manual aloud in class, and, worst of all, precious time spent on grammatical drill, the singers should emerge from a diction class ''warmed up'' from having intoned the vowel-sounds or, better yet, complete song texts. Chapter 4 of this manual is dedicated to a description of textual preparation, intoning, and the application of diction to interpretation itself. The instructor must tirelessly correct and refine the sounds, make use of the accompanying record, and insist upon the utilization of cassette tape recorders whenever possible. Oral and written exercises have been provided throughout. They are intended to occupy the singer outside of class, as well as to enable the instructor to keep track of his students' comprehension. (An answer key is provided in the back of the book.) If the singers can *sing* passably well in French upon leaving the course, meaningful progress has been made. (A little class recital in place of an exam serves as a great incentive to young performers.) Those who want to speak, read, or write in French should take the appropriate academic courses.

Lists of songs and operatic arias have been provided in chapter 7. These should aid the singer, voice or diction teacher, and coach in the search for and selection of the proper repertoire for a specific voice. Alphabetical vowel and consonant charts also can be found in the Appendix, for quick reference to phoneticization of letters, single and in combination.

But the classroom is not the only territory where this manual will be useful. It is intended as well for the private studio. Here the singer alone or with the aid of a coach, conductor, or voice teacher, can consult it repeatedly. The basic aim of the manual is to confirm the importance of a beneficial union between healthy vocal production and clear, uncomplicated diction. No mysteries, no secret formulas, and, above all, no separatism! Singing diction is the vocalization of a text, vocalization is the singing of words and their sounds; such a combined study must be perpetuated throughout a singer's career, not truncated with the completion of degree work. Before an audition, a recital, or an appearance in an operatic production, for the duration of a career, progress can and should be made in one's diction and its vocal delivery.

Teachers of French not acquainted with this specialized area of their field also may find this manual helpful when called upon to ''coach a singer's pronunciation.'' For some reason, singers assume that anyone who can speak French should be able to coach them in diction. They forget that the most important aspect of their delivery—singing itself—will of necessity shift the emphasis in the instruction.

Yes, I am American born. I was fortunate enough to have lived in France for several years and to have dutifully studied the French language and literature, as well as instrumental and vocal music (French and non-French alike) before the idea of ''diction'' ever came to mind. Only when asked to give a course in the subject did I find myself concentrating upon it *per se.* In retrospect, I realize that a compatriot can be more in tune with the dilemma Americans face when confronted with diction study. My own questions, confusions, problems, and controversies regarding good diction were luckily cushioned with fluency in the language and a background of study and life experience. As a teacher, I now understand that anticipation of difficulty via firsthand exposure is sometimes more useful than complete ignorance of it. I would not have had it any other way. This should encourage those of you who are subject to the same self-interrogation. As Americans, you understand more about your compatriots than anyone else.

Most of the insights presented here are the results of my collaboration, as pianist and coach, with the eminent French baritone, *doyen* and *maître* of French art song, Pierre Bernac. His personality, as a man, as an artist, and as a teacher, has been my inspiration, source of knowledge, and support in the writing of this book, as well as in my own personal study. Since 1970 I have had the privilege of accompanying and coaching his master classes in the United States, Canada, and abroad. He has patiently gone over every page of this manual; he has corrected and counseled me when necessary; and he has encouraged me in many moments of duress. In turn, I have attempted to illuminate every corner of this study with his teaching and example in mind. Few disciples have had the good fortune to have had such a consummate and generous *maître* as I.

Next, I want to thank Miss Alice Tully who, through the Alliance française de New-York, has been most supportive and interested in this project over the years.

I would like to acknowledge Robert Taibbi from the recording studio at the Juilliard School who so expertly and patiently engineered the taping of the enclosed record. The singer is Guy Merola, a student of mine at the Manhattan School. Guy gave of his time, energy, and vocal ability with a professionalism rarely encountered in one so young. I also wish to express my gratitude for their advice and interest in my work to the following: Marguerite Meyerowitz, Daniel Ferro, Judith Raskin, Sabine Rapp, Dr. Emmy Joseph, Dorothy Uris, Frits Noske, Thérèse Casadesus Rawson, Chris Macatsoris, Carol Ann Kimball, Mary Beth Armes, Paul Sutton, and, last but not at all least, my students at both the Curtis Institute of Music and at the Manhattan School and countless friends and colleagues throughout the country who have brought both gaps and superfluities to my attention.

T.G.

1

An Introduction to Singing in French

Diction, the Missing Link

There are many approaches to the study of diction depending upon the means, nature, and level of the communication involved. A diction lesson may be useful to the actor, the television announcer, the chairman of the board, or to a politician. In each case, the method and nature of study will be different. An individual may wish to rid his speech of an impediment or a regional accent. Again, a specialized approach will be necessary.

Courses in "diction" are offered to singers throughout the country, very often as electives and as part of their "academic" study. They are all too often considered necessary evils. Some highly reputable institutions consider the study of English diction unnecessary and even demeaning to the American-born, English-speaking singer. Courses in the diction of a foreign language are usually cluttered with a misguided emphasis on grammar and vocabulary and, occasionally, a flimsy set of general rules for pronunciation. Such courses and attitudes serve to demonstrate the widespread ignorance concerning the role of diction in singing.

Yes, the singer, too, needs to have a specialized approach to diction study, whatever the language in question may be. Singers must undertake the study of the singing of their own language, as well as that of several foreign languages: the "big three" (in alphabetical order)—French, German, and Italian—and others, notably Spanish and Russian. The latter should not be excluded, since a respectable percentage of the basic repertoire involves these languages as well. How formidably vast this study becomes when one very obvious fact is overlooked: the singer must above

1

all learn to *sing* comfortably and intelligibly in these languages, not necessarily to pronounce them, read them, or converse in them.

The singer's highly specialized and stylized method of vocal production and delivery—*singing*—dictates a similarly specialized and stylized approach to the study of language. This is the study of "singing diction," the term to be used here to differentiate it from other diction study. The study of singing diction has many of the same aspects as general diction study, but it is differentiated from the latter by the added aspect of learning how to *sing* in an intelligible and vocally comfortable way the sounds of any given language.

Singing diction is the missing link in the chain of vocal study. It bridges the gap between language and vocal delivery itself by defining the sounds upon which the voice is to be transmitted. The sonorities and shapes of words and their sounds are to the singer what steps and patterns are to the dancer and what colors and strokes are to the painter. The sound of a word is the vehicle upon which vocalization is conveyed. It makes the essential connection between basic vocal production and the end result: correctly produced, pleasing, intelligible, and expressive singing. The sounds and the meanings of words can color and highlight the voice, shape and align its approach to a phrase, choreograph and sketch its path.

The presence of language most significantly distinguishes vocal music from all other music. The role of words in the singing process is equal in technical and expressive importance to those of production, support, resonance, and phrasing. Since the uniform production or occasional modification of a vowel-sound is an integral part of the study of singing diction, even a vocalise or a coloratura display piece cannot escape its sphere of influence. The singer should make diction his ally and consider it as a means of definition and simplification. Diction is musical; diction is vocal; diction is expressive. Only when it is studied with the same zeal as the other aspects of vocal and musical training and is properly integrated into the study process will the singer discover the missing link that singing diction can be for him.

So, good singing diction has two purposes:

1. to facilitate and clarify the singing process by a definition and mastery of the sounds to be sung; and
2. to communicate the sounds, meanings, and overall message of a text in an intelligible, natural, and appropriately expressive way.

Furthermore, singing diction has three essential aspects, all equal in importance:

1. *pronunciation,* or the conversion of the letters of a word into the proper vocal sounds as represented by the symbols of the International Phonetic Alphabet (I.P.A.);

2. *vocalization,* or the distinct and natural singing of these sounds in all registers of the voice with responsible modification where absolutely necessary, the aim always being toward intelligibility and natural, unhindered vocal production; and
3. *interpretative expression,* or the effective communication of the meaning, mood, and character of the text as set to music.

The French heu *and the English* um

When a Frenchman is at a loss for words, which happens more often than one might expect, he rounds his lips in the position of a pout and drones on "heu" for a moment, a sound that approximates the *-er* of English but which is much more frontal and without the final *r*. This rounded, definitely frontal utterance is the "at ease" position of the French mouth and clearly illustrates the typical placement of French vocalic emission and resonance, which is somewhere between the upper front teeth and the base of the nose. In contrast, the English-speaking conversationalist fills his void with a heady "um" or a throaty "ah." His lips are flat and the resonance tends to remain somewhere beneath or in back of the nose.

French is a frontal, highly placed language. English, especially American English, is median, somewhat contained and occasionally dropping in its placement. The Frenchman's lips are highly active in the formation of words and his vocalic flow is buoyantly resonated in the upper teeth-to-nose area of his face. Yet French is truly devoid of the raspy nasality of some American accents. The Frenchman coos and clicks onward at what seems to be breakneck speed due to the legato character of his tongue, whose syllabic flow is only slightly more rapid than that of English. To a foreign ear, the absence of both a strong tonic accent, or the heavy stressing of a syllable in the word at the expense of others, likens French to the patter of a typewriter. The Frenchman's voice seems to rise and descend in a highly predictable, monotonous melody devoid of cadences and resolutions.

But listen to French! It sings, it floats, it groans, it purrs, and it titillates the ear with its crisp, clean consonants, its pure, highly resonated, frontal vowel-sounds. The French and English languages are both tongues of exceptional beauty and share many etymological similarities. But they are, in their essential resonances, as different as the people who created them. Americans, with their own set of characteristic speech habits, will find themselves using a previously neglected set of facial muscles and resonating chambers when pronouncing French words and phrases. Singers, with their heightened vocal awareness, will experience these sensations even more acutely. The singer's study of French will necessarily involve a greater adjustment and technical precision than that of the conversationalist. He must master the singing of these sounds with authenticity, but without vocal discomfort or loss of personal timbre.

The International Phonetic Alphabet (IPA)

The International Phonetic Alphabet (IPA) is a system of phonetic symbols representing fixed sounds that appear in languages. Each language employs only certain of the IPA symbols according to the sounds making up the language. Some languages share common sounds and symbols. One should be reluctant, however, to transfer the use of the same symbol from one language to another without the guidance of an expert. The sounds of these symbols may vary slightly from language to language. After all, the languages evolved naturally before any such system was heard of. For this reason, the singer must adapt his use of the IPA to each language being studied, for, although basic similarities are most certainly present between vowel-sounds in two different languages that are represented by the same phonetic symbol, they may differ significantly with respect to resonance and coloration. Beware of systems that rely on equivalents in English or other languages. It is just not that simple. Languages cannot be expected to share identical vowel-sounds just because of a set of phonetic symbols, as helpful as they may be. In this manual, the phonetic symbols under examination, and the sounds they represent, are applicable to French *only,* except when, in rare instances, they can be safely compared to sounds in other languages.

In French singing diction there are thirty-six sounds represented by a corresponding number of phonetic symbols: fifteen vowel-sounds, eighteen consonant-sounds, and three semiconsonant sounds. IPA symbols will of course be used extensively in this manual. These symbols must *always* be enclosed in brackets, whether single ([a], [ø],) or multiple ([b o t e]). Whole lines of verse should be enclosed in *one* set of brackets if comprising a single, uninterrupted musical phrase:

> Dans ton coeur dort un clair de lune.
> [d ɑ̃ t õ k œ r d ɔ r œ̃ k l ɛ r d œ l y n œ]
> (In your heart there sleeps a moonlight.)

Phonetic symbols should always be made clearly and exactly. A slight variation in the formation of the symbol might make for ambiguity. Never write phonetic symbols in script or capitalize them for any reason unless the symbol happens to be a capital, which is very rare in French. "Bright *a*" ([a]) must not be confused with "dark *a*" ([ɑ]), and so on. The symbol [œ] must always be drawn "Siamese-style" and not [oe], since the latter symbols represent *two* different neighboring vowel-sounds. All punctuation such as commas, apostrophes, periods and the like are foreign to phonetic spelling and must not appear in phoneticizations. Phonetic symbols are pictures of exact sounds, not of inflection, stress, or duration.

Two diacritical marks may be used within the brackets of a phoneticization. The first, [/], may be used to indicate a *hiatus* or any break between neighboring sounds:

> Hélas! hélas!
> [e l ɑ s / e l ɑ s]
> (Alas! alas!)

The second, [→], may indicate a sizable prolongation of a vowel-sound and serves to phoneticize the effect of a legato:

> Ah, fuyez! douce image!
> [ɑ → f ɥ i j e → d u → s i m a → ʒ ə]
> (Ah, be gone! sweet image!)

French: A Legato Language

When singing in French, the basic tenet of *bel canto* must be strictly and constantly observed: legato. Although almost everyone knows that legato involves a connected, smooth, and uninterrupted production of sound, this vocal ideal is rarely linked to singing diction as it should be. Also, there seems to be considerable confusion as to what a true legato is and how it can be achieved.

An understanding of what vowels and consonants are, and their proper relationship, is necessary to the realization of a true legato. A vowel (*ah, ee, oh,* and so on) is a free, unobstructed, defined vocal sound produced by the breath, which becomes voice at the vocal cords, passes through the mouth, and ultimately takes on its particular vocalic definition through the various and precise positions assumed by the lips and tongue upon emission. The word *vowel* comes from the Latin word *vox,* meaning "voice." A consonant (*tuh, vuh, muh,* and so on) is the stoppage, blockage, or friction, partial or complete, of the breath sufficient to cause audible separation of the vocalic flow. The word *consonant* comes from the Latin word *consonare,* meaning "to sound with."

> **A true legato is the uniform production of pure vowel-sounds for the duration of their assigned note-values, these pure vowel-sounds being separated and ushered in by rapid, late, and clear consonants that, in turn, must never be allowed to shorten or alter the preceding or following vowel-sound.**

To illustrate the principle of legato and its relationship to the flow of vowel- and consonant-sounds, the opening phrase of Henri Duparc's well-known song "Chanson triste" shall be examined here.

"Chanson triste," H. Duparc-J. Lahor

As demonstrated on the accompanying recording, (Recording Illustration A) in line one only the vowel-sounds are intoned in an uninterrupted stream of vocalized sound. These vowel-sounds must be as distinct but at the same time as uniformly "placed" as possible. It is misleading to assume that good diction is founded on exaggerated, highly differentiated vowel-sounds. Instead, neighboring vowel-sounds should always be closely matched in singing by a conscious examination of what they have in common. The first five vowel-sounds of this line are all very closely related, all being centered around the basic *heu* position. Their individual differences may be subtly and distinctly underlined in order to make the text intelligible, but *never* at the expense of the uniformity of the vocalized flow of sound. The vowel of the word *clair* is the only unrounded one of the phrase; in its "raw" state it is bright and wide. But to exaggerate these aspects of the vowel-sound [ɛ] would be a mistake, just as it would be to conceal them entirely. Also, the vowel-sound of the *u* of the word *lune* is the most closed and pointed of the line of verse that speaks of a heart filled with sleeping moonlight. It would be a jolt to the mood and vocal flow of the phrase to fail to match this [y] of *lune* as closely as possible to the surrounding open, mellow vowel-sounds while at the same time retaining just enough of its intrinsic quality for the sake of intelligibility. "Sing*ing* diction," yes, by all means, but never "sing*ers*' diction" and the self-conscious exaggerations such a term implies!

In the second line of the example above, the consonants have been slipped in *rapid, late,* and *clear,* on the same stream of vocalic sound.

French consonants must be:

rapid, not prolonged or dwelled upon;
late, never anticipated or shortening the preceding vowel-sound, but "postponed" as long as possible, serving only to usher in the following vowel-sound; and
clear, not mumbled, fuzzy, or inaudible.

As can be seen by the phoneticization and heard by the intoning and singing of the second line, consonants in singing exist only in relation to the vowel. They serve to separate and propel the vowel-sounds without ever inhibiting or arresting their flow.

Even and especially in fast-moving, wordy, so-called staccato recitations the legato principle is applicable. A vocal staccato is the reverse of an instrumental one because words are involved: in singing it is the attack on the consonant that creates the effect of staccato; on an instrument it is the release of the sound (or vowel, in vocal terms). The singer must render his consonants even more rapid, late, and clear than before to provide the incisive, wordy nature of the vocal staccato. More important, at the same time, he must elongate and *sing* as much as possible the vowel-sounds so that the voice is at all times resonant and audible and the text intelligible. (See the section on "Vocal Staccato" in chapter 5.)

Consonant-Vowel Flow

Beginning students of French often complain that the language seems to "run together" and that, unlike English and German, there are no clear separations between words of a French sentence. Although but a superficial impression, it is true that the tendency to melt words together makes French the legato language that it is. Singers need not complain of this characteristic, for it makes the language eminently singable and a good starting point for the mastery of a true legato. The legato character of the French language is due to the regular and practically uninterrupted alternation of consonant and vowel flow within the individual word and from word to word as well. This word-to-word flow is achieved by means of three linking devices.

1. *Liaison* is the sounding of a normally silent final consonant in a word that is followed by another word beginning with a vowel or a mute *h*. (See the following section for a discussion of the mute *h*.) Note how liaison is marked in the following example:

Elle est ici avec un homme.
[ε l ε t i s i a v ε k œ̃ ɔ m ə]
(She is here with a man.)

Here, the *t* of *est* and the *n* of *un* are said to be "in liaison" with the following vowel-sounds. Normally, these final consonants would be silent, as in the following example:

> Elle es*t* venue avec u*n* cadeau.
> [ɛlɛvœnyavɛkɛ̃ekado]
> (She has come with a gift.)

That is because these same final consonant-letters are here followed by consonant-sounds. But, to avoid the meeting of two vowel-sounds, as in the first example sentence, these final consonants are pronounced as if they were the first letters of the following words. As always, the consonant in liaison must be rapid, late, and clear, smoothly ushering in the new vowel-sound, never altering or shortening the preceding one. Liaison is more frequently and stylistically used in singing diction than in everyday speech, and is generally modeled after the usage of the French classical theater. Its application is governed by a few set rules, grammar and syntax, euphony and good taste. Liaison is further discussed in chapter 3.

2. *Elision* is the omission of a final, unstressed *-e* in a word that is followed by a word beginning with a vowel or a mute *h*. Note how elision is marked in the following example:

> Ell*e* est ici depuis un*e* heure.
> [ɛ→lɛ→tisidœpyi→zy→nœrə]
> (She has been here for an hour.)

Here, the final *-e*'s of *elle* and *une* are said to be "elided," a basic rule of French versification, since they are followed respectively by a vowel-sound and a mute *h*. The consonant-sound preceding the elided *e* is delayed until just before the following vowel-sound of the next word. In this example, the [l] of *elle* is sounded with the [ɛ] of *est,* thus allowing the [ɛ] of *elle* to occupy the total duration of its syllable. Above all, liaison is not to be confused with elision. The two words are not interchangeable, nor is elision a translation of liaison. Whereas liaison is the addition of a consonant-sound that is otherwise unsounded, elision is the contraction of a vowel-sound that is otherwise sounded. Elision is common to both everyday speech and to singing diction, and is relatively inflexible. The final *-e* and its musical setting and phoneticization are more thoroughly discussed under [œ] below.

3. *Normal Linking-Up* is the carrying over of a normally sounded final consonant into a word beginning with either a vowel or a consonant. Note how normal linking-up is marked in the following examples:

> Il est ici.
> [ilɛtisi]
> (He is here.)

Dans ton coeur dort un clair de lune.

[d ɑ̃ → t õ → k œ → r d ɔ → r ɑ̃̃ → k l ɛ → r d œ l y → n œ]

(In your heart there sleeps a moonlight.)

In the first example, the *l* of *il* is said to be "normally linked-up" with the following vowel-sound, in rapid, late, and clear fashion, as always. Although its effect is the same, normal linking-up should not be confused with liaison, since each is governed by a different set of rules concerning phonetic changes. (See chapter 3, "Phonetic Changes Due to Liaison.") For example, an *-s* that is in liaison becomes [z], but an *-s* that is normally linked-up remains [s]:

sans amour	sens extasiés
[s ɑ̃ z a m u r]	[s ɑ̃ s ɛ k s t ɑ z i e]
(without love)	(senses in ectasy)

Here, the normally silent, final *-s* of *sans* is in liaison with the first syllable of *amour*, and is sounded as [z]. But the final *-s* of *sens*, normally pronounced as [s], remains [s] when linked with *extasiés*. Sounding the final *-s* of *sens* as [z] in this expression would render "sans extasier," which is sheer nonsense meaning something roughly akin to "without giving ecstasy." In the second example above ("Dans ton coeur dort un clair de lune"), the normally pronounced *r* of *dort* (do *not* link the *t* in liaison!) is linked with the [ɑ̃̃] of *un*, and the *r* of *clair* with the [d] of *de*. Similarly the *r* of *coeur* is sounded immediately before the [d] of *dort*. Consonant-sounds must be normally linked-up with ensuing consonant-sounds just as they are with ensuing vowel-sounds in the interest of the legato. Remember: rapid, *late,* and clear.

Hiatus, Mute and Aspirate h

Hiatus is the meeting of two vowel-sounds, either in the same word (as in *chaos* [k a o], meaning "chaos") or in two different words (as in *tu es* [t y e], meaning "you are," and in *peu à peu* [p ø a p ø]; meaning "little by little"). Hiatus is often indicated by the presence of the diæresis in such words as *Noël* [n ɔ ɛ l], *Azaël* [a z a ɛ l], and *naïf* [n a i f]. Although the tendency in French is toward a constant alternation of consonant- and vowel-sound, hiatus most certainly does occur upon occasion. Above all, it must not cause any real interruption in the legato. When in the same word, or in different, closely related words, there should be no glottal click interrupting the vocalic flow:

cru/auté	lui/et/elle
[k r y o t e]	[l y i e ɛ l ə]
(cruelty)	(he and she)

Nor should a forbidden liaison be made just to prevent hiatus:

> Le print<u>emps</u> ~~ps~~ <u>e</u>st triste.
> [l œ p r ɛ̃ t ɑ̃ ɛ t r i s t ə]
> (The springtime is sad.)

Here, the liaison is forbidden on a singular noun, the word *printemps* meaning "springtime." But, the absence of liaison is *no* reason to interrupt the legato vocalic flow. Instead, the vowels should occupy, each in turn, the full note-value assigned them, with no glottal click in between.

Occasionally, for the sake of textual clarity, or because of the presence of an aspirate *h* (to be discussed immediately below), a gentle separation may be made between the neighboring vowel-sounds of two different words that create the hiatus, or even between the consonant-sound that would normally be linked by elision or liaison and the ensuing vowel-sound. This latter separation may be due to punctuation or the need to avoid confusion in the meaning of the text:

> Elle/à la mer; nous/au tombeau.
> [ɛl/a→la→m ɛr/nu/o→tõ→bo]
> (It, to the sea; we, to the tomb.)
>   ("Beau soir," Debussy-Bourget)

Here, a slight separation after *elle* avoids the ambiguous intrusion of [lala] in the line of verse. The separation of *nous* from *au* can be justified by the clarifying punctuation in the English translation:

> Comm<u>e</u> une larme,/il s'évapore.
> [k ɔ→m y→n œ→la→r m/i→l s e→v a→p ɔ→r œ]
> (Like a tear, it vanishes.)
>   ("Le Secret," Fauré-Silvestre)

Here, although Fauré does not indicate such a separation in his setting of the line, the comma and the syntax cry out for a slight separation between *larme* and *il*. To say *larme il* would be tantamout to saying "tear it" in English.

> une/honte   la/haine
> [y n œ/õ t ə]   [l a/ɛ n ə]
> (a disgrace)   (hatred)

In the above examples, both *h*'s are *aspirate,* which does not really mean what it suggests. The letter *h* in French is almost never sounded (or aspirated) as it is in the English word "how." But in French an aspirate *h* forbids liaison and elision. Furthermore, its presence may justify a slight reattacking of the vowel-sound following it, as shown in the above examples.

Anyone who does not speak French fluently cannot expect to detect the difference between a word beginning with an aspirate *h-* and one beginning with an *h-* that is mute. To do so, he must consult the dictionary. Only an initial *h-* can be potentially aspirate, such as the *h-* in the word *honte;* the *h*'s in the word *brouhaha* could never be aspirate. To ascertain the presence of an aspirate *h*, look up in the dictionary the word in question that begins with *h*. If it is preceded in the dictionary by an asterisk (*), an apostrophe ('), or a dagger (†), the word definitely begins with an aspirate *h*. If, however, there is no such sign in the dictionary before the word beginning with *h*, the initial *h-* is mute. Whereas an aspirate *h* forbids them, a mute *h* permits liaison, elision, and contraction:

un homme	une horreur	l'honneur
[œ n ɔ m ə]	[y n ɔ r œ r]	[l ɔ n œ r]
(a man)	(a horror)	(honor)

Only in operatic outbursts such as "Je te hais!" ("I hate you!") might the aspirate *h* be truly aspirated as in English *how* or German *hell*. This sound, however, is not typical to French and should be used sparingly and only for reasons of expressive emphasis.

This discussion of the interruption of the flow of vocalic sound (or the *legato*) is not to encourage an indiscriminate use of hiatus. Some singers and coaches show an exaggerated, even misguided respect for punctuation, especially commas, at the expense of the vocalic and textual flow. A comma does *not* necessarily indicate an interruption of the legato, either in French or in English. Both the hiatus and the "punctuating breath" are threats to a good legato if used irresponsibly and to extremes. Downright butchery occurs if, in the following line, a slight break or breath is allowed for each comma. The English translation should amply explain why.

Voici des fruits, des fleurs, des feuilles, et des branches.
[v w a → s i → d ɛ → f r ɥ i → d ɛ → f l œ → r d ɛ → f œ j œ → z e → d ɛ → b r ɑ̃ → ʃ œ]
(Here are fruits, flowers, leaves, and branches.)
("Green," Debussy—Fauré-Verlaine)

Nor do other punctuation marks always call for breaks in the phrase:

Ah! s'il était ici!
[a → s i → l e → t ɛ → t i s i]
(Ah! if only he were here!)
(*Faust,* Gounod)

Only meaning and expression may determine breaks in a musical line, not mere punctuation, just as in everyday speech.

Syllabic Division

To determine the pronunciation of a French word, a fundamental knowledge of syllabic division is desirable, especially since most musical scores, including those printed in France, give incorrect or unclear division. Some simple rules govern the division of syllables in the French word. They are best grouped according to vowels and consonants.

VOWELS

As a general rule, syllabic division in French is made *after* the vowel-sound. In other words, most French syllables end in vowel-sounds, not in consonant-sounds as they do in English. A syllable in French contains *at least one and only one* vowel-sound.

- French vowel-sounds may be represented in spelling by one vowel letter:

  a/ma/bi/li/té   i/nu/ti/le
  [a m a b i l i t e]   [i n y t i l ə]
  (friendliness)   (useless)

- French vowel-sounds may be represented in spelling by more than one vowel-letter, by two or three, and even four at a time:

  trou/ba/dour   beau/té
  [t r u b a d u r]   [b o t e]
  (troubadour)   (beauty)

  coeur   queue
  [k œ r]   [k ø]
  (heart)   (tail)

- Consecutive vowel-letters are usually grouped together, as above, in the same syllable, *except:*

  1. When the second vowel-letter is marked by a diæresis (¨)

     na/ïf   A/za/ël
     [n a i f]   [a z a ɛ l]
     (naïve)   (Azaël)

  2. When *é* or *è* (acute- and grave-accented *e*) is preceded or followed by a vowel-letter:

     po/è/te   bien-ai/mé/e
     [p ɔ ɛ t ə]   [b j ɛ̃ n (e) m e ə]
     (poet)   (beloved)

3. In combinations *aill, eill, euill, œill, ouill, ueill,* where division occurs after the vowel-sound and before *ill:*

tra/va/ill<u>e</u>r	a/be/ill<u>e</u>	f<u>eu</u>/ill<u>e</u>
[t r a v a j e]	[a b e j ə]	[f œ j ə]
(to work)	(bee)	(leaf)

gr<u>e</u>/n<u>ou</u>/ill<u>e</u>	<u>œ</u>/ill<u>e</u>t	c<u>ue</u>/ill<u>i</u>r
[g r ə n u j ə]	[œ j ɛ]	[k œ j i r]
(frog)	(carnation)	(to gather)

4. When two or more vowel-letters are preceded by a consonant plus *l* or *r*, in which case division is made between the vowel-letters:

cr<u>u</u>/<u>e</u>l	bl<u>eu</u>/<u>e</u>t
[k r y ɛ l]	[b l ø ɛ]
(cruel)	(cornflower)

5. When letter *y* occurs between two vowel-letters, and in the word *pays* and its derivatives, where it is phonetically equivalent to *-ii-:*

voyage	pays
(v<u>oi</u>-i<u>age</u>)	(p<u>ai</u>-is)
[v w a j a ʒ ə]	[p (e) i]
(voyage)	(country)

6. In combination *-ao-, ao-,* which is usually divided:

ch<u>a</u>/<u>os</u>	<u>A</u>/<u>oua</u>
[k a o]	[a w a]
(chaos)	(Aoua!)

Exceptions:

S<u>aô</u>ne	<u>aoû</u>t	s<u>aou</u>l
[s o n]	[u]	[s u]
(Saône)	(August)	(drunk)

p<u>ao</u>n	p<u>ao</u>/nn<u>e</u>	p<u>ao</u>/nn<u>e</u>r
[p ã]	[p ɑ n ə]	[p ɑ n e]
(peacock, m.)	(peacock, f.)	(to strut)

CONSONANTS

As a general rule, syllabic division in French is made *before* the consonant-sound. Of course, a consonant cannot constitute a syllable without being accompanied by a vowel-sound.

- A single consonant-sound, whether represented by one or more letters, occurring between two vowel-sounds, belongs to the syllable of the *second* vowel-sound:

jo/li	ca/cher	bo/nheur
[ʒɔli]	[kaʃe]	[bɔnœr]
(pretty)	(to hide)	(happiness)

- Double consonants, with few exceptions, should be treated as one and divided accordingly:

a/ller	ca/sse/tte
[ale]	[kasɛtə]
(to go)	(strongbox)

- Only those double consonants in initial combinations *ill-*, *imm-*, *inn-*, and *irr-* are doubled and must be divided accordingly. In this case, the consonant-sound is merely prolonged:

il/lu/sion	im/mense
[illyzjõ]	[immãsə]
(illusion)	(immense)

- Double consonants in initial combinations *enn-* and *emm-* are usually divided but not doubled, since the first of each indicates the presence of a nasal vowel:

en/nui	em/me/ner
[ãnɥi]	[ãmœne]
(boredom)	(to take along)

Exception:

e/nne/mi
[ɛnœmi]
(enemy)

- Double consonants *-gg-* and *-cc-* are divided only when followed by *e* or *i*:

sug/gé/rer	ac/cep/ter	ac/ci/dent
[sygʒere]	[aksɛpte]	[aksidã]
(to suggest)	(to accept)	(accident)

When not followed by *e* or *i*, they are both relegated to the same syllable:

a/ggra/ver	Ba/cchus
[agrave]	[bakys]
(to aggravate)	(Bacchus)

- Division usually occurs between any two neighboring consonants:

par/ler   en/fant
[parle]   [ãfã]
(to speak) (child)

Except between a consonant followed by *l* or *r*:

ta/bleau   a/près   se/cret
[tablo]   [aprɛ]   [sœkrɛ]
(picture)   (after)   (secret)

And except in the following consonant combinations that produce *one* consonant-sound:

ch: tou/cher   **nh:** i/nhu/main
     [tuʃe]   [inymɛ̃]
     (to touch)   (inhuman)

th: go/thi/que   **gn:** Sei/gneur
     [gɔtikə]   [sɛɲœr]
     (Gothic)   (Lord)

ph: Sa/pho   **sc:** de/scen/dre
     [safo]   [desãdrə]
     (Sappho)   (to go down)

- Three consecutive consonant-letters are usually divided between the first and second letters:

cher/cher   mal/gré   res/plen/dir
[ʃɛrʃe]   [malgre]   [rɛsplãdir]
(to look for) (in spite of) (to shine forth)

But not in combinations affected by the rules already given above:

ath/lè/te   A/phro/di/te   a/ffli/ger
[atlɛtə]   [afrɔditə]   [afliʒe]
(athlete) (Aphrodite)   (to afflict)

- Since the letter *x* is usually representative of two different consonant-sounds, it is generally cut in half:

e/xil   e/xce/llent
[ɛgzil]   [ɛksɛlã]
(exile)   (excellent)

But not in most numerical words:

soi/xan/te
[swasãtə]
(sixty)

Stress and Word Rhythm

In most languages with which the singer is concerned, one syllable in every word or word-group receives more weight or emphasis than the others. This weight or emphasis is known as *stress*, and the syllable receiving it is called the stressed or accented syllable. The intermittent occurrence of stressed syllables within a line of verse is known as word rhythm or prosody.

A stress on a syllable so heavy that it affects the vowel quality and length of the surrounding syllables is known as a *tonic accent*. An example in English is the syllable *in-* of the word *interest*. It dominates the word, so to speak, and the remaining syllables fall away from it.

In French, there is no tonic accent comparable to that of Italian, German, or English. Unlike English, the stress in a French word habitually falls on the final or last vowel-sound, but never on final, unstressed -*e*, -*es*, or -*ent* sounding as [œ] or [ə]. Compare the following words in English and French, noting the differences in stress and syllabic equality between the two languages as shown by the note-values. Whether spoken or sung, French syllabic equality is more even and regular than that of English (see Recording Illustration B):

ENGLISH   FRENCH

(fi)<u>del</u>(ity)   fi<u>dé</u>lité

<u>a</u>(morous)   am<u>ou</u>reux

<u>in</u>(teresting)   in<u>té</u>ress<u>ant</u>

Word-groups follow the same principle in French: the stress falls on the last sounded vowel of the word-group, except final, unstressed -*e*, -*es*, and -*ent*. Compare the English "That is impossible!" to the French "C'est impossible!" Note, however, that for emphasis in both languages stress may be changed by accenting the first syllable of the word *impossible*. Most important of all, the tonic accent in English diminishes the length and resonance of the surrounding syllables, whereas the stress on the final syllable in French has no diminishing or varying effect on the preceding syllables.

All of this is to warn the singer not to insert whimsical stresses into a sung line of French verse by exaggerating or distorting the rhythm. Marking the beat with the voice is also foreign to all vocal styles except perhaps nursery rhymes and some folk music. Such monotony of stress is deadly in its effect on the legato, on the expressive delivery of the text, and is plainly unmusical and tiresome to the ear. Instead, a consistent vocalization of all the vowel-sounds and their corresponding syllables is the key to a good legato in French. If the composer has demonstrated a good sense of prosody, the stressed words or syllables will emerge of their own accord. Sometimes, unimportant words may fall on the "strong beat" of the measure, but this is no reason to stress them. Good phrasing and legato diction must resist the "tyranny of the bar line."

Equalization of the syllabic flow by occasional stress where appropriate is the ideal here. In singing dotted and triplet patterns (♩. ♪ ♩. ♪, ♪ ³♪ ♪ ³♪, etc.) the longer note should not be accented at the expense of the shorter one unless the music is of a martial, folksy, or highly declamatory nature. In general, it is a good idea to underline carefully the syllable assigned to the shorter note. Anticipate it slightly, and vocalize it fully to insure the legato and the natural evenness of the French syllabic flow. In the following examples, in which the prosody is somewhat weak, note how a gentle underlining of the short note can "iron out" a rhythmic jerkiness inappropriate to both the text and the musical phrase (see Recording Illustration C):

"Les Berceaux," G. Fauré—Sully-Prudhomme

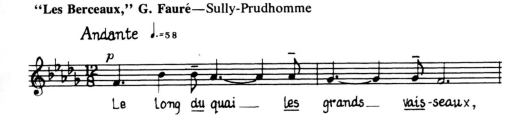

"Connais-tu le pays," *Mignon,* **A. Thomas**

Remember that this underlining of the shorter note-values is a means of smoothing out and equalizing syllabic flow. It must not be misused to create false accents within the musical phrase.

Scores, Editions, Printing Procedures, and Errors

A good musician and a serious student of diction must always start with the premise that there is no such thing as an edition without errors. Some have fewer than others, but none can be completely trusted. A "reliable edition" is one that has been carefully checked against other editions by experts thoroughly acquainted with the repertoire. First editions are sometimes the least accurate. Anthologies, so common and so widespread in the United States, are the most suspect, especially the large-print variety "edited by X" or "with an English version by Y." Beware of unacknowledged transpositions and *ossia* interpolations. They can both betray and deform the true character of a composition and, more often than not, would not have been condoned by the composer.

Some points to remember when deciphering the texts in French vocal scores, whether published in France or not are:

- A capitalized word is not always an important one or a proper noun. The first word of a line of verse is traditionally capitalized in the printing of poetry and will appear so in the musical score.
- Composers and editors (both French and non-French) do not always syllabify words correctly. Furthermore, they often fail to insert dashes between syllables to show that they belong to the same word. It is always beneficial to see the text in its original poetic format. Some editions provide such information for this reason and should be consulted.
- Due to lack of space, accent-marks are traditionally omitted over capital letters in print. Thus, the word *étoile* may appear as *Etoile* when capitalized, but it still sounds the same as when uncapitalized.
- Original punctuation is often omitted or incorrectly inserted in scores. Again, verification with the isolated poetic text in a literary source is the best procedure.
- Very often there are inaccuracies and outright errors in translations provided in some editions. Always check them in the dictionary or with a qualified expert before believing in them. A smooth, even faithful translation need not necessarily be word-for-word. Such a literal translation inserted into the score may help the singer be aware of the meaning of each word he is singing. But when reading a translation out loud a fluent one is preferable, or one that is faithful to the original but reads well at the same time.
- Some words, alas, are truly untranslatable. It is not always an affectation to say that there is no real English equivalent for a certain French word. For example, the word *ennui* means "boredom," "slight depression," and "worry" all wrapped into one word.
- And finally, the "translation" provided directly beneath the original French text in the score should be considered an "English version,"

not a translation. This is a sad remnant of the time when art song was sung in paraphrase translations that rhymed, a blatant dismissal of the fact that the poem existed in its own right before the music set to it, and that it was the poem in its original language and poetic form that inspired and guided the composer. Fortunately, today the world has been sufficiently "internationalized" so that Schubert songs are no longer sung in French translation for after-dinner entertainment and the poetry of Verlaine is no longer paled by genteel Victorian couplets.

2
Singing the Sounds of the French Language

The Fifteen Vowel-sounds in French

Below is a numbered list of the fifteen vowel-sounds in French that gives for each vowel the phonetic symbol, its "name," and words that contain the vowel-sound in question. (Consult Recording Illustration D.)

[′] - accent grave
(closed)

[＼] - accent ague
(open)

THE FOUR TONGUE VOWELS

1. [i]	"phonetic *i*"	midi, il lit, cygne
2. [e]	"closed *e*"	été, aimer, nez
3. [ɛ]	"open *e*"	belle, mère, mais
4. [a]	"bright *a*"	la table, art

THE FOUR LIP VOWELS

5. [ɑ]	"dark *a*"	âme, passer
6. [ɔ]	"open *o*"	mort, robe, aurore
7. [o]	"closed *o*"	mot, beau, faux
8. [u]	"phonetic *u*"	doux, où, grenouille

THE THREE MIXED VOWELS

9. [y]	"phonetic vowel *y*"	lune, dur, but
10. [ø]	"o-slash"	deux, feu, queue
11. [œ]	"oh-ee"	fleur, coeur, œil
[ə]	"schwa"	lune, bien-aimée

THE FOUR NASAL VOWELS

12. [ɑ̃]   "dark *a* nasal"   <u>en</u>fant, <u>sem</u>bler
13. [õ]   "closed *o* nasal"   <u>bon</u>, <u>tom</u>ber
14. [ɛ̃]   "open *e* nasal"   v<u>in</u>, p<u>ain</u>, s<u>im</u>ple
15. [œ̃]   "oh-ee nasal"   <u>un</u> parf<u>um</u>, h<u>um</u>ble

The vowel chart below indicates the relationships between the vowels. In the top row are the eight basic vowel-sounds. The first four are governed by tongue position, the four adjacent are formed by the lips. Below these eight vowel-sounds, the three sets of solid lines that meet connect those combinations of tongue and lip positions, which, respectively, produce the three mixed vowel-sounds. The four dotted lines connect the basic vowel-sound or the mixed vowel-sound with its nasal counterpart.

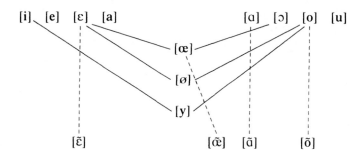

WAYS OF CLASSIFYING VOWELS

There are seven groupings among the fifteen vowel-sounds in French.

1. *Tongue and Lip Vowels.* The formation of four French vowel-sounds is governed exclusively by the tongue: [i], [e], [ɛ], [a]. These four vowel-sounds are commonly called "front" vowels by phoneticians. Similarly, the following four vowel-sounds are formed mainly by the progressive rounding of the lips: [a], [ɔ], [o], [u]. These four vowels are commonly called "back" vowels by phoneticians, a term obviously out of place in the study of singing diction.

2. *Mixed Vowels.* The three vowels [y], [ø], and [œ] are called "mixed" because their formation is dependent upon the simultaneous positioning of the tongue and of the lips. These three vowels are also called "mixed rounded vowels" and "rounded front vowels" by the phoneticians. Along with [œ], number eleven in the list on page 21, is given the neutral vowel-sound [ə], or "schwa," which is simply an abbreviated version of [œ] that never occupies a full syllable, is always unstressed, and is of split-second duration.

3. *Nasal Vowels.* The last four vowel-sounds in the list on page 22 are produced by the resonating of three basic vowel-sounds and one mixed vowel-sound in the nasal cavities behind the nose. They are [ɑ̃], [õ], [ɛ̃], and [œ̃].

4. *Closed and Open Vowels.* There are seven vowel-sounds that are more closed than open: [i], [e], [o], [u], [y], [ø], and [õ]. This closed quality may be effected by either the tongue or the lips, or by both simultaneously. In vocal terms, a "closed" vowel should be thought of as more "focused" or "pointed" when sung. Singers must abandon the erroneous concept of the closed vowel as being restricted, constricted, and "enclosed" in the mouth or throat. On the contrary, they are the easiest to project when properly executed. For good singing diction, a "closed" vowel must never be pinched or "swallowed," but instead matched as closely as possible with neighboring vowels that are more or less open to insure the uniformity of the vocalic flow.

Five vowels and three corresponding nasal vowels can be considered "open": [ɛ], [a], [ɑ], [ɔ], [œ], [ɑ̃], [ɛ̃], and [œ̃]. Their openness is dependent upon either a wider opening between the tongue and the upper back molars or less rounding of the lips. These vowels, although usually considered to be comfortable and preferable to sing, are the ones most apt to be "spread" or to lose "focus" when being sung. Every effort must be made to preserve the uniformity of the vocalic flow from open to closed vowel by correct focusing and resonance of the open vowel when in the midst of neighboring closed vowel-sounds.

5. *Rounded and Unrounded Vowels.* Six vowel-sounds and two corresponding nasals are more "rounded" than the rest. In forming them, the lips are thrust forward in varying degrees in the shape of a circle. These vowels are [ɔ], [o], [u], [y], [ø], [œ], [õ], and [œ̃]. American singers are often guilty of "flattening out" rounded vowels. Also, they frequently fail to preserve the roundness of the vowel during its emission by a slackening in the lip position. This is perhaps due to speech habits and the diphthongal character of the English language itself, and plus the fact that the lip muscles may not be properly trained to achieve and retain relaxed but consistent rounding. The over-rounding of vowel-sounds is equally objectionable for obvious reasons: first, defective pronunciation and the resultant lack of intelligibility, and second, unhealthy vocalization that can lead to hooty, constricted, or throaty singing.

Five vowel-sounds and one corresponding nasal require no rounding of the lips for their formation: [i], [e], [ɛ], [a], [ɑ], and [ɛ̃]. When these unrounded vowels occur next to rounded vowel-sounds, they are sometimes pronounced incorrectly due to an unwarranted rounding of the lips during their emission. Some singers round all their vowel-sounds indiscriminately, either for "vocal reasons" (that all-encompassing, lame excuse) or because they think that this is "French," probably an impression received from the prosaic Gallic pout observed in the parodied imitations of a French accent so prevalent in American films and on the stage. This annoying (and amateurish) habit, a true vocal and linguistic mannerism, only results in vocal monotony and hootiness, not to mention lack of intelligibility. For example, a rounded [i] sounds like [y], making "Je dis" sound like "Je dus." A rounded [ɛ] resembles [œ], thus confusing "père" and "peur," and so on. Only for reasons of vowel modification to achieve vocal facility should any degree of rounding be exercised on unrounded vowels, and then only with the guidance of a trained ear.

6. *Contrasting Vowel-pairs.* There are four contrasting vowel-pairs, three in the "closed-open" category, one in the "bright-dark" category. These vowel-sounds receive their identity by contrast rather than as isolated sounds:

	CLOSED	OPEN
the two "*e*'s"	[e]	[ɛ]
the two "*o*'s"	[o]	[ɔ]
the two "*eu*'s"	[ø]	[œ]

	BRIGHT	DARK
the two "*a*'s"	[a]	[ɑ]

Some Guiding Rules for the Formation of Vowels

THE TIP OF THE TONGUE

In the formation of all fifteen vowel-sounds in French, the tip of the tongue must always be gently placed behind the two front lower teeth, without undue pressure and never arching forward, however. In this way, the middle and sides of the tongue are free and in position to participate in the formation of each vowel.

THE SIDES AND THE MIDDLE OF THE TONGUE

The sides of the tongue may be called upon to rise slightly to or toward the upper back molars. They must do so without any undue rising of the middle of the tongue toward the hard palate. And although the middle of the tongue may approach the hard palate in the formation of some vowels, it must *never* actually touch the hard palate. Any positioning of the tongue must be effected with utmost rapidity and precision both to insure accuracy of vowel quality and to avoid diphthongization. Also, the position of the tongue must be maintained for the duration of the vowel-sound (or note-value), quietly and with relaxation.

THE ROUNDING OF THE LIPS

When the lips are to be rounded, they must leave the teeth in the shape of a circle as in the act of whistling. Depending upon the vowel, this circle will be larger or smaller in diameter. All lip-rounding must be effected with relaxation, precision, and rapidity. To test lip relaxation, stroke the rounded lips briskly with the index finger. Any resistance on the part of the lips will reveal the slightest trace of tension. Since lip-rounding in English is generally less extreme and, above all, less sustained, rounded French vowels may initially cause the English-speaking singer slight discomfort or self-consciousness. Hitherto neglected lip muscles may be called upon in the formation of the rounded French vowels. While avoiding tension at all cost, the degree of lip-rounding must be exact to insure the desired vowel quality, and positioning must be split-second to avoid diphthongization. Then, once the position of rounding is assumed, it must not vary for the duration of the syllable or note-value.

THE JAW

The jaw should *never* be directly applied to the formation of any vowel-sound. It must be left absolutely loose in the formation of all vowel-sounds. While totally mobile and free, the jaw must never be unnecessarily dropped or pushed downward in the formation of any vowel-sound. For any unrounded vowel, the lips may assume the natural "ah" position while the sides of the tongue insure the formation of the vowel-sound. There should be no clenching of the jaw for closed or rounded vowel-sounds. When in the process of rounding, the lips should be thought of as separate from the jaw, which, of course, they are. In the formation of the closed, rounded vowel-sounds, the jaw must not drop unnecessarily; such a motion will make relaxed and effective lip-rounding that much more difficult. In the formation of the more open, rounded vowel-sounds, the circle of the lips and the desired degree of rounding determine the degree of jaw release, not the reverse. It is most often the jaw, not the tongue or lips, which serves as a source of undesirable tension in the singing process. Articulation of any kind is the function of the smallest part of the anatomy. Singers must consciously form vowel-sounds with their tongues and lips, not their jaws or throats, just as a pianist articulates notes with his fingers, not his arms or neck. It is precisely these larger parts that produce discomfort when they are allowed to participate in a process in which they have no place.

GLOTTAL ATTACKS

Except in rare instances, there should be no glottal attack at the outset of any French vowel. This glottal snap, so common in American speech (for example, the society matron's "Actually, . . .") may be avoided by preceding the vowel-sound with a slight aspiration, or a little "h," or simply by thinking "h" upon emission. Occasionally, a very gentle glottal separation may be appropriate for expressive or phonetic reasons as was demonstrated earlier in the section on hiatus, the mute and aspirate *h*.

VOWEL MODIFICATION

Vowel modification is based on pure common sense and good artistry, but it must not be attempted until after the vowel-sounds are secure in the singer's ear and mouth. The vowel-sounds place (focus, resonate) the voice in different ways. With each vowel-sound there is a particular resonance, level, and direction of the flow of vocal sound. The singer must first acquaint himself thoroughly with the essential characteristics of each vowel-sound. Only then can he responsibly and intelligently know how to modify it in the different registers of the voice.

The basic rule of vowel modification in singing is quite simple: the higher the range or tessitura, the less the articulation of the vowel-sound by the tongue and/or lips. In other words, tongue vowels are less fronted and lip vowels are less rounded in the upper reaches of the voice. The degree to which the articulations by the tongue and the lips may be reduced will, of course, depend upon the individual singer who must keep two objectives in mind when modifying vowel-sounds: vocal comfort and vocalic intelligibility. In any case, these two considerations must go hand-in-hand in all responsible vowel modification which, above all, must not be simplistically confused with "vowel substitution" where the original vowel-sound is replaced by a completely unrelated one. Tasteful coloring and projection of any vowel in any register is a mark of vocal and linguistic sophistication and may be arrived at only after a certain degree of mastery in both areas. Painters learn to use their basic colors before venturing into the realm of the nuanced hue. So it is with singers.

Phoneticization, Formation, and Singing of the Vowel-sounds

THE TONGUE VOWELS

1. [i]   m<u>i</u>d<u>i</u>   [m i d i]
2. [e]   <u>é</u>t<u>é</u>   [e t e]
3. [ɛ]   b<u>e</u>lle   [b ɛ l ə]
4. [a]   l<u>a</u>   [l a]

The four tongue vowels have two things in common:

1. *The fronting of the tongue:* All four vowels require, each to a different degree, the fronting of the sides of the tongue toward the upper back molars and the fronting of the middle of the tongue toward, but never to, the hard palate. For all four vowel-sounds, the lips should maintain the "ah" position and avoid any trace of a forced smile which only tends to spread the vowel-sound. Keep the tip of the tongue gently anchored behind the lower front teeth in the articulation of all vowel-sounds.

2. *Resonance, space and placement:* All four tongue vowels are directed toward the eyes and immediately around them in the region of the face referred to as the "mask." From [i] all the way to [a], this point of resonance must be maintained for authenticity. Also, all four tongue vowels must maintain the space of "ah." Without this space, the tongue cannot be sufficiently fronted to articulate an authentic French [i] or [e]. Likewise, without the point of resonance high in the mask, in the place of [i], neither [ɛ] nor [a] will be authentically French. Thus, the four tongue vowels share the same space and placement in their resonances.

1. Phonetic *i* [i]   Model word: m<u>i</u>d<u>i</u> [m i d i] (noon)

FORMATION:

Lips in natural "ah" position with the sides of the tongue fronted so that they come into contact with the upper back molars. Avoid any unnecessary smiling or thickening of the tongue, any closing or tensing of the jaw. Check to see if the width of a thumb will fit between the teeth. Keep placement of resonance high in the mask, but maintain the space of "ah." Avoid dropped [i] of English *see* in French *si.*

SPELLINGS:

(N.B.: Spellings represent all possible vowel-letters or combinations thereof in any given syllable. Nasalization not considered until nasal vowels.)

i, ï, î	*as a general rule,* when only vowel in syllable, except when nasalized (see [ɛ̃])	Bilitis [bilitis] (Bilitis) île [ilə] (island)	Thaïs [tais] (Thaïs)
ie	*when final, always*	la vie [lavi] (life)	Sylvie [silvi] (Sylvia)
	when medial, in forms and derivatives of verbs in *-ier,* but not in final *-ier:* oubli/er hi/er [ublie] [jɛr] [iɛr] (to forget) (yesterday)	j'oublierai [ʒublire] (I shall forget)	
y, ÿ	*as a general rule,* when it is the only vowel-letter in a syllable, except when nasal (see [ɛ̃])	lys [lis] (lily) Louÿs [lwis] (Louÿs)	Styx [stiks] (Styx)

2. Closed *e* [e]

Model word: été [ete] (summer)

FORMATION:

Lips in natural "ah" position with the sides of the tongue fronted so that they come into contact with the upper back molars as for [i], but with the blade (or the middle) of the tongue slightly less fronted and more relaxed. Avoid any unnecessary smiling or spreading of the lips, any thickening of the tongue, closing or tensing of the jaw. Check to see if the width of a thumb will fit between the teeth. Keep placement of resonance high in the mask, but maintain the space of "ah." Avoid the diphthong of English *gay* in French *gai.* This vowel-sound is extremely close in sound and formation to [i], indeed much closer than is usually believed, but it must not be confused with it. The point of resonance for [e] is slightly broader than, but just as high as, for [i]. Some singers may find it helpful to begin with [i] to insure the proper placement for [e]. But the similarities between the vowel-sounds should not render them identical, for they are absolutely distinct from one another.

SPELLINGS:

é	*as a general rule*	désiré [d e z i r e] (desired)	étoilé [e t w a l e] (starry)
e	before final, silent -d, -ds, -r, -z	pied [p j e] (foot)	je m'assieds [ʒ œ m a s j e] (I sit down)
		aller [a l e] (to go)	parlez [p a r l e] (speak)
	in initial combinations *eff-, ess-, dess-, desc-* (may be phoneticized [(e)] to indicate slightly less closed quality; see [œ] for any exceptions)	effet [(e)f ɛ] (effect)	essaim [(e)s ɛ̃] (swarm)
		dessein [d(e)s ɛ̃] (design)	descendre [d(e)s ã d r ə] (to go down)
	in a few isolated words	et [e] (and)	clef [k l e] (key)
		eh [e] (eh!)	ressusciter [r e s y s i t e] (to resurrect)
	in short words like *les, des,* etc. (normally [ɛ]), closes to [(e)] in vocalic harmonization when immediately followed by [e], [i] or [y]	les_étoiles [l(e)z e t w a l ə] (the stars)	des rues [d(e)r y] (streets)
ai	when final in verb forms (normally [ɛ])	j'ai [ʒ e] (I have)	je serai [ʒ ə s ə r e] (I will be)
	in *vocalic harmonization* (see Chapter 5) where unstressed *ai,* normally [ɛ], closes to [(e)] when immediately followed by [e], [i] or [y]	bien-aimé [b j ɛ̃ n(e)m e] (beloved)	laisser [l(e)s e] (to leave)
		plaisir [p l(e)z i r] (pleasure)	baiser [b(e)z e] (kiss)

in a few isolated words and their derivatives

je v<u>ai</u>s
[ʒ œ v e]
(I go)

je s<u>ai</u>s
[ʒ œ s e]
(I know)

il s<u>ai</u>t
[i l s e]
(he knows)

g<u>ai</u>
[g e]
(gay)

qu<u>ai</u>
[k e]
(quay)

<u>ai</u>gu
[e g y]
(acute)

<u>æ</u>, <u>œ</u>   in a few words of Greek origin

<u>æ</u>gypan
[e ʒ i p ã]
(nymph)

Ph<u>œ</u>bé
[f e b e]
(Phoebe)

3. Open *e* [ɛ]   Model word: b<u>e</u>lle [b ɛ l ə] (beautiful)

FORMATION:

Lips in natural "ah" position with the corners relaxed to avoid tension or spreading. The sides of the tongue barely touching the upper back molars, much less fronted than for [e]. Placement same as for [i] and [e], thus insuring a higher and brighter resonance than for its English counterpart. (French *belle* is higher, brighter and somewhat more fronted than English *bell.*) Avoid diphthong of English *lay* in French *les.*

SPELLINGS:

<u>è</u>, <u>ê</u>, <u>ë</u>   *as a general rule*

p<u>è</u>re
[p ɛ r ə]
(father)

r<u>ê</u>ve
[r ɛ v ə]
(dream)

No<u>ë</u>l
[n ɔ ɛ l]
(Noel)

<u>e</u>   *when followed by one or more consonants, silent or sounded, in the same syllable (except when followed by silent, final -d, -ds, -r, or -z; see* [e])

il <u>e</u>st
[i l ɛ]
(he is)

l'<u>e</u>st
[l ɛ s t]
(the east)

l<u>e</u>s
[l ɛ]
(the)

ét<u>e</u>rn<u>e</u>l
[e t ɛ r n ɛ l]
(eternal)

		elle [ɛ l ə] (she)	faiblesse [f ɛ b l ɛ s ə] (weakness)
	when followed by a double consonant (except in some initial combinations; see [e] and [œ] and in combination *enn* and *emm;* see [a], [ɑ̃])		
		mettre [m ɛ t r ə] (to put)	guerre [g ɛ r ə] (war)
ei, ey, eai	*as a general rule* (except when nasalized; see [ɛ̃])	reine [r ɛ n ə] (queen)	neige [n ɛ ʒ ə] (snow)
		Leguerney [l œ g ɛ r n ɛ] (Leguerney)	je songeais [ʒ œ s õ ʒ ɛ] (I was musing)
ai, aî	*as a general rule* (for exceptions, see [e] and [œ]) (may be [(e)] in vocalic harmonization)	mais [m ɛ] (but)	était [e t ɛ] (was)
		connaître [k ɔ n ɛ t r ə] (to be acquainted with)	
aie, aies aient ay, aye, ayes	*as a general rule,* in all positions (*ay* may be [(e)] in vocalic harmonization)	haie [ɛ] (hedge)	tu essaies [t y (e) s ɛ] (you try)
		Souzay [s u z ɛ] (Souzay)	pays [p (e) i] (country)
		ils étaient [i l z e t ɛ] (they were)	je paye [ʒ ə p ɛ j ə] (I pay)

4. Bright *a* [a]   Model words: la table [l a t a b l ə] (the table)

FORMATION:

Lips in natural "ah" position, front sides of tongue slightly toward upper back molars and away from floor of mouth. Do not drop or back the tongue, thus insuring resonance in the same place as [i], [e] and [ɛ]. Keep corners of lips quiet to avoid spreading the vowel, with soft palate high so that resonance can be directed upward into the mask. Avoid dark American "ah" of "father" and, above all, the [æ] of American "cat." No excessive nasal resonance—aim for the eyes. This "bright a" of

French can be safely compared to the [a] of Italian. Nine out of every ten "ah"-vowels in French are bright; the exception is dark [ɑ]. Without a truly high, bright [a], any singer's French will lack authenticity.

SPELLINGS:

a, à	as a general rule (for exceptions, see [ɑ])	là [l a] (there)	madame [m a d a m ə] (madame)
â	is normally [ɑ]; only in rare verb endings	nous donnâmes [n u d ɔ n a m ə] (we gave)	
ao	rare, when followed by -nn-,	paonne [p a n] (peacock, f.)	paonner [p a n e] (to strut)
e	rare, only in combinations -emm- and -enn-, when medial	[femme] [f a m ə] (woman) fréquemment [f r e k a m ɑ̃] (frequently)	[solennel] [s ɔ l a n ɛ l] (solemn)
oi, oy	as [wa], as a general rule (for exceptions, see [ɑ] on page 34)	oiseau [w a z o] (bird) gloire [g l w a r ə] (glory)	voir [v w a r] (to see) royal [r̄ w a j a l] (royal)
oe, eoi	as [wa], rare, only in a few words Note: Ligature œ may sound as [e] (see page 30) or as [œ] (see page 45).	moelle [m w a l ə] (marrow)	s'asseoir [s a s w a r] (to sit down)

EXERCISES

1. Intone (see Chapter 4 for description of intoning) the following slowly and legato, with one breath per set of brackets:

[i →] [e →] [ɛ →] [a →] [f i f e f ɛ f a] [f e f ɛ f a f i]
[f ɛ f e f i f a] [i → e →] [e → ɛ →] [ɛ → a →]
[i → e → ɛ → a] [a → ɛ → e → i →]

2. Carefully copy the following text, including all accent marks and underlines, skipping a line between each line of verse. Then, above each

underlined vowel-sound, insert the proper representative phonetic symbol in brackets.

> Lydia, sur tes roses joues
> Et sur ton col frais et si blanc
> Roule étincelant
> L'or fluide que tu dénoues;
> Le jour qui luit est le meilleur
> Oublions l'éternelle tombe
> Laisse tes baisers de colombe
> Chanter sur ta lèvre en fleur.
> Un lys caché répand sans cesse
> Une odeur divine en ton sein;
> Les délices comme un essaim
> Sortent de toi, jeune déesse
> Je t'aime et meurs, ô mes amours,
> Mon âme en baisers m'est ravie
> O Lydia, rends-moi la vie,
> Que je puisse mourir toujours!
>   "Lydia," G. Fauré-Leconte de Lisle

THE LIP VOWELS

5. [ɑ]   âme   [a m ə]
6. [ɔ]   mort   [m ɔ r]
7. [o]   mot   [m o]
8. [u]   doux   [d u]

Beginning with [ɑ], which involves slight lip-rounding in the position of a pout, the subsequent three vowels in this category are formed by a progressive rounding of the lips with the tongue flat and its tip anchored against the lower front teeth. While lip-rounding is a voluntary, visible action and can be easily controlled, the backing of the tongue is all too often the involuntary, invisible culprit in the formation of the lip vowels and must be avoided assiduously. As the lips round progressively from [ɑ] to [u], always remember to sing them over a flat tongue. For more on lip rounding, see page 25 above.

5. Dark *a* [ɑ]   Model word: âme [a m ə] (soul)

FORMATION:

Lips slightly rounded in the pout position with the tongue flat as when saying "ah" for the doctor. Resonance under the soft palate.

SPELLINGS:

a	when followed by intervocalic *s* or *z* sounding as [z]	ext<u>a</u>se [ɛkstɑzə] (ecstasy)	g<u>a</u>zon [gɑzõ] (lawn)
	Note: The *a* is usually dark in most words and names ending in *as* or *aille(s)*, and in isolated words and their derivatives (only the most common in the repertoire are given here; check dictionary)	Hél<u>a</u>s! [elɑs] (Alas!)	p<u>a</u>ille [pɑjə] (straw)
		di<u>a</u>ble [djɑblə] (devil)	s<u>a</u>bre [sɑbrə] (sabre)
		esp<u>a</u>ce [ɛspɑsə] (space)	j<u>a</u>dis [ʒɑdis] (formerly)
		d<u>a</u>mner [dɑne] (to damn)	cad<u>a</u>vre [kadɑvrə] (cadaver)
â	*as a general rule* (except in verb endings)	<u>â</u>me [ɑmə] (soul)	ch<u>â</u>teau [ʃɑto] (castle)
<u>oi</u>, <u>oie</u>, <u>oy</u>	as [wɑ], generally after a consonant plus *r*, and in isolated words (check dictionary)	cr<u>oi</u>re [krwɑrə] (to believe)	pr<u>oie</u> [prwɑ] (prey)
		cr<u>oy</u>ant [krwɑjã] (believer)	b<u>oi</u>s [bwɑ] (wood)

Open *o* [ɔ]   Model word: m<u>o</u>rt [mɔr] (dead)

FORMATION:

Lips rounded open and away from teeth, in the "aw" position of English vowel in *more.* Tongue absolutely flat, tip behind lower front teeth. Avoid closing the lips on "ooh" upon release, retaining "aw" position until the new consonant- or vowel-sound. Above all, avoid the unrounded vowel-sound of American *hot.*

SPELLINGS:

o	*as a general rule,* and usually when followed by a pronounced consonant (see [o] for exceptions) or vowel-sound in same word	robe [r ɔ b ə] (dress)	frivole [f r i v ɔ l ə] (fickle)
		Noël [n ɔ ɛ l] (Noel)	poète [p ɔ ɛ t ə] (poet)
au	*only when followed by r* (otherwise is [o]) and in two isolated words, *mauvais* and *Paul*	aurore [ɔ r ɔ r ə] (dawn)	laurier [l ɔ r j e] (laurel)
		mauvais [m ɔ v ɛ] (bad)	Paul [p ɔ l] (Paul)
-um	when final, in a few words of foreign origin (otherwise is [œ̃])	minimum [m i n i m ɔ m] (minimum)	maximum [m a k s i m ɔ m] (maximum)
		album [a l b ɔ m] (album)	rhum [r ɔ m] (rum)
-eo-	after *g* and before a pronounced consonant	Georges [ʒ ɔ r ʒ ə] (George)	

7. Closed *o* [O]   Model word: m<u>o</u>t [m o] (word)

FORMATION:

Lips very rounded in the shape of the phonetic symbol and aim slightly downward away from teeth with upper lip gently curled over lower lip. Avoid closing on "ooh" upon release or delayed rounding of lips, giving the diphthong of English *mow.* Avoid throatiness or "rounding" of throat and keep the tongue flat with the tip against the lower front teeth.

o	*when final in word*	écho [e k o] (echo)	Roméo [r o m e o] (Romeo)
	when followed by a silent, final consonant (except nasalizing m or n as in mon nom)	mot [m o] (word)	trop [t r o] (too much)
	(may open to [ɔ] in liaison or when unstressed in word trop:) trop‿aimable trop souffert [t r ɔ p ɛ m a b l ə] [t r ɔ s u f ɛ r] (too kind) (too much suffered)	héros [e r o] (hero)	Gounod [g u n o] (Gounod)
	when followed by intervocalic s or by -tion	rose [r o z ə] (pink)	émotion [e m o s j õ] (emotion)
	in a few isolated words (only most common in repertoire given here; check dictionary)	odeur [o d œ r] (scent)	oasis [o a z i s] (oasis)
		grosse [g r o s ə] (fat)	fosse [f o s ə] (pit)
ô	*as a general rule*	drôle [d r o l ə] (funny)	le nôtre [l ə n o t r ə] (ours)
au	*as a general rule,* **except when followed by** *r* **and in words** *mauvais* **and** *Paul* **(see [ɔ])**	autour [o t u r] (around)	chaud [ʃ o] (warm)
		saule [s o l ə] (willow)	fléau [f l e o] (scourge)
eau	*as a general rule*	l'eau [l o] (water)	beauté [b o t e] (beauty)
aô, oa	rare	Saône [s o n ə] (Saône)	toast [t o s t] (toast)

8. Phonetic *u* [u]   Model word: d<u>ou</u>x [d u] (soft)

FORMATION:

Lips very rounded as for [o], but aimed slightly upward as in a "smooch." No dropping of the jaw. Avoid diphthongizing effect due to delayed lip-rounding, throatiness or "rounding" of throat. Keep tongue flat with tip gently anchored against lower front teeth.

SPELLINGS:

<u>ou</u>, <u>où</u>, <u>oû</u>	*as a general rule*	l<u>ou</u>p [l u] (wolf) d<u>ou</u>x [d u] (soft)	<u>où</u> [u] (where) g<u>oû</u>ter [g u t e] (snack)
-<u>oue</u>(-)	when final, or when medial before a single consonant-letter	Ind<u>oue</u> [ɛ̃ d u] (Hindu girl)	je j<u>ou</u>erai [ʒ ə ʒ u r e] (I shall play)
<u>aou</u>, <u>aoû</u>	*as a general rule* (but not in *Aoua!* [awa])	<u>aoû</u>t [u] (August)	s<u>aou</u>l [s u] (drunk)

EXERCISES

1. Intone the following, slowly and legato, with one breath per set of brackets:

[i] [e] [ɛ] [a] [ɑ →] [ɔ →] [o →] [u →] [fɑ → fɔ → fo → fu →]
[fu → fo → fɔ → fɑ →] [ɑ → ɔ → o → u →] [u → o → ɔ → ɑ →]
[poze] [ɛkstazə] [elɑs] [ʃɑto] [krwɑrə] [frivɔlə] [pɔɛtə]
[ɔrɔr] [mɔvɛ] [eko] [tro] [rozə] [otɔnə] [fleo] [bote] [gute]
[ebluir] [brujar] [pardɔnemwa] [silvuplɛ]
[purkwamatilkite]

2. Carefully copy the following text, including all accent marks and

underlines, skipping a line between each line of verse. Then above each underlined vowel-letter(s) insert the proper representative phonetic symbol(s)
in brackets.

> Dans un sommeil que charmait ton image
> Je rêvais le bonheur, ardent mirage;
> Tes yeux étaient plus doux, ta voix pure et sonore,
> Tu rayonnais comme un ciel éclairé par l'aurore.
> Tu m'appelais et je quittais la terre
> Pour m'enfuir avec toi vers la lumière;
> Les cieux pour nous entr'ouvraient leurs nues,
> Splendeurs inconnues, lueurs divines entrevues,
> Hélas! triste réveil des songes!
> Je t'appelle, ô nuit, rends-moi tes mensonges;
> Reviens radieuse, ô nuit mystérieuse!
>   ("Après un rêve," G. Fauré-Bussine)

THE MIXED VOWELS

9.	[y]	lune	[l y n ə]
10.	[ø]	deux	[d ø]
11.	[œ]	fleur	[f l œ r]
	[ə]	lune	[l y n ə]

The mixed vowels have the following characteristics in common:

1. They are all formed by the simultaneous production of a tongue vowel
and a lip vowel:

> Tongue position of [i] plus lip position of [ɔ] = [y]
> Tongue position of [ɛ] plus lip position of [o] = [ø]
> Tongue position of [ɛ] plus lip position of [ɔ] = [œ], [ə]

2. They are all *rounded* vowels since two of the rounded lip vowels are
necessary in their formation.

3. They are all *front* vowels since two of the frontal tongue vowels are
necessary in their formation.

The only essential difference between the three mixed vowel-sounds is
their degree of closedness or openness. The most closed of the three is [ø];
[y] is slightly less closed yet much more fronted than [ø]; and [œ] is definitely an open vowel.

All the mixed vowels are *front* and *round*. The last one [œ] is *front, open,* and *round.*

9. Phonetic *y* [y]   Model word: l<u>u</u>ne [l y n ə] (moon)

FORMATION:

Tongue in [i] position, lips in [ɔ] position. The most important ingredient of a good [y] is [i], especially in the higher registers. The [ɔ] element of [y], effected by the lips, takes on an added importance in the middle and lower areas of the voice. But it is the presence of the tongue position of [i] that will guarantee the [y] in all registers; upon this [i] the rounded lips may gently superimpose [ɔ] to create the illusion of [y]. Never pinch or over-round this vowel. Such constriction closes off the sound and also creates an incompatibility with surrounding vowel-sounds and their uniform, legato flow.

Diphthongization will be the undesired result of a delayed positioning of the tongue and lips in the formation of [y]. These articulatory parts must assume their position simultaneously, just a split-second before emission. Likewise, these positions must be retained until emission ceases or until the ensuing consonant introduces the new vowel-sound.

PRACTICE:

[i ɔ i ɔ i ɔ i ɔ]	Note that as the tongue rises at the sides to the upper back molars, the lips flatten; and that as the lips round, the tongue lowers at the sides.
[i y i y i y i y]	Note the stationary position of the tongue while the lips alternately round and flatten. The lip-rounding must be gentle and unforced.
[ɔ y ɔ y ɔ y ɔ y]	Note the stationary position of the lips, while the sides of the tongue alternately rise and lower to and away from the upper back molars.

SPELLINGS:

<u>u</u>, <u>û</u>, <u>ü</u>(e), -<u>ue</u>(-)	*as a general rule,* when the only vowel-letter in a syllable (if nasalized is [œ̃], see [œ̃])	d<u>u</u> [d y] (of the)	d<u>û</u> [d y] (had)

une   murmurer
[y n ə]   [m y r m y r e]
(a, an)   (to murmur)

cru/el   vue
[k r y ɛ l] [v y]
(cruel)   (sight)

il tue/ra
[i l t y r a]
(he will kill)

Esaü   ciguë
[e z a y]   [s i g y]
(Esau)   (hemlock)

but note that *u* is usually silent after *g* and *q* (see [ɥ], [w] for exceptions):

langu/ir   langu/eur
[l ɑ̃ g i r]   [l ɑ̃ g œ r]
(to languish)   (languor)

qu/i   qu/eue
[k i]   [k ø]
(who)   (tail)

eu, eû   rarely, and only in forms of the verb *avoir* and in isolated words

j'ai eu   il eût
[ʒ e y]   [i l y]
(I had)   (he had)

gageure
[g a ʒ y r ə]
(wager)

10. O-slash [ø]   Model word: deux [d ø] (two)

FORMATION:

Tongue in [ɛ] position, lips in [o] position. In contrast with [y], it is the lip position of [o] that insures this vowel's formation. The tongue position of [ɛ] takes on an added importance in the upper register when the lip position may be slightly relaxed for vocal comfort, if necessary. The [o] position of the lips is especially important in the middle and lower registers. As with [o], excessive dropping of the jaw should be avoided, since this makes lip-rounding more difficult. The rounding for [ø] can be arrived at by an energetic whistle positioning of the lips. Without the appropriate degree of lip-rounding, [ø] will not be authentic. Be sure that the lips leave the teeth in their rounding. Avoid excessive tongue-raising or [ø] will sound too much like [y]. Whereas [y] is essentially a tongue vowel, [ø] is essentially a lip vowel. Remember: find the whistle position for [ø]!

Delayed positioning of the tongue and lips will result in diphthongization. Instead, these must assume their positions simultaneously, a split-second before emission. These positions must be maintained until emission ceases or until the ensuing consonant that introduces the new vowel-sound.

PRACTICE:

[ɛ o ɛ o ɛ o ɛ o]	Note that as the tongue gently rises at the sides to the upper back molars, the lips flatten, and that as the lips round, the tongue lowers at the sides.
[ɛ ø ɛ ø ɛ ø ɛ ø]	Note the stationary position of the tongue while the lips alternately round to the whistle position and then flatten.
[o ø o ø o ø o ø]	Note the stationary, rounded position of the lips, while the tongue alternately rises and lowers. Care must be taken to avoid pinching [ø] through an excessive raising of the sides of the tongue.

SPELLINGS:

eu	when final in word	feu [f ø] (fire)	adieu [a d j ø] (farewell)
	when followed by silent, final consonant(s), usually *t* and *x*	deux [d ø] (two)	il pleut [i l p l ø] (it is raining)
	in final *-euse*, *-eute*, *-eutre*	heureuse [(ø) r ø z ə] (happy)	meute [m ø t ə] (mob)
		neutre [n ø t r ə] (neutral)	
	in a few isolated words	meule [m ø l ə] (hayrick)	meunier(-ère) [m ø n j e] [-ɛ r ə] (miller)
	in vocalic harmonization, when unstressed [œ] followed by stressed [ø] closes to [(ø)]	heureux [(ø) r ø] (happy)	

	in derivatives of the above	deuxième [d ø z j ɛ m ə] (second)	
oeu	when final in word	voeu [v ø] (vow)	
	when followed by silent, final consonant(s)	noeud [n ø] (knot)	des boeufs [d ɛ b ø] (oxen)
ueu(e)	after *g* or *q* (where first *u* is silent) when followed by silent, final consonant or as final *-ueue* in final *-ueuse*	fougueux [f u g ø] (fiery) moqueuse [m ɔ k ø z ə] (mocking)	queue [k ø] (tail)
e	only in vocalic harmonization when unstressed [œ], given as [ə] in the dictionary, is followed by stressed [ø]; to be phoneticized as [(ø)]	cheveux [ʃ (ø) v ø] (hair)	

11. Oh-ee [œ]   Model word: fleur [f l œ r] (flower)

FORMATION:

Tongue in [ɛ] position, lips in [ɔ] position. This vowel-sound is perhaps the most characteristic and common of the French language, yet often the least understood and the least accurately executed.

Remember that [œ] has three definite characteristics:

Front. This may be insured by proper rounding of the lips and the slight fronting of the tongue. Failure to do so will result in [ɑ] or [ɔ].

Open. Too often [ø] is heard instead of [œ] in such words as *coeur, feuille, le,* etc. Also, the word *de* [d œ] must not sound like *deux* [d ø].

Round. Failure to round the lips in the formation of [œ] will result in the sound of the English vowel in the word *rub*, definitely too flat for a French [œ].

PRACTICE:

[ɔ ɛ ɔ ɛ ɔ ɛ ɔ ɛ]   Note that the sides of the tongue lower as the whole tongue backs for [ɔ], and that the sides of the tongue rise as the whole tongue fronts for [ɛ].

[ɔ œ ɔ œ ɔ œ ɔ œ]   Note that the lips remain stationary in the position of
[ɔ] as the tongue alternately lowers and rises.

[ɛ œ ɛ œ ɛ œ ɛ œ]   Note that the tongue remains stationary in the position
of [ɛ] as the lips alternately round and flatten.

The [œ] and [ɔ], or Schwa

In conversational French, as well as in sung French, [œ] may be long (or
stressed), as in the word *peur* [pœːr], or short (unstressed), as in the word
jeune [ʒœn]. The only difference between these two is one of duration. The
word *peur* takes almost twice the time to say as the word *jeune*.

But one of the greatest discrepancies between spoken and sung French
occurs in the use of the *schwa* ([ə]). This sound may be best described as a
shortened [œ] and is used in the dictionary to phoneticize the vowel-sound
of the word *le* and the first two vowel-sounds of the word *devenir.* This
sound is rounded, but unstressed, and of split-second duration.

Singers must be careful to distinguish between a *schwa* that is a true
schwa and one that must be sounded in singing as a short or unstressed [œ].
In singing, the conversational [ə] rarely occurs within the phrase. It may appear at the end of the phrase, habitually on a very short note, tied or untied,
followed by a rest. Only in this position can final *-e, -es, -ent* be sounded as a
genuine *schwa* in singing, either as a round "uh" or simply as a light expulsion of quasi-vocalized breath after the well-sounded consonant, as shown in
the following examples.

"Fleurs," *Fiançailles pour rire,* **F. Poulenc** – L. de Vilmorin

Carmen (Act III), **G. Bizet**

In the first example, the final *-e* of *cheminée* is sounded as the brief "uh" mentioned above, rounded but unstressed, and of split-second duration. In the second example, the final *-e* of *elle* amounts to a small expulsion of breath after the well-sounded [l].

However, when what is phoneticized in the dictionary as [ə] is assigned a note of any considerable duration, whether within or at the end of a phrase, the vowel-sound of this syllable ceases to be a true [ə]. Instead, it takes on the rounder, more frontal quality of unstressed or short [œ]. For example, in the phrase *le coeur de ce petit* the traditional phoneticization would be [lə k œ r d ə s ə p ə t i], and in the rapid click of French conversation, two of the *schwa*'s would be typically dropped: [lə k œ d ə s p t i]. When sung on note-values of any considerable duration, at least more than split-second, the *schwa* takes on the rounder, more frontal quality of unstressed or short [œ], thus occupying the time allotted to a normal syllable, and must be phoneticized as such:

It would not do to elongate the *schwa* by singing "luh coeur duh suh puhtit," nor would it be any more appropriate to shorten the note-values and thereby destroy the legato of the French vocalic flow. It is this frequency of the *schwa* sounded as short, unstressed [œ] in singing that renders it crucial to the legato. Only the short [œ] can project and carry the same amount of vocalized sound in the appropriate frontal position as the vowels of neighboring syllables. Without it, French sounds uneven, lacks true legato, and is simply less "singable." Above all, it must be kept in mind that the IPA was not conceived with the singing process in mind. The IPA is, after all, only a system. To be useful and applicable to singing, certain adjustments must be made in it. This conversion of the [ə] to short [œ] is one of the most crucial of these adjustments.

SPELLINGS (OF [œ]):

<u>eu</u>	when followed by a pronounced consonant (except in final *-euse, -eute, -eutre,* or in vocalic harmonization; see [o])	fl<u>eu</u>r [f l œ r] (flower)	s<u>eu</u>l [s œ l] (only)
		p<u>eu</u>ple [p œ p l ə] (people)	av<u>eu</u>gle [a v œ g l ə] (blind)
	when followed by [j] (or *-ill-, -il*)	f<u>eu</u>ille [f œ j ə] (leaf)	d<u>eu</u>il [d œ j] (mourning)

o<u>eu</u>	when followed by a pronounced consonant (except *-se*, see [ø])	c<u>oeu</u>r [k œ r] (heart)	<u>oeu</u>f [œ f] (egg)
<u>ueu</u>	after *g* and *q* (where first *u* is silent) and followed by a pronounced consonant (except final *-se*; see [ø])	lang<u>ueu</u>r [l ɑ̃ g œ r] (languor)	vainq<u>ueu</u>r [v ɛ̃ k œ r] (conquering)
<u>ue</u>	only in combinations *cueil-* and *-gueil* when medial and *que* when not followed by double consonant and when final	c<u>ue</u>illir [k œ j i r] (to gather) org<u>ue</u>il [ɔ r g œ j] (pride)	q<u>ue</u>relle [k œ r ɛ l ə] (quarrel) q<u>ue</u> [k œ] (that)
<u>œ</u>	only in combinations *oeil*, *oeill-*	<u>œ</u>il [œ j] (eye)	<u>œ</u>illet [œ j ɛ] (carnation)
<u>e</u>	(phoneticized as [ə] in dictionary) *when final in syllable and not followed by double consonant, or when final in word* (for exceptions see [e], initial combinations)	c<u>e</u>ci [s œ s i] (this) ch<u>e</u>velure [ʃ œ v œ l y r œ] (head of hair)	j<u>e</u> [ʒ œ] (I)
	in initial *ress-* (except in *ressusciter* is [e])	r<u>e</u>ssembler [r œ s ɑ̃ b l e] (to resemble)	r<u>e</u>ssentir [r œ s ɑ̃ t i r] (to feel)
	in initial *dess-* of two isolated words (normally [(e)])	d<u>e</u>ssus [d œ s y] (over)	d<u>e</u>ssous [d œ s u] (under)
	in final unstressed *-es* (plural endings of nouns and adjectives, verb endings) but never in short words like *les* (see [ɛ])	les bell<u>es</u> fill<u>es</u> [l ɛ b ɛ l œ f i j œ] (the beautiful girls) m'aim<u>es</u>-tu? [m ɛ m œ t y] (do you love me?)	
	in final unstressed *-ent* of third person plural verb endings (in other words may be [ɑ̃] or [ɛ̃]; see these)	ils parl<u>ent</u> [i l p a r l œ] (they speak) vienn<u>ent</u>-ils? [v j ɛ n œ t i l] (are they coming?)	

Note: See below concerning syllabification of final -e, -es, -ent and methods of determining presence of [ə] or short [œ] according to the musical setting.

<u>ai</u>	rare, only in forms of the verb *faire* (to make, do) beginning with unstressed *fais-* followed by stressed syllable, and derivatives (note that *je fais* is [ʒ œ f ɛ])	nous f<u>ai</u>sons [n u f œ z õ] (we are making) je f<u>ai</u>sais [ʒ œ f œ z ɛ] (I was making) malf<u>ai</u>sant [m a l f œ z ã] (evil-minded)
<u>on</u>	only in the first syllable of the word *monsieur*, phoneticized as [ə] in the dictionary and often closed to [(ø)]	m<u>on</u>sieur [m œ s j ø] or [m (ø) s j ø] (sir)

PRONUNCIATION AND SYLLABIFICATION
OF FINAL -e, -es, -ent

Below are listed the following: the conjugation and English translations of the verb *parler* (to speak or talk) in the present indicative tense and some underlined examples of final, unstressed -e, -es as they appear in nouns, pronouns, and adjectives:

Parler (to speak, to talk)

SINGULAR		PLURAL	
1. je parl<u>e</u>	(I speak)	nous parlons	(we speak)
2. tu parl<u>es</u>	(you speak)	vous parlez	(you speak)
3. il parl<u>e</u>	(he speaks)	ils parl<u>ent</u>	(they speak)
ell<u>e</u> parl<u>e</u>	(she speaks)	ell<u>es</u> parl<u>ent</u>	(they speak)

Ils écout<u>ent</u> mais n'entend<u>ent</u> rien aux mots qu<u>e</u> nos bouch<u>es</u> s<u>e</u>
disent.
(They listen but understand nothing of the words that our lips say
to each other.)
("Sérénade italienne," Chausson-Bourget)

Les lign<u>es</u>, les couleurs, les sons devienn<u>ent</u> vagu<u>es</u>.
(The outlines, the colors, the sounds become vague.)
("Soir," Fauré-Samain)

All of the underlined syllables in the above examples are examples of the final -e, -es, -ent sounding as [ə] or short [œ]. Note that in the conjugation of the verb *parler* the endings of the first, second, and third person singular and of the third person plural forms are *all* pronounced the same. In conversation, they would all be dropped, with only [p a r l] sounding for all four, which is *not* the case in French poetic versification, a traditional system of syllabification followed by both poets and composers of vocal music.

Again, a major difference between spoken and sung French must be considered by the singer. Note that in the examples above, all the final, unstressed syllables are followed by words beginning with a consonant. The French line of verse is governed by *syllabic count*. Every final -e, -es, -ent that appears before a word beginning with a consonant must be counted as a syllable and is accordingly set to a note by the composer (except in rare instances discussed below). Of course, if the final -e is immediately followed by a word beginning with a vowel-sound, this final -e will be elided. For example:

Elle me parle.   Elle me parlé en français.
[ɛ l œ m œ p a r l œ]   [ɛ l œ m œ p a r l ɑ̃ f r ɑ̃ s ɛ]
(She speaks to me.)   (She speaks to me in French.)

Similarly, the final -es and -ent of verb endings must be syllabified and sounded as short [œ] within the line when followed by a consonant-sound or a vowel-sound (in which case the final -s or -t is sounded in liaison):

Tu parles trop!   Tu parles en français.
[t y p a r l œ t r o]   [t y p a r l œ z ɑ̃ f r ɑ̃ s ɛ]
(You talk too much!)   (You speak in French.)

Elles parlent toujours.   Elles parlent encore.
[ɛ l œ p a r l œ t u ʒ u r]   [ɛ l œ p a r l œ t ɑ̃ k ɔ r ə]
(They always talk.)   (They are still talking.)

These final, unstressed syllables may not be capriciously dropped or elided in singing, unless, of course, the composer has specifically indicated by means of notation that they be omitted, which sometimes, but rarely, occurs in the vocal music of a few composers (see below).

Remember also that final, unstressed -ent may be phoneticized as [ə] or short [œ] only in third person plural verb endings. Beware of final -ient, a third person *singular* verb ending sounding as [j ɛ̃], or final -ent in nouns, adjectives, and adverbs sounding as [ɑ̃]:

Il vient fréquemment.   Le mouvement est lent.
[i l v j ɛ̃ f r e k a m ɑ̃]   [l œ m u v œ m ɑ̃ ɛ l ɑ̃]
(He comes frequently.)   (The tempo is slow.)

SINGING FINAL, UNSTRESSED -e, -es, -ent: [œ] OR [ə]?

It is the musical notation that dictates the vocalization of a final, unstressed
-e, -es, -ent and the subsequent distinction between [œ] and [ə]. In either
case, none of these syllables must ever be accented. Tempo and literary
style play significant roles in determining the phonetic quality and duration of these final, weak syllables as well as notation. At any rate, most
composers are quite clear as to how they wish these syllables to be
sounded; it is merely a question of deciphering their indications, which,
although at times are rather specific, are often ignored.

   Sound final -e, -es, -ent as short, unstressed [œ] at the end of the phrase if:
   1. They are assigned a new note on a pitch different from the preceding
pitch.

"Le Secret," G. Fauré-A. Silvestre

   2. They are assigned an *untied* note of sizable duration on the same
pitch as the note before, especially in a slow-to-moderate tempo and also
when followed by a rest sufficient to obtain a good breath for the next
phrase.

"Le Secret," G. Fauré-A. Silvestre

   3. Sometimes even a tied note may be sounded as [œ] if the tempo and
mood so permit or indicate, and especially if there is a rest following that
is sufficient for a good breath for the following phrase.

"Il pleure dans mon coeur," Debussy-Verlaine

Sound final *-e*, *-es*, *-ent* as [ə] at the end of the phrase if:

1. They are assigned a short tied note of the same pitch as the preceding note, especially when followed by a rest that allows just enough time for a breath, no rest at all, and/or a vocally taxing note or phrase. In this case sing the vowel-sound preceding the final, weak syllable for the combined value of the tied notes, then the [ə] or, if there is a consonant, sound it as well as the [ə]:

Carmen **(Act III), G. Bizet**

"Il pleure dans mon coeur," *Ariettes oubliées*, **C. Debussy-P. Verlaine**

2. They are assigned a short, *untied* note of the *same* pitch as the preceding note and are immediately followed by a new phrase with no rest sufficient for breathing. The consonant, if there is one, must be clearly sounded. Then, in place of sounding the final, weak syllable as short

[œ], supply a split-second [ə] and make time for the optional breath in preparation for the next phrase:

"Ici-bas," G. Fauré—Sully-Prudhomme

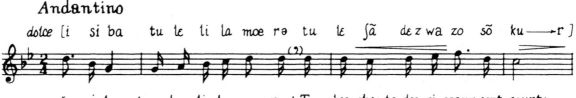

3. They are assigned a grace note, a most specific request for an [ə] by the composer:

"Le Dromadaire," *Le Bestiaire,* **F. Poulenc**-G. Apollinaire

Manon **(Act III), J. Massenet**

When a vowel-sound, not a consonant-sound, precedes the final, weak syllable and this syllable is assigned a grace note, exclude it entirely:

Carmen **(Act III), G. Bizet**

Sound final *-e*, *-es*, *-ent* as short, unstressed [œ] within the phrase if assigned a note and followed by a word beginning with a consonant. Note that final *-e* is elided if followed by a word beginning with a vowel-sound; the notation will again testify to this, as shown in the following musical examples:

Faust (Act I), C. Gounod

Lia's recitative and aria, L'Enfant prodigue, C. Debussy

Do not sound final *-e*, *-es*, *-ent* at all (as either [ə] or [œ]) within the line if they are assigned a short tied note or no note at all. This is common in the works of Maurice Ravel and a few others, the intended effect being one of natural declamation. Here, the consonant preceding the final, weak vowel is well-sounded and immediately linked to the next consonant- or vowel-sound:

"Asie," *Shéhérazade,* M. Ravel-T. Klingsor

"Le Paon," *Histoires naturelles,* **M. Ravel-J.** Renard

Also, within the line, final *-e*, *-es*, *-ent* and even medial *-e-* are sometimes contracted in the text itself with the notation seconding these contractions. In this case, they are not sounded and accordingly not phoneticized, except when they are assigned a grace note or a short tied note before a rest or when they are final in the line or phrase:

Louise **(Act II), G. Charpentier**

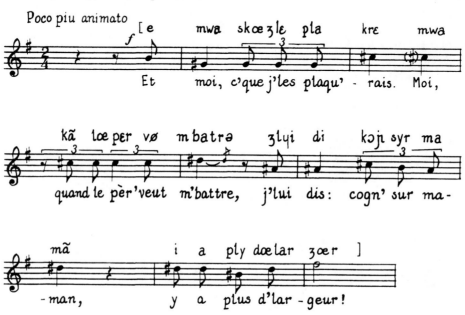

VOCALIZATION OF THE HIATUS OCCURRING IN FINAL [i œ], [e œ], AND [y œ]

As already stated, hiatus, or the sounding of the two neighboring vowel-sounds, occasionally occurs in French. One of the most common incidences of such hiatus appears when stressed [i], [e], or [y] is followed by a short, unstressed [œ] at the end of a musical phrase. In all three of these combinations, the sides of the tongue must be raised to the upper molars for the stressed vowel, then lowered directly to form the ensuing [œ] with *no* [i] or [j] in between (thus incorrectly rendering [e i œ] or [e j œ]). The passage from the stressed vowel-sound to the unstressed [œ] must be direct and immediate with no sound in between. The most common combination is [e œ] as it occurs in the following example:

"De Rêve," *Proses lyriques,* C. Debussy

If the [e] of *navrée* is properly executed, half the battle is already won. The raised position of the sides of the tongue for [e] should discourage any further tongue-raising before the lower tongue position for the unstressed [œ]. Any additional tongue-raising before [œ] will create [e i œ] or [e j œ], which are decidedly unacceptable. The [œ] must, of course, never be accented or stressed here. Also, the singer should formulate the [œ] by rounding the lips and a gentle dropping of the tongue and jaw. Some singers erroneously attempt to produce such an [œ] "inside" the mouth. This will only lead to lack of clarity and bad vocal habits. Others insist on singing [ø] in place of [œ] here; this is equally incorrect. Finally, if the desired effect is [i ə] or [e ə], sound a round, split-second [œ] after the stressed vowel for the *schwa*.

EXERCISES

1. Intone the following, slowly and legato, with one breath per set of brackets:

[i →e →ɛ →a →] [ɑ →ɔ →o →u →] [f y →] [f ø →] [f œ →]
[s y →ø →] [s y →œ →] [y →ø →œ →] [i →y →i →]
[e →ø →e →] [ɛ →œ →ɛ →] [i →œ →] [e →œ →] [y →œ →] [i ə]
[e ə] [ø r ø] [l œ v ø p u r l a v i œ] [d j ø ʒ y s t œ] [s i t y l œ v ø]
[l a f l œ r d œ m a v i ɛ f ɛ r m e œ] [v u m œ d i t œ d œ m œ t ɛ r ə]
[p u r l œ k œ r k i l u b l i ə]

2. Carefully copy the following text, including all accent marks and underlines, skipping a line between each line of verse. Then, above each underlined vowel-letter insert the proper representative phonetic symbol in brackets. Use the Debussy setting of *Il pleure dans mon coeur* to determine the sounding of final *-e*. Final *e*'s that are not underlined should be elided. Be able to intone all underlined vowels.

Il pleure dans mon coeur
Comme il pleut sur la ville
Quelle est cette langueur
Qui pénètre mon coeur?
O bruit doux de la pluie
Par terre et sur les toits!
Pour un coeur qui s'ennuie
O le bruit de la pluie!

Il pleure sans raison
Dans ce coeur qui s'écoeure.
Quoi! nulle trahison?
Ce deuil est sans raison.
C'est bien la pire peine
De ne savoir pourquoi,
Sans amour et sans haine,
Mon coeur a tant de peine.

THE NASAL VOWELS

12.	[ɑ̃]	enfant	[ɑ̃fɑ̃]
13.	[ɔ̃]	bon	[bɔ̃]
14.	[ɛ̃]	vin	[vɛ̃]
15.	[œ̃]	un parfum	[œ̃parfœ̃]

Three important principles govern the nasal vowels and their production:

1. *Over-nasalization is neither good singing nor good French.* In a sense, "nasalization" is a misnomer, and, indeed, a misleading term for the singer. A "nasal" vowel is correctly resonated in the nasal cavities which are located behind the nose, in the "yawn," more or less in the center of the head. It must *never* be placed solely in the nose! A correctly resonated nasal vowel-sound has *added* richness and depth. This is achieved when one-third of the vocalic flow is allowed to resonate in the nasal cavities, right above the soft palate and behind the nose. The soft palate is gently dropped in the process, thus permitting entry into these

resonating chambers in the center of the head. The process has often been compared to "covering the tone" and, as stated above, "singing in the yawn." The major part of the vocalic flow, however, must continue to emanate from the mouth. A nasalized vowel should not shift the basic placement or timbre of the voice, but instead is a heightening, coloring, and enrichment of the singer's normal production. The misconception that "nosey nasals" will "Frenchify" one's French will only lead to a parody of the language. One has only to listen to an educated Frenchman's conversation to understand that nasality per se is absent from his speech. Indeed, many French people, and for that matter Europeans in general, find American speech to be excessively "nasal," or at best "twangy." It is therefore self-incriminating for well-meaning Americans to sing French "nasal" vowels with this alleged American nasality, besides being linguistically incorrect and vocally unhealthy. Admittedly, some French singers of the "cabaret" variety revel in an exaggeration of the nasal vowels. This is entirely appropriate to a certain style of singing in French popular song or *chanson,* of which Edith Piaf is the model. But comparable differences between the "popular" and "legit" vocal styles can be cited in the United States, as in any country. Even the exponents of French art song display added nasal resonance from time to time, but only for expressive or coloristic effect, for mood, or even intended vulgarity on occasion. Such additional nasality must be used sparingly and, above all, artistically and responsibly. Do not try to "out-French the French" with your nose—you may find yourself being accused of sounding "too American" (as if there could be nothing worse)!

2. *The most distinctive feature of each of the four nasal vowels is its basic vowel quality, not its nasalization.* How often the word "nasal" appears scribbled over a syllable in a singer's score. Nasal *what?* Such a notation completely disregards the fact that it is the basic vowel quality that is being nasalized that determines the syllable's particular pronunciation and consequently the meaning of the word. Imagine an indiscriminate nosey "honk" for each of the following words, each of whose pronunciation is differentiated by a definite vowel quality and not by nasal resonance:

lent   [l ɑ̃]   (slow)
long   [l ɔ̃]   (long)
lin   [l ɛ̃]   (flax)
l'un   [l œ̃]   (the one)

It is *not* just nasalization, but *what* vowel-sound is being nasalized that counts here.

3. *The* m *or* n *that follows every nasalized vowel-letter (or all nasalized vowel-letters) is silent.* A nasal vowel is just that, a *vowel,* not a vowel-plus-a-consonant, a sort of *m* or *n,* or the faint "ng," a consonant-

sound nonexistent in French that so many non-French singers seem to enjoy attaching to the end of the nasalized syllable. Some dictionaries, not to be recommended, even suggest this quasi-Oriental (but hardly French) sound in their clumsy "phoneticizations." Like any vowel formed in accordance with the principle of legato, the nasal vowel must fill the duration of its assigned note-value, unaltered and unshortened. There may very well be a consonant-sound following the nasalized vowel, but it will probably be in the following word or syllable. The one and only time that nasalizing *n* may be sounded is when it is in liaison with the following vowel. Nasalizing *m* is never sounded under any circumstances. When underlining nasal-vowel spellings in the text, be sure to include the nasalizing *m* or *n*.

RULE: Any vowel-letter(s) followed by *m* or *n* is usually nasalized unless this *m* or *n* is followed by:

1. a vowel-letter or vowel-sound in the same word, or
2. an *m*, *n*, or *h* in the same word.

So, whereas the vowel-sound of the word *sein* [s ɛ̃] (breast) is nasalized, the name of the river flowing through Paris, the Seine, is not, since the *n* is followed by a vowel-letter. The first syllable of the word *important* is [ɛ̃] in French, but in the word *immense* [i m m ɑ̃ s ə] the same syllable is not nasalized due to the double *-mm-*. The same goes for *intense* [ɛ̃ t ɑ̃ s ə] and *innocent* [i n n ɔ s ɑ̃]. And although the word *bon* [b õ] is most definitely nasalized, the same letters in the word *bonheur* [b ɔ n œ r] are not, due to the *h* following them.

PRACTICE

Decide which of the vowel-letters in the following words would be nasalized and, according to the RULE, give the reason why:

enfant	inutile	bonté	inhumain	dompter	damner
faim	femme	songe	sonner	tomber	automne
plein	pleine	dans	danser	canot	pain
gaine	immédiat	Jeanne	inné	fantôme	intime

12. Dark *a* nasal [ɑ̃] 　　　　Model word: <u>en</u>fant [ɑ̃ f ɑ̃] (child)

FORMATION:

Dark *a* nasal is slightly more rounded than basic [ɑ], approaching "aw" or [ɔ]. Care must be taken not to flatten or back the vowel; the result is an unpleasant nasal rasp with displaced resonance. Rather, [ã] is somewhat rounded, frontal, and "tall." Of course, over-rounding will result in [õ] and must be avoided.

SPELLINGS (Remember the Rule):

en, an, em, am	*as a general rule*	cependant [s œ p ã d ã] (however)	temple [t ã p l ə] (temple)
		champ [ʃ ã] (field)	
	not in final *-ien*, or in final *-iens*, *-ient* of verb forms (see [ɛ̃])		
	not in a few proper nouns and words of foreign origin (see [ɛ̃]):		
	Carmen Poulenc [k a r m ɛ n] [p u l ɛ̃ k] (Carmen) (Poulenc)		
	but, contrary to the RULE, [ã] appears in all words beginning with *emm-* or *enn-* (except *ennemi* [ɛ n œ m i])	ennui [ã n ɥ i] (boredom)	
		emmener [ã m œ n e] (to take away)	
	also, contrary to the RULE, [ã] appears in a few composite words beginning with *en-* plus a vowel-letter	enivré [ã n i v r e] (intoxicated)	
		enorgueillir [ã n ɔ r g œ j i r] (to make proud)	
		s'enamourer [s ã n a m u r e] (to fall in love with)	
aen, aën, aon, ean	*as a general rule,* with rare exceptions	Saint-Saëns [s ɛ̃ s ã s] (Saint-Saëns)	Messiaen [m e s j ã] (Messiaen)
		Jean [ʒ ã] (John)	paon [p ã] (peacock, m.)

13. Closed *o* nasal [õ]   Model word: b<u>on</u> [b õ] (good)

FORMATION:

Give the basic vowel [o] resonance in the nasal cavities. This vowel is customarily and quite inaccurately given in the dictionary as [ɔ̃], which sounds closer to [ɑ̃] as in *banc* than the nasalized *o* of *bon*. Always close the nasalized *o* and phoneticize it accordingly.

SPELLINGS (Remember the Rule):

<u>on</u>, o<u>m</u>   *as a general rule*

m<u>on</u>	l<u>ong</u>
[m õ]	[l õ]
(my)	(long)
t<u>om</u>beau	b<u>on</u>té
[t õ b o]	[b õ t e]
(tomb)	(kindness)

but, denasalization may occur in liaison with *bon*:

B<u>on</u> appétit!
[b ɔ n a p e t i]
(Eat hearty!)

<u>eon</u>   *as a general rule*

pig<u>eon</u>
[p i ʒ õ]
(pigeon)

14. Open *e* nasal [ɛ̃]   Model word: v<u>in</u> [v ɛ̃] (wine)

FORMATION:

In nasalizing [ɛ̃], the singer must soften the basic vowel-sound by resonating it in the "uh." Above all, do not allow the basic vowel-sound either to spread or be accompanied by a nasal raspiness. Aim for a mellow, rich sound. This vowel-sound can be most unattractive if the resonance is not properly distributed. ("uh" = the vowel-sound of English 'the')

SPELLINGS (Remember the Rule):

<u>in</u>, i<u>m</u>, <u>yn</u>, y<u>m</u>   *as a general rule*

br<u>in</u>	<u>in</u>fini
[b r ɛ̃]	[ɛ̃ f i n i]
(sprig)	(infinite)
s<u>im</u>ple	Jocel<u>yn</u>
[s ɛ̃ p l ə]	[ʒ ɔ s l ɛ̃]
(simple)	(Jocelyn)

		sympathie [s ɛ̃ p a t i] (liking)	thym [t ɛ̃] (thyme)
ain, aim, ein, eim	*as a general rule*	pain [p ɛ̃] (bread)	faim [f ɛ̃] (hunger)
		ceinture [s ɛ̃ t y r ə] (belt)	Reims [r ɛ̃ s] (Reims)
en	although usually [ɑ̃], may be [ɛ̃] in final *-ien*(*s*)	bien [b j ɛ̃] (well)	liens [l j ɛ̃] (bonds)
	in final *-ient* of third person singular forms of such verbs as *venir, tenir,* etc.	il vient [i l v j ɛ̃] (he comes)	on tient [õ t j ɛ̃] (one holds)
	in a few proper nouns	Poulenc [p u l ɛ̃ k] (Poulenc)	Abencérages [a b ɛ̃ s e r a ʒ ə] (Abencerages)
		Benjamin [b ɛ̃ ʒ a m ɛ̃] (Benjamin)	
oin [w ɛ̃], uin [ɥ ɛ̃] or [ɛ̃]	*as a general rule*	loin [l w ɛ̃] (far)	point [p w ɛ̃] (point)
		juin [ʒ ɥ ɛ̃] (June)	coquin [k ɔ k ɛ̃] (rogue)

15. *OH-ee* nasal [œ̃]   Model words: un parfum [œ̃ p a r f œ̃]
(a fragrance)

FORMATION:

Begin by intoning the model word for [œ], *fleur* [f l œ r]. One by one, leave off the consonant-sounds, thus isolating the vowel-sound. Then resonate this in the nasal cavities. The resulting sound should be [œ̃], the French word *un*. One must be sure to nasalize [œ], not [ɛ], in the formation of this nasal vowel. Conversational French may condone this interchange of basic vowel quality, but in singing French a definite distinction must be made between them. Also remember that any [œ], nasalized or not, must be *front, open,* and *round.*

SPELLINGS (Remember the Rule):

un, um	as a general rule	un parfum	humble
		[œ̃ p a r f œ̃]	[œ̃ b l ə]
		a fragrance	(humble)
		lundi	
		[l œ̃ d i]	
		(Monday)	
eun	only in the expression:	à jeun	
		[a ʒ œ̃]	
		(fasting)	

EXERCISES

1. Intone the following, slowly and legato, with one breath per set of brackets:

[i→e→ɛ→a→] [ɑ→ɔ→o→u→]
[y→ø→œ→] [fɑ̃→] [fõ→] [fɛ̃→] [fœ̃]
[fifɑ̃fefɑ̃fɛfɑ̃fafɑ̃] [fɑfɑ̃fɔfɑ̃fofɑ̃fufɑ̃] [fyfɑ̃føfɑ̃fœfɑ̃]

(Repeat the above line, substituting the three other nasal vowels—[õ], [ɛ̃], and [œ̃]—for [ɑ̃].)

[i→ɑ̃→] [e→ɑ̃→] [ɛ→ɑ̃→] [a→ɑ̃→]
[ɑ→ɑ̃→] [ɔ→ɑ̃→] [o→ɑ̃→] [u→ɑ̃→]
[y→ɑ̃→] [ø→ɑ̃→] [œ→ɑ̃→]

(Repeat the above three lines, substituting the three other nasal vowels—[õ], [ɛ̃], and [œ̃]—for [ɑ̃].)

2. Copy the texts given below, skipping a line between each line of verse. Underline all vowel-sounds (always underline nasalizing *m* or *n* that follows the nasalized vowel-letters as part of the vowel-sound), and determine their phonetic quality by inserting the proper phonetic symbol above the line. Phoneticize all final -*e*'s as [œ] unless they are elided with the following vowel-sound. Indicate all elisions.

   a. Instant charmant où la crainte fait trêve,
      Où nous sommes deux, seulement!
     Tiens, Manon, en marchant, je viens de faire un rêve!
      (*Manon*, Massenet)

b. En vain pour éviter les réponses amères,
En vain tu mêleras,
Cela ne sert à rien,
Les cartes sont sincères,
Et ne mentiront pas!
  (*Carmen,* Bizet)

c. Je veux vivre
Dans ce rêve
Qui m'enivre
Longtemps encor!
  (*Roméo et Juliette,* Gounod)

d. Je n'en dis rien. Cela peut nous paraître étrange,
parce que nous ne voyons jamais que l'envers des
destinées, l'envers même de la nôtre. . . . Il avait
toujours suivi mes conseils jusqu'ici, j'avais cru
le rendre heureux en l'envoyant demander la main de
la princesse Ursule. . . . Il ne pouvait pas rester seul,
et depuis la mort de sa femme il était triste d'être
seul; et ce mariage allait mettre fin à de longues
guerres, à de vieilles haines. . . . Il ne l'a pas voulu
ainsi.
  (*Pelléas et Mélisande,* Debussy)

Phoneticization, Formation, and Singing of the Semiconsonants

A semiconsonant sound has some of the characteristics of both vowels and consonants. For example, the letter *y* in the English word *you* produces the semiconsonant sound [j]. The *y* here functions as a consonant since it ushers in the vowel-sound. Although it lacks any real blockage or friction, its semi-vocalic nature cannot qualify it as a vowel, since it does not constitute a syllable. (See Recording Illustration E.)

THE SEMICONSONANTS

1. [ɥ]   n<u>ui</u>t
2. [j]   d<u>i</u>eu
3. [w]   s<u>oi</u>r

All three of the French semiconsonants have three things in common:

1. They are always *before* the vowel-sound of the syllable.

2. They are introductory closures that open into or glide into the more open vowel-sound, which in turn occupies the duration of the note-value.

3. They never, in themselves, constitute a syllable. When they become vowel-sounds (and/or when they are assigned a note) they lose their qualities as semiconsonants, each being transformed into a particular vowel-sound.

1. Semiconsonant *y* [ɥ]

Model word: n<u>ui</u>t [n ɥ i] (night)

FORMATION:

Technically speaking, [ɥ] is a split-second [y] (formed by the tongue position of [i] and the lip position of [ɔ]) at the very beginning of the syllable. The vowel-sound it ushers in must occupy the duration of the syllable and the note-value. Above all, the singer must not settle for [w] instead of [ɥ]. This can always be guaranteed by the presence of [i] and its tongue position in every [ɥ]. Each combination presents its own difficulty:

1. [ɥi]. Concentrate on singing [i] throughout the duration of the syllable, from its very beginning to its end. Begin the syllable on [i], with the lips rounded to a [ɔ]. While sustaining the [i], draw the lips back from the [ɔ] position to their natural, unrounded state. The higher the note, the less rounded the [ɔ]; the lower the note, the more rounded the [ɔ]. If the [i] is not present at the very outset of the syllable, the result will be [wi], which is not acceptable. Practice singing *huis* [ɥi], *puis* [pɥi], *pluie* [plɥi], and *bruit* [brɥi].

2. [ɥe]. Concentrate on singing [e] for the duration of the syllable, from its very beginning to its end. Begin the syllable on [e], with the lips rounded to a [ɔ]. While sustaining the [e], draw the lips back from the [ɔ] position to their natural, unrounded state. The higher the note, the less rounded the [ɔ]; the lower the note, the more rounded the [ɔ]. If the [e] is not present at the very beginning of the syllable, the result will be [we]. As with [ɥi], the superimposed [ɔ] of [ɥe] is of split-second duration and must occur over the [e] that is always present in the syllable. Practice singing *tué* [tɥe] and *nuée* [nɥe].

3. [ɥɛ]. Sing a split-second [y] at the outset of the syllable, gliding into the [ɛ] by simultaneously lowering the tongue, releasing the jaw, and unrounding the lips. Again, it is helpful to conceive of the syllable as being composed entirely of [ɛ], with a touch of [y] superimposed over [ɛ] at the beginning of the syllable. There must be no intermediary sound or diphthong such as [ɥiɛ] between the two sounds. Beware of singing [we] in-

stead of [ɥe]. Practice singing *muet* [mɥɛ], *annuaire* [anɥɛr], and *tuais* [tɥɛ].

4. [ɥa]. The same procedure applies as for [ɥɛ], except that [a] is substituted for [ɛ]. Care must be taken not to insert [w] between the semiconsonant and the vowel-sound [ɥwa]. Practice singing *suave* [sɥavə] and *nuage* [nɥaʒə].

5. [ɥø] and [ɥœ]. Here, the semiconsonant and the predominating vowel-sound are very closely related in formation; therefore, great care must be taken to distinguish between them. A split-second [y] at the outset of the syllable must glide into a slightly less rounded and closed [ø], as in the last syllable of *luxueux* [lyksɥø]. In the case of [ɥœ], the split-second [y] at the beginning of the syllable glides into a considerably less rounded and more open [œ] as in *lueur* [lɥœr]. The glide from the semiconsonant to the vowel-sound must be smooth enough to conceal the seam at which the former ends and the latter begins. Yet, upon emission, the semiconsonant must be distinctly more closed than the resultant vowel-sound. Practice singing the words *luxueux* [lyksɥø] and *lueur* [lɥœr].

SPELLINGS:

u   in the following combinations of vowel-letters:

  in *ui, uie* remember *u* is silent after *g* and *q* except in the word *aigu* [egy] and derivatives

puis	pluie
[pɥi]	[plɥi]
(then)	(rain)
juin	aiguille
[ʒɥɛ̃]	[egɥijə]
(June)	(needle)

  in *ua, uai*; remember *u* is silent after *g* and *q*, but may be [w] in this combination; see [w]

suave	sanctuaire
[sɥavə]	[sɑ̃ktɥɛrə]
(suave)	(sanctuary)

  in *ué, ueu*, and medial *-ue-*; remember in final *-ue* is [y] or, if after *g* or *q* is [œ]:

vue	que
[vy]	[kœ]
(sight)	(that)

habitué	lueur
[abitɥe]	[lɥœr]
(accustomed)	(glimmer)
luxueux	muet
[lyksɥø]	[mɥɛ]
(luxurious)	(mute)

  in *uy* (after a single consonant); if after consonant plus *l* or *r* is [y]:

bruyère	fuyez
[bryjɛrə]	[fɥije]
(heather)	(flee)

remember *u* is silent after *g* or *q:*

G*u̸*y

[g i]

(Guy)

Note: If letter *u*, normally sounding and phoneticized as [ɥ], is provided a note in the score, it is sounded and phoneticized as [y]:

♪ | ♩. ♪   ♪ ♪ | ♩. ♪

l<u>e</u>s nu<u>age</u>s   or   l<u>e</u>s nu-<u>a</u>-ges

[l ɛ n ɥ a ʒ œ]   [l ɛ n y a ʒ œ]

(the clouds)   (the clouds)

2. Yod [j]

Model word: d<u>ie</u>u [d j ø] (god)

FORMATION:

The same as for letter *y* of English *you*.

SPELLINGS:

i, ï	preceded by a single consonant in the following combinations of vowel-letters; *ia, ïa, iai, iau, ie, iè, ié, io, ieu, ïeu* (not in medial *-ie-* in some verbs and derivatives, see [i]; not in final *-ie*, see [i])	d<u>i</u>able [d j a b l ə] (devil)	na<u>ï</u>ade [n a j a d ə] (water-nymph)
		l<u>i</u>aison [l j ɛ z õ] (liaison)	m<u>i</u>auler [m j o l e] (to mew)
		b<u>ie</u>n [b j ɛ̃] (well)	b<u>iè</u>re [b j ɛ r ə] (beer)
		pass<u>i</u>on [p ɑ s j õ] (passion)	pit<u>i</u>é [p i t j e] (pity)
		ad<u>i</u>eu [a d j ø] (farewell)	a<u>ï</u>eux [a j ø] (elders)
<u>il</u>, <u>ill</u>, <u>ll</u>	in final *ail, eil, euil, œil* and *ueil, il* sounds as [j] before a vowel-sound; *ill* sounds as [j] in medial *aill, eill, euill, ouill, ueill* and *œill* but as [ij] otherwise; note division in examples	l'œ<u>il</u>‿ouvert [l œ j u v ɛ r] (with open eye)	deu<u>il</u>‿éternel [d œ j e t ɛ r n ɛ l] (eternal mourning)

trava/**iller**   abe/**ille**
[travaje]   [abɛjə]
(to work)   (bee)

feu/**ille**   grenou/**ille**
[fœjə]   [grənujə]
(leaf)   (frog)

cue/**illir**   œ/**illet**
[kœjir]   [œjɛ]
(to gather)   (carnation)

fi/**lle**   jui/**llet**
[fijə]   [ʒɥijɛ]
(daughter)   (July)

Exceptions:

1) when followed by a consonant-sound or final in line (before a rest), final -il sounds as diphthong "clipped i" [ⁱ]:

soleil couchant   O deuil!
[sɔlɛⁱkuʃã]   [odœⁱ]
(setting sun)   (Oh mourning!)

But: Ce deuil est sans raison.
[sœdœjɛsãrɛzõ]
(This mourning has no reason.)

2) in final il(s) after a consonant, the i is [i] and the l is sometimes silent, sometimes sounded:

gentil	fusil	grésil	sourcil
[ʒãti]	[fyzi]	[grezi]	[sursi]
(nice)	(gun)	(hail)	(eyebrow)
cil	fil	fils	fils
[sil]	[fil]	[fil]	[fis]
(eyelash)	(thread)	(threads)	(son(s))

3) in the following words and their derivatives, -ill- sounds as [il]:

mille	ville	tranquille
[milə]	[vilə]	[trãkilə]
(thousand)	(city)	(tranquil)
pupille	Séville	(but [sevijə]
[pypilə]	[sevilə]	when rhyming
(eye)	(Sevilla)	with *séguedille*)

y   when followed by a vowel-letter in the same word

tes yeux   rayon
[tɛzjø]   [rɛjõ]
(your eyes)   (beam)

Note: If letter i, normally phoneticized and sounding as [j], is provided a note in the score, it is phoneticized and sounded as [i]:

cu-ri**eux**   or   cu-ri-**eux**
[kyrjø]   [kyriø]
(curious)   (curious)

3. Semiconsonant *w* [W]   Model word: s**oir** [swar] (evening)

FORMATION:

The *w* of English *we*.

SPELLINGS:

o<u>i</u>	as	*as a general rule*	<u>oi</u>seau	cl<u>oî</u>tre
o<u>î</u>	[w a],		[w a z o]	[k l w a t r ə]
o<u>y</u>	[w a]		(bird)	(cloister)
e<u>oi</u>				

v<u>oy</u>age   s'ass<u>eoi</u>r
[v w a j a ʒ ə]   [s a s w a r]
(voyage)   (to sit down)

<u>oua</u>	([w a])	in these combinations, *ou* sounds as [w] when initial or
<u>ouai</u>	([w e], [w ɛ])	medial and after a vowel- or single consonant-sound
<u>oue</u>	([w e], [w ɛ],	
	[w ɑ̃]) [w ɛ̃])	
<u>oué</u>	([w e])	
<u>oui</u>	([w i])	
<u>ouie</u>	([w i])	
<u>oueu</u>	([w ø], [w œ])	
<u>ouÿ</u>	([w i])	But not in *ouill*, final *oue*, *oues*, *ouent* or in medial

A<u>oua</u>!   <u>oua</u>is!
[a w a]   [w ɛ]
(Aoua!)   (yeah!)

f<u>oue</u>t   <u>oue</u>st
[f w ɛ]   [w ɛ s t]
(whip)   (west)

R<u>oue</u>n   j<u>oue</u>r
[r w ɑ̃]   [ʒ w e]
(Rouen)   (to play)

oue followed by a single consonant:

m<u>ou</u>/iller	je j<u>oue</u>	je j<u>oue</u>/rai
[m u j e]	[ʒ ə ʒ u]	[ʒ ə ʒ u r e]

enr<u>oué</u>   <u>oui</u>
[ɑ̃ r w e]   [w i]
(hoarse)   (yes)

épan<u>oui</u>r   enf<u>oui</u>e
[e p a n w i r]   [ɑ̃ f w i]
(to bloom)   (buried)

<u>u</u>   only in combination *-ua-* after *q* and *g*, and only in a few words, mostly of foreign origin

aq<u>u</u>arelle   q<u>u</u>atuor
[a k w a r ɛ l ə]   [k w a t ɥ ɔ r]
(watercolors)   (quartet)

Note: If letters *ou*, normally phoneticized and sounded as [w], are provided a note in the score, they should be phoneticized and sounded as [u]:

alg<u>u</u>azil
[a l g w a z i l]
(Spanish police)

♪ | ♩. ♪   ♪ ♪ | ♩. ♪

a-lo<u>ue</u>-tt<u>e</u>   or   a-lo<u>u</u>-<u>e</u>-tt<u>e</u>
[a l w ɛ t œ]   [a l u ɛ t œ]
(lark)   (lark)

EXERCISES

1. Intone the following in the usual manner:

[d ɥ i] [d ɥ e] [d ɥ ɛ] [d ɥ ɛ̃] [d ɥ a] [d ɥ ɑ̃] [d j e] [d j ɛ] [d j a] [d j ɑ]
[d j ɔ] [d j o] [d j u] [d j ø] [d j œ] [d j ɑ̃] [d j ɛ̃] [d j õ] [d w e] [d w i] [d w ɛ]
[d w a] [r w ɑ] [d r w ɑ] [k r w ɑ] [s w ɛ̃] [o ʒ u r d ɥ i]
[d œ p ɥ i l œ ʒ u r u ʒ œ m œ s ɥ i d ɔ n e œ]

2. Carefully copy the following text, "Villanelle" (T. Gautier) from *Les Nuits d'été* of Berlioz, including all accent marks, skipping a line between each line of verse. Underline all vowel-sounds and circle all semiconsonant sounds. Use the score to aid in determining semiconsonant sounds. Mark all elisions. Also, use the score to determine the phoneticization of final, unstressed *-e*, *-es*. Then, above each underlined vowel-sound and circled semiconsonant sound, insert the proper representative phonetic symbols, one set of brackets per line. Be able to intone the phoneticization.

Quand viendra la saison nouvelle,
Quand auront disparu les froids,
Tous les deux, nous irons, ma belle,
Pour cueillir le muguet aux bois.
Sous nos pieds égrenant les perles,
Que l'on voit, au matin, trembler,
Nous irons écouter les merles siffler.
Le printemps est venu, ma belle;
C'est le mois des amants béni;
Et l'oiseau satinant son aile,
Dit des vers au rebord du nid.
Oh! viens donc sur ce banc de mousse
Pour parler de nos beaux amours,
Et dis-moi de ta voix si douce toujours!
Loin, bien loin, égarant nos courses,
Faisons fuir le lapin caché;
Et le daim au miroir des sources,
Admirant son grand bois penché;
Puis, chez nous, tout heureux, tout aises,
En paniers enlaçant nos doigts,
Revenons rapportant des fraises des bois!

Phoneticization, Formation, and Singing of the Consonants

Below is a numbered list of the eighteen consonant-sounds in French that gives the phonetic symbol and a model word for each consonant-sound. (For a review of consonant formation in singing in French, see above, pages 5–9.) (See Recording Example F.)

EXPLOSIVES

1. [b]   base   (phonetic *b*, voiced)
         [b ɑ z ə]
         (basis)

2. [p]   <u>p</u>asser   (phonetic *p*, voiceless)
         [p ɑ s e]
         (to pass)

3. [d]   <u>d</u>on   (phonetic *d*, voiced)
         [d õ]
         (gift)

4. [t]   <u>t</u>our   (phonetic *t*, voiceless)
         [t u r]
         (tower)

5. [g]   <u>g</u>uide   (phonetic *g*, voiced)
         [g i d ə]
         (guide)

6. [k]   é<u>ch</u>o   (phonetic *k*, voiceless)
         [e k o]
         (echo)

FRICATIVES

7. [v]   <u>v</u>ase   (phonetic *v*, voiced)
         [v ɑ z ə]
         (vase)

8. [f]   <u>f</u>ort   (phonetic *f*, voiceless)
         [f ɔ r]
         (strong)

9. [z]   ro<u>s</u>e   (phonetic *z*, voiced)
         [r o z ə]
         (rose)

10. [s]   <u>s</u>on   (phonetic *s*, voiceless)
         [s õ]
         (sound)

11. [ʒ]   rou<u>g</u>e   (zsa-zsa *z*, voiced)
         [r u ʒ ə]
         (red)

12. [ʃ]   bou<u>ch</u>e   (snaky *s*, voiceless)
         [b u ʃ ə]
         (mouth)

NASALS

13. [m]   <u>m</u>ode   (phonetic *m*, voiced)
         [m ɔ d ə]
         (fashion)

[mm]	i<u>mm</u>ense [i m m ɑ̃ s ə] (immense)	(phonetic double *m*, voiced)
14. [n]	fi<u>n</u>e [f i n ə] (fine)	(phonetic *n*, voiced)
[nn]	i<u>nn</u>ombrable [i n n õ b r a b l ə] (innumerable)	(phonetic double *n*, voiced)
15. [ɲ]	cy<u>gn</u>e [s i ɲ ə] (swan)	(*yod-n*, voiced)

LATERAL

16. [l]	<u>l</u>ion [l j õ] (lion)	(phonetic *l*, voiced)
[ll]	i<u>ll</u>usion [i l l y z j õ] (illusion)	(phonetic double *l*, voiced)

FLIPPED, ROLLED, UVULAR

17. [r]	la <u>r</u>ue [l a r y] (the street)	(phonetic flipped *r*, voiced)
[r r]	ho<u>rr</u>ible [ɔ r r i b l ə] (horrible)	(phonetic rolled *r*, voiced)
18. [R]	Pa<u>r</u>is [p a R i] (Paris)	(phonetic uvular *r*, voiced)

(Consult Recording Illustration F for the Eighteen Consonant-sounds.)

All consonant-sounds in French have the following characteristics:

1. They are either *voiced* or uttered simultaneously with sound from the vocal cords, such as [b], [v], [z], [r], or *voiceless*, or those uttered without sound from the cords, or whispered, such as [s], [p], [t], or [f].

2. They are *rapid, late,* and *clear,* and definitely more *energetic* than their English counterparts. The French consonant propels the ensuing

vowel-sound and must never alter or shorten the preceding vowel-sound.

3. They are *unaspirated,* that is, neither preceded nor followed by an escape of air as in English *peep*. (Compare French *pipe*.)

4. They are *single,* as a general rule, even when spelled with two (or double) consonant-letters. There are very few exceptions. (See [ll], [mm], [nn], and [rr].)

Before beginning a study of the eighteen consonant-sounds, here are some of the terms that will be used in this section to describe consonantal formation:

1. *labial*—formed with both lips, the same as "bilabial" if no other articulatory organ is involved, as for [b] and [m]—no tongue movement.

2. *dental*–formed with the tongue and the upper teeth, as for [d] and [t].

3. *labio-dental*–formed with the lower lip and the upper teeth, as for [v] and [f].

4. *alveolar*–formed by contact of the tongue with the gum ridge (in which are fixed the upper front teeth), as for [z] and [s].

5. *alveolar-palatal*–formed by contact of the tongue with the border area between the gum ridge (in which are fixed the upper front teeth) and the hard palate (or the roof of the mouth), as for [ʒ] and [ʃ].

6. *palatal*–formed by contact of the tongue with the hard palate (or roof of the mouth), as for [g] and [k].

7. *uvular*–formed by vibrating contact between the back of the tongue and the uvula, or the v-shaped piece of flesh that hangs from the soft palate, as for [R].

THE EXPLOSIVES

VOICED	VOICELESS
1. [b]	2. [p]
3. [d]	4. [t]
5. [g]	6. [k]

Note that numbers 2, 4, and 6 are merely numbers 1, 3, and 5 without voice. These consonant-sounds require "explosion," or sudden, deliberate eruption of sound. In the case of the *voiced* explosives, the cords vibrate (voice begins) when the articulatory organs assume a position (*closure*) that is complete, continues through blockage (*stop*), until the explosion (*release*) of the consonant. These consonants are *unaspirated,* totally voiced, whether at the beginning, middle, or end of a word, and tend to be clearer, more resonant, and more energetic than their English counterparts. The formation of the *voiceless* explosives is basically the same as for those that are voiced, except that there is no voice accompanying their emission. They, too, must be kept "dry," neat and precise, energetic, and without any leakage of air, or aspiration.

	SPELLING	FORMATION	EXAMPLES	
1. [b]	b, bb	Voiced, with bilabial stoppage	bois [b w a] (wood)	abbaye [a b (e) i] (abbey)
2. [p]	p, pp	Voiceless, with bilabial stoppage	pipe [p i p ə] (pipe)	appel [a p ɛ l] (call)
	b (before s, t)		absent [a p s ɑ̃] (absent)	obtenir [ɔ p t ə n i r] (obtain)
3. [d]	d, dd	Voiced, with dental stoppage: tip of tongue at point where teeth and gum ridge meet. (Avoid using middle of tongue and rim of gum ridge and/or hard palate)	dot [d ɔ t] (dowry) addition [a d i s j õ] (check)	
4. [t]	t, tt	Voiceless, with dental stoppage; same as for [d]	table [t a b l ə] (table) flatter [f l a t e] (to flatter)	
	d (only in liaison)		grand‿arbre [g r ɑ̃ t a r b r ə] (big tree)	
5. [g]	g (before a, o, u, or consonant)	Voiced, with palatal stoppage: middle of tongue on middle of hard palate; avoid backing of English [g]; as frontal as possible	gâter [g ɑ t e] (to spoil) bague [b a g ə] (ring)	agonie [a g ɔ n i] (agony) gros [g r o] (fat)
	gg (before e, e, è as [gʒ], or before consonant as [g])		suggérer [s y g ʒ e r e] (to suggest)	aggraver [a g r a v e] (to aggravate)
	c (in second and derivatives only)		second [s ə g õ] (second)	

	SPELLING	FORMATION	EXAMPLES	
	x (in initial *ex-* plus vowel-sound as [gz]; also when initial in names, see page 215)		exil [ɛgzil] (exile)	exhaler [ɛgzale] (to exhale)
6. [k]	c (before *a, o, u* or consonant)	Voiceless, with palatal stoppage; same as for [g] (More frontal than English counterpart)	calme [kalmə] (calm)	cocu [kɔky] (cuckold)
			encore [ɑ̃kɔrə] (still)	action [aksjõ] (action)
	cc (before *a, o, u* or consonant is [k]; before *i, e* is [ks]; note division)		a/ccord [akɔr] (chord)	a/ccuser [akyze] (to accuse)
			ac/cident [aksidɑ̃] (accident)	ac/cent [aksɑ̃] (accent)
	q		qui [ki] (who)	cinq [sɛ̃k] (five)
	cq		grecque [grɛkə] (Greek)	Jacques [ʒɑkə] (Jacques)
	ch (rare, in words of Greek and Italian origin)		choeur [kœr] (choir)	écho [eko] (echo)
			chrétien [kretjɛ̃] (Christian)	orchestre [ɔrkɛstrə] (orchestra)
	g (in liaison; rare)		sang_impur [sɑ̃kɛ̃pyr] (impure blood)	
	k		açoka [asɔka] (hibiscus)	Karnak [karnak] (Karnak)
	x (in initial *ex-* plus consonant and when medial is [ks]; see also page 75)		extase [ɛkstɑzə] (ecstasy)	vexer [vɛkse] (to vex)

THE FRICATIVES

VOICED	VOICELESS
7. [v]	8. [f]
9. [z]	10. [s]
11. [ʒ]	12. [ʃ]

Note that numbers 8, 10, and 12 are merely numbers 7, 9, and 11 without voice. These six consonant-sounds are called "fricatives" because they are produced by audible friction of the breath against some part of the articulatory organs of the mouth. Whereas the stoppage of the explosive consonant is complete, fricative stoppage is partial and sustained. It can be safely stated that the formation of these consonant-sounds in French is the same as for their English counterparts.

	SPELLING	FORMATION	EXAMPLES	
7. [v]	v	Voiced, with labio-dental stoppage; upper teeth on lower lip	vérité [v e r i t e] (truth)	
	f (in liaison)		neuf heures [n œ v œ r ə] (nine o'clock)	
	w (in some words of foreign origin and proper nouns)		wagon [v a g õ] (rail coach)	Wallonie [v a l ɔ n i] (Walloon uplands)
8. [f]	f, ff, ph	Voiceless, with labio-dental stoppage; same as for [v]	if [i f] (yew) effet [(e) f ɛ] (effect)	rafale [r a f a l ə] (squall) Aphrodite [a f r ɔ d i t ə] (Aphrodite)
9. [z]	s (between vowel-letters or -sounds, and in liaison)	Voiced, with alveolar stoppage; middle of tongue on gum ridge, tip of tongue just behind front teeth	rose [r o z ə] (rose) mes amis [m e z a m i] (my friends)	baiser [b (e) z e] (kiss) isolé [i z ɔ l e] (alone)

	Spelling	Formation	Examples	
	x (in some numerical words, and in liaison; also in initial *ex-* plus vowel-letter or -sound)		deuxième [døzjɛmə] (second)	exact [ɛgzakt] [ɛgza] (exact)
			six ans [si͜zɑ̃] (six years)	exhaler [ɛgzale] (to exhale)
	z		Azaël [azaɛl] (Azael)	
	zz		le jazz [lœdʒaz] (jazz)	
10. [s]	s (when initial, or when preceded or followed by a consonant; often sounded when final; see index to consonant-letters for further examples)	Voiceless, with alveolar stoppage, same as for [z]	sous [su] (under)	Salomé [salɔme] (Salome)
			jasmin [ʒasmɛ̃] (jasmin)	désespoir [dezɛspwar] (despair)
			hélas [elɑs] (alas)	jadis [ʒɑdis] (formerly)
	ss (always)		laisser [l(e)se] (to let)	frisson [frisõ] (shiver)
	ç (before *e, i, y*)		ceci [sœsi] (this)	cygne [siɲə] (swan)
	ç (always, with cedilla)		français [frɑ̃sɛ] (French)	reçu [rœsy] (received)
	cc (before *e, i,* or *y* is [ks])		accent [aksɑ̃] (accent)	Occident [ɔksidɑ̃] (Occident)
	sc (before *e, i,* or *y*)		scintiller [sɛ̃tije] (to sparkle)	descendre [d(e)sɑ̃drə] (to go down)
	t (when medial and before [j]; see index)		patient [pasjɑ̃] (patient)	émotion [emosjõ] (emotion)

	SPELLING	FORMATION	EXAMPLES	
	x̱ (in most numerical words)		six̱ [s i s] (six)	dix̱ [d i s] (ten)
	(in initial *ex-* plus consonant is [k s]		ex̱quis [ε k s k i] (exquisite)	
	(in medial *-ex-*, always)		tex̱te [t ε k s t ə] (text)	
	(final in several words, is [k s], see index)		Béatrix̱ [b e a t r i k s] (Beatrice)	
11. [ʒ]	g̱ (before *e*, *i*, *y*)	Voiced, with alveolar-palatal stoppage; rim of tongue curled against gum ridge, lips quite rounded; avoid [d ʒ]	mirag̱e [m i r a ʒ ə] (mirage) Eg̱yptien [e ʒ i p s j ɛ̃] (Egyptian)	g̱ivre [ʒ i v r ə] (frost)
	g̱g (before *e*, *i*, *y* is [g ʒ])		sug̱gestion [s y g ʒ ε s t j õ] (suggestion)	
	j̱ (always)		j̱e [ʒ œ] (I)	déj̱à [d e ʒ ɑ] (already)
12. [ʃ]	c̱h (except in a few words, see [k])	Voiceless with alveolar-palatal stoppage; same as for [ʒ]; avoid [t ʃ]	c̱hose [ʃ o z ə] (thing)	cloc̱he [k l ɔ ʃ ə] (bell)
	s̱ch (rare)		s̱chisme [ʃ i s m ə] (schism)	

THE NASALS

VOICED

13. [m] [mm]
14. [n] [nn]
15. [ɲ]

Note that all the nasal consonants are voiced. These consonants are called "nasal" because in their formation the breath passes through and resonates in both the mouth and nasal cavities. As with all voiced consonants in French, the voice begins upon closure and continues through blockage until the release, which must be energetic and rapid.

	SPELLING	FORMATION	EXAMPLES	
13. [m]	m (when followed by vowel-letter or -sound)	Voiced, with labial stoppage	amour [a m u r] (love)	climat [k l i m a] (climate)
	(usually silent when followed by *n*, always silent when nasalizing: *autom̸ne, parfum̸*)		hymne (excep.) [i m n ə] (hymn)	
	mm (except in initial *imm-*)		femme [f a m ə] (woman)	homme [ɔ m ə] (man)
[mm]	imm- (only when initial)	Voiced, with labial stoppage; a prolonged [m]	immense [i m m ɑ̃ s ə] (immense)	
14. [n]	n (when followed by vowel-letter or -sound, silent when nasalizing except when in liaison)	Voiced, with dental stoppage; tip of tongue against upper front teeth	inutile [i n y t i l ə] (useless)	bonheur [b ɔ n œ r] (happiness)
	nn (except in initial *inn-*)		donner [d ɔ n e] (to give)	
	mn (*m* is usually silent, *n* always pronounced)		autom̸ne [o t ɔ n ə] (autumn)	dam̸ner [d ɑ n e] (to condemn)
[nn]	inn- (only when initial)	Voiced, with dental stoppage; a prolonged [n]	innombrable [i n n õ b r a b l ə] (innumerable)	
15. [ɲ]	gn (almost always, with notable exceptions sounding [g n]: *Magnificat stagnant gnome*)	Voiced, with palatal stoppage; middle of tongue, *not* tip, against front of hard palate; avoid [n j]	Seigneur [s ɛ ɲ œ r] (Lord)	ignorer [i ɲ ɔ r e] (to not know)

LATERAL

VOICED

16. [l]   [ll]

This consonant is called "lateral" because in its formation the breath passes out of the mouth along the sides of the tongue. Avoid the backed [l] of English by articulating the French [l] with the tip of the tongue against the edges of the upper front teeth. Keep the middle and back of the tongue away from the gum ridge and the hard palate. The soft palate must remain absolutely loose and inactive in the formation of French [l]. In spite of the term "lateral," this is a most *frontal* consonant in French.

	SPELLING	FORMATION	EXAMPLES	
16. [l]	l (almost always, but may be silent when final; see [j])	Voiced, with dental stoppage activated by tip of tongue on edge of upper front teeth	lilas [lilɑ] (lilac)	il [il] (he)
	ll (except in initial *ill*-)		aller [ale] (to go)	
[ll]	ill- (only when initial)	Same as for [l], but prolonged	illusion [illyzjɔ̃] (illusion)	

FLIPPED, ROLLED, UVULAR

VOICED

17. [r]   [rr]
18. [R]

Correct and effective flipping of an *r* demands that the tongue be relaxed and nimble throughout execution and that the consonant be fully voiced. A flipped *r*, which is the predominant sort used in sung French, is articulated by the tip of the tongue flapping once across voiced breath against the rim dividing the gum ridge and the hard palate. For those who find the flipping of an *r* difficult, it might be helpful to start with a light [d], gradually relaxing the stoppage and placing the tip of the tongue as high on the gum ridge as possible, and eventually on the rim. Remember that [d] is an explosive with complete blockage and dental stoppage, while [r] has fricative qualities, with incomplete blockage and sustained stoppage. The rule is to *relax* and to use only the *tip* of the tongue.

A rolled *r* is actually several flipped *r*'s in succession, or a sort of "trill." It is the sound children make when playing with toy cars. If you can flip an *r*, but cannot seem to roll one, try flipping a few *r*'s in close succession. After this, attempt to vibrate several together in a vigorous air flow which, as with [r], must be voiced. Again, *relax* and use only the *tip* of the tongue *lightly* against the division between the gum ridge and the hard palate. The sides of the tongue should barely touch the sides of the hard palate, as if to brace the relaxed tip.

A uvular *r* is formed by the vibration of the uvula, or the *v*-shaped piece of flesh hanging from the soft palate. The uvula is vibrated by vocalized breath against the back of the tongue. The French uvular *r* is high and delicate, very unlike that of German, Yiddish, or several mid-Eastern and Oriental languages. Its articulation can be approximated as being almost directly under the nose. Even though most French people use the uvular *r* while speaking, it is the flipped *r* and occasionally the rolled *r* that is used *by the French themselves* in singing opera, oratorio, and songs. The uvular *r*, however, is indeed used in the music-hall, cabaret, and in folk-style, and may be sparingly inserted into some contemporary songs of a Parisian "street scene" cast for an intended note of colorful vulgarity. But, as a rule, French and non-French singers alike avoid this troublesome and unstylistic consonant when singing the opera, concert and recital repertoire simply because it is somewhat bothersome in a vocal sense, hinders the *legato,* and has a distinctly commonplace ring when sung. Use it only when advised to do so by a qualified expert and, again, resist trying to be more "French" than the French themselves.

	SPELLING	FORMATION	EXAMPLES	
17. [r] (flipped)	r, rr (*r* may be silent when final)	Voiced, with alveolar stoppage (see above)	rire [rirə] (to laugh)	guerre [gɛrə] (war)
[rr] (rolled)	r, rr (*r* may be silent when final); only in words of forceful emotion	Voiced, with alveolar stoppage; a prolonged, trilled [r] (see above)	brûle [brrylə] (burn)	terrible [tɛrriblə] (terrible)
	irr- (only when initial)		irrémédiable [irremedjablə] (irremediable)	
	-rr- (in a few verbs to distinguish between the imperfect and present conditional tenses)		je mourrais (pres. cond.) [ʒœmurrɛ] (I would die)	

	SPELLING	FORMATION	EXAMPLES
18. [R] (uvular)	r, rr	Voiced, with uvular stoppage (to be avoided as a rule in opera and art song; (see above)	Paris [p a R i] (Paris) marrant [m a R ã] ("a riot")

EXERCISES

1. Completely phoneticize *all* sounds (vowels, semiconsonants, consonants) of the text of the song "Beau soir" by Claude Debussy. See the section on phoneticization of a song or an aria in Chapter 4 before doing this. (See pp. 97-98.)

2. Insert the phoneticization into the musical score of the song and intone it, legato, in rhythm, and in tempo. Again, refer to Chapter 4 before doing so.

3
Liaison

Liaison is far more frequent in sung French than in conversation. An acceptable, even required, liaison in song often sounds stilted in everyday speech. Contemporary conversational French avoids many optional liaisons that only a generation ago were commonly heard. There was a time when one's use of liaison revealed breeding and background (or a lack of the same); today, liaison appears as a rule only when "compulsory," and sometimes not even then, for fear of sounding affected or outdated. Therefore, it is important to understand that the rules governing liaison change with the times and with the context or setting of the delivery. Because most of the texts of the French vocal repertoire are of nineteenth- and early twentieth-century origin, or even earlier, the liaisons made in them should and do adhere to the literary and theatrical practices of those periods. Liaison in opera and song is generally made according to the rules set by the Comédie française (the French National Theater) and poetic declamation. For all these reasons, the average Frenchman who is not familiar with these styles of delivery may find some liaisons made by singers to be unnecessary, pompous, even archaic. Indeed, singers do sometimes make ill-advised and quite preposterous liaisons that obscure or even change the meaning of the text. Just one example of erroneous use of liaison should suffice: "un homme et une femme" means "a man and a woman." The *t* of the word *et* must *never* be sounded in liaison. If it *is* sounded, the resulting meaning of the above phrase becomes: "a man *is* a woman," a literal slip-of-the-tongue that would surely not go unnoticed.

A brief explanation of what liaison is may be found in Chapter 1 of this manual. Liaison may occur only between a normally silent final consonant and an ensuing vowel-sound, for example, "Elle est ici." In this sentence, the *t* of *est* is said to be "in liaison" with the *i* of *ici*. (The *e* of *elle* has been *elided,* an example of *elision* and *not* liaison!) Under no circumstances may the *s* of the word *est* be pronounced or thought to be "in liaison." A liaison can only be made on a *final,* normally silent consonant, *not* a medial one.

Oddly enough, the best way to begin to study liaison is to learn when *not* to make one. These rules are largely based on Pierre Bernac's magnificent book *The Interpretation of French Song* (1970, Praeger; 1978, Gollancz-Norton reprint in softcover), wherein are included over two hundred song texts. For each text, Bernac suggests or discourages the use of liaison, and it is from these indications that these guiding principles have been drawn. Today Bernac stands alone in his scrupulously tasteful, traditional, but enlightened approach to liaison. Born in 1899, he was able to imbue himself in a musical-literary atmosphere that had all but disappeared by the Second World War. Yet his language, like his artistry, is never dated. His favorite recommendation to the young singer is, "And please, do not sing this song in the bad taste of my youth," referring, of course, to the offensive and tasteless self-indulgence rampant in vocal art in the early years of this century. And this sense of taste, founded at the same time upon tradition and modern awareness, must be extended to the linguistic realm of vocal study through a stylized use of vowel quality and of liaison.

Forbidden Liaisons

Forbidden liaisons are exactly that: they must not be made. Unlike optional liaisons, those that are forbidden are not made in either singing or conversation. Like compulsory liaisons that are sounded, forbidden liaisons contribute to the intelligibility of the text by their very absence. Indeed, their inclusion often results in absurdity or ambiguity, as illustrated earlier.

There are eight instances where liaison is unconditionally forbidden. Do not make a liaison:

1. Over a rest or breath within the vocal line:

Carmen (Act II), G. Bizet

Except when the rest separates two grammatically related words or syllables of the same word within the phrase that are separated by a punctuating lift within the legato (rather than by a breath or rest that interrupts the flow):

Roméo et Juliette (Act I), C. Gounod

2. Before an aspirate *h* (see Chapter 1):

> Qui dans les halliers humides te cueille!
> [ki→dɑ̃→lɛ→/alje→zy→mi→dœ→tœ→kœjœ]
> (Who in the damp thickets gathers you!)
> ("La Rose," Fauré-L. de Lisle)

Note that a slight separation may be made before the vowel following the aspirate *h*.

3. After a noun in the singular:

> Le printemps est triste et ne peut fleurir.
> [lœ→prɛ̃→tɑ̃→ɛ→tri→ste→nœ→pø→flœrir]
> (The springtime is sad and cannot flower.)
> "Le Temps des Lilas," Chausson-Bouchor)

Note that no separation is made between the [ɑ̃] of *-temps* and the [ɛ] of *est*.

> La nuit a des douceurs de femme.
> [la→nɥi→a→dɛ→du→sœ→rdœ→fa→mœ]
> (The night has womanly softness.)
> ("De Rêve," Debussy)

Except:

a. In some common expressions:

nuit et jour	mot à mot	de temps en temps
[nɥitɛʒur]	[motamo]	[dœtɑ̃zɑ̃tɑ̃]
(night and day)	(word for word)	(from time to time)

b. On a few singular nouns, notably *enfant*, *voix*, and *bois*, especially

in opera, and often to separate two similar or identical vowel-
sounds. A gentle, hardly perceptible consonant is sufficient here:

cet enfant a dormi   enfant abandonnée
[sɛtɑ̃fɑ̃(t)adɔrmi]   [ɑ̃fɑ̃(t)abɑ̃dɔneœ]
(this child slept)   (abandoned child)
   (*Faust*, Gounod)   (*Hérodiade*, Massenet)

Note that although this light liaison on *enfant* is traditional, it is
not advised by Bernac; note also the parentheses around [t] above and [z]
below to indicate lightness of attack.

Obéissons quand leur voix appelle.
[ɔ→be→i→sõ→kɑ̃→lœ→rvwa→(z)a→pɛlœ]
(Let us obey when their voice calls.)
   (*Manon*, Massenet)

Bois épais
[bwɑ(z)epɛ]
(Dense wood)
   (*Amidis*, Lully)

4. After the conjunction *et*, meaning ''and'':

lui et elle   et alors?
[lɥieɛlə]   [ealɔr]
(he and she)   (and then?)

5. Before most interjections and numerical words (see below, ''Special
Words and Liaison''):

Il a dit oui.   les onze hommes
[iladiwi]   [lɛ/õzɔmə]
(He said yes.)   (the eleven men)

6. On words ending in *-rd*, *-rs*, *-rt*. Instead, normally link the sounded *r*
with the following vowel-sound:

Dans ton coeur dort un clair de lune.
[dɑ̃→tõ→kœ→rdɔ→rɛ̃→klɛ→rdœ→ly→nœ]
(In your heart there sleeps a moonlight.)
   (''Chanson triste,'' Duparc-Lahor)

sur le bord arrivée
[sy→rlœ→bɔ→ra→ri→ve]
(arrived upon the shore)
   (''Chanson perpétuelle,'' Chausson-Cros)

Cela ne sert à rien.
[s œ → l a → n œ → s ɛ → r a → r j ɛ̃]
(That is useless.)
 (*Carmen*, Bizet)

à travers un immense espoir
[a → t r a → v ɛ → r œ̃ → n i → m m ɑ̃ → s ɛ → s p w a r]
(through an immense hope)
 (*La Bonne Chanson*, Fauré-Verlaine)

Except:

a. To show pluralization of final -*rs*:

Si mes vers avaient des ailes
[s i → m ɛ → v ɛ → r z a → v ɛ → d ɛ → z ɛ → l œ]
(If my verses had wings)
 (''Si mes vers avaient des ailes,'' Hahn-Hugo)

b. Sometimes on the word *toujours* (see below, ''Special Words and Liaison'')

c. In inversion of third person singular verb forms and their pronoun subject:

Meurt-on de volupté?
[m œ → r t õ → d œ → v ɔ → l y → p t e]
(Does one die of pleasure?)
 (*Chansons madécasses*, Ravel-Parny)

7. In enumerations of any kind:

Ils vont, ils viennent.	Femmes, hommes, enfants
[i l v õ / i l v j ɛ n ə]	[f a m ə / ɔ m ə / ɑ̃ f ɑ̃]
(They go, they come.)	(Women, men, children)

8. On proper nouns:

Paris est beau.	Manon enchanteresse!
[p a r i ɛ b o]	[m a n õ ɑ̃ ʃ ɑ̃ t œ r ɛ s œ]
(Paris is beautiful.)	(Enchantress Manon!)

Optional Liaisons

The recitalist and concert singer seem to be more scrupulous in their use of liaison than the opera singer. The abuse of liaison in opera is probably due to foreign influence and the shopworn excuses of ''tradition'' and vocal facility. But nothing can justify what the French call a ''barbarous'' liaison. Bernac says, "There are a great number of cases when the liaison is optional, and left to the taste of the performer." This is dangerous territory, where sound taste, common sense, and a thorough knowledge and feel for the French language and its literature are required. This is not to intimidate the already awe-struck English-speaking singer faced with the intricacies of French pronunciation, but it is a word to the wise.

Bernac goes on to say that more liaisons might be made in a lyrical song text than in a folk song (in a Duparc song as opposed to one of the Ravel's *Greek Songs,* for example):

> Aimer à loisir, aimer et mourir
> [(e) m é r a l w a z i r / (e) m e r e m u r i r]
> (To love at leisure, to love and die)
>   ("Invitation au voyage," Duparc-Baudelaire)

> Pour le nouer autour de tes cheveux
> [p u → r l œ → n u → e → o → t u → r d œ → t ɛ → ʃ (ø) v ø]
> (To tie it around your tresses)
>   ("Le Réveil de la mariée," *Chansons populaires grecques,* Ravel)

He also discourages the use of liaison when it would create sounds more disagreeable to the ear than its absence, or when it makes for ambiguity, unintelligibility, or comical alliteration:

> Dans tes yeux/alors, je boirai
> [d ã → t ɛ → z j ø → / a l ɔ → r ʒ œ → b w a → r e]
> (In your eyes then, I shall drink)

> Tant de baisers/ et de tendresses
> [t ã → d œ → b (e) → z e → / e → d œ → t ã → d r ɛ → s œ]
> (So many kisses and tendernesses)
>   (*Chanson triste,* Duparc-Lahor)

Here, both liaisons are avoided to reduce the recurrence of [z] within the line, as well as to put the words "alors" and "et de tendresses" in expressive relief by means of gentle separations and reattacks on the vowels with no real halting of the legato.

One of the most common misconceptions regarding liaison is that it cannot occur over a comma. There are several kinds of commas: some separate closely related words; others separate entire clauses and quite unrelated material. In the following lines, liaison is advised over the comma. The words in liaison are short introductory ones that are closely linked in meaning, syntax, and mood with the following words:

> Puis, elle s'épanche
> [p ɥ i z ɛ l œ s e p ã ʃ œ]
> (Then, it overflows)
>   ("Le Jet d'eau," Debussy-Baudelaire)

Mais, hélas, les plus longs amours sont courts
[m ɛ →z e →l ɑ →s l ɛ →p l y →l õ →z a →m u →r s õ →k u r]
(But, alas, the longest loves are short)
("Adieu," Fauré-Grandmougin)

But, in the following line, the liaison is discouraged since it obscures and weakens the text. The words "Oh, my beloved" gain in impact by being put into expressive relief by avoiding liaison and gently separating the vowel sounds:

Mais,/ô mon bien-aimé, pour mieux sécher mes pleurs
[m ɛ /o →m õ →b j ɛ̃ →n (e) →m e →/p u →r m j ø →s e →ʃ e →m ɛ →p l œ r]
(But, oh my beloved, in order to better dry my tears)
(*Samson et Dalila,* Saint-Saëns)

Syntax, or sentence structure, is equally important in determining the presence or absence of liaison. Grammatically unrelated words should *not* be in liaison:

Et le charme des soirs à ta belle âme est cher
[e →l œ →ʃ a r →m œ →d ɛ →s w a →r a →t a →b ɛ →l ɑ →m ɛ →ʃ ɛ r]
(And the charm of the evenings to your beautiful soul is dear)
("Rencontre," Fauré-Grandmougin)
Le temps des lilas et le temps des roses est passé
[l œ →t ɑ̃ →d ɛ →l i →l a →e →l œ →t ɑ̃ →d ɛ →r o →z œ →ɛ →p ɑ →s e]
(The time of lilacs and the time of roses is past)
("Le Temps des Lilas," Chausson-Bouchor)

In the first example ("Rencontre"), the normal word order would be "Et le charme des soirs est cher à ta belle âme." Poetic word order often juxtaposes clauses and raises havoc with normal syntax. This can be seen easily in the English translation. *Soirs* is not linked to *à ta belle âme* because this prepositional phrase is governed by the word *cher*. Even in the normal word order given above, *soirs* would not be linked to *est* because this singular verb form is the predicate of the singular subject *charme*. As a general rule, plural nouns and singular verbs (or singular nouns and plural verbs) should not be in liaison with each other. This is further demonstrated in the second example from "Le Temps des Lilas" by the words *roses* and *est*. Also, the conjunction *et* connects *temps* and *temps* and should not be in liaison with the word *lilas* preceding it.

Yes, it sounds complicated, and it is. But a little hard thinking will show that liaison is based largely on common sense and a desire for intelligibility. For the singer who does not speak French, a good word-for-word translation will aid in deciding upon the use of liaison with respect to syntax.

Compulsory Liaisons

In conversation as well as in singing, some liaisons are unavoidable, or compulsory. Most of these liaisons are based on grammatical structure. Some of the most common are listed below:

ALWAYS MAKE A LIAISON BETWEEN	EXAMPLES
a plural noun and a neighboring adjective defining it	des jours heureux [d ɛ ʒ u r z (ø) r ø] (happy days) de grands arbres [d œ g r ɑ̃ z a r b r ə] (tall trees)
a plural noun and its verb	mes espoirs ont fui [m ɛ z ɛ s p w a r z ɔ̃ f ɥ i] (my hopes have fled)
a plural noun and a preposition introducing its modifier	beaux yeux aux flammes douces [b o z j ø z o f l a m œ d u s œ] (beautiful eyes with gentle flames)
a plural noun and a conjunction linking another plural noun to it	hommes et femmes [ɔ m œ z e f a m ə] (men and women)
pronouns and their verbs (also in inversion)	ils ont [i l z ɔ̃] (they have) tout est [t u t ɛ] (all is) nous avons été [n u z a v ɔ̃ z e t e] (we have been) Ont-ils été? [ɔ̃ t i l z e t e] (Have they been?)
a direct object pronoun preceding its governing verb form	Je les ai vus. [ʒ œ l ɛ z e v y] (I saw them.)
composite verb forms	Il est allé. [i l ɛ t a l e] (He went.)

Always Make a Liaison Between	Examples
	Je veux être [ʒœvǿzɛtrə] (I want to be)
verbs and articles or predicate adjectives	Je vois un enfant. [ʒœvwazœ̃nɑ̃fɑ̃] (I see a child.)
	ils restent agenouillés [ilrɛstœtaʒœnuje] (they remain kneeling)
verbs and prepositions introducing modifiers	il m'apprend à jouer [ilmaprɑ̃taʒue] (he teaches me to play)
verbs and their adverbs	que viennent encore [kœvjɛnœtɑ̃kɔrə] (may there come still)
infinitives and closely linked words and modifiers	pour laisser arriver le soir [purl(e)serarivelœswar] (to allow the evening's arrival)
	rêver en paix [rɛverɑ̃pɛ] (to dream in peace)
verbs and conjunctions that connect others verbs of the same subject	il chantait et buvait [ilʃɑ̃tɛtebyvɛ] (he was singing and drinking)
articles and adjectives preceding the nouns they modify and with other related adjectives	un homme [œ̃nɔmə] (a man)
	des enfants [dɛzɑ̃fɑ̃] (children)
	un autre petit élève [œ̃notrœpœtitelɛvə] (another little pupil)
adjectives in certain expressions, and with prepositions connecting modifiers	petit à petit [pœtitapœti] (little by little)
	pendus à ma ceinture [pɑ̃dyzamasɛ̃tyrə] (hung on my belt)

ALWAYS MAKE A LIAISON BETWEEN	EXAMPLES
adjectives linked by conjunctions (singular and plural)	langoureux et las [lãgurøzelɑ] (languorous and weary)
	petits ou grands [pœtizugrã] (little or big)
an adverb and the adjective, participle, or adverb it modifies	bien entendu [bjɛ̃nãtãdy] (of course)
	beaucoup aimé [bokup(e)me] (much loved)
an adverb preceding and modifying an infinitive	pour bien écrire [purbjɛ̃nekrirə] (to write well)
a preposition and its object	sans amour [sãzamur] (without love)
	devant un obstacle [dœvãtœnɔpstaklə] (before an obstacle)
a conjunction and the subject pronoun of the clause or verb	quand il pleut [kãtilplø] (when it rains)
	quand est-il parti? [kãtetilparti] (when did he leave?)

Phonetic Changes Due to Liaison

CONSONANTS

The letters $d, f, g, n, r, s, t, x,$ and z are those most subject to liaison. Of those, only four, $n, r, t,$ and $z,$ remain the same phonetically as [n], [r], [t], and [z] when in liaison. The remaining five change phonetically when in liaison, as shown below:

LETTER	IN LIAISON BECOMES	EXAMPLES
d̲	[t]	un grand arbre [œ̃ g r ɑ̃ t a r b r ə] (a tall tree)
f̲	[v]	neuf ans [n œ v ɑ̃] (nine years)
g̲	[k]	sang impur [s ɑ̃ k ɛ̃ p y r] (impure blood)
s̲	[z]	les anges [l ɛ z ɑ̃ ʒ ə] (the angels)
x̲	[z]	dix ans [d i z ɑ̃] (ten years)

Remember that only a consonant that is normally silent and final is subject to liaison and these phonetic changes. If the consonant is pronounced (and final) normally, and regardless of whether followed by a vowel-sound or not, it does not change phonetically (see Chapter 1).

VOWELS

Only two vowel-sounds change when the consonant following them is in liaison. They are [o] and [õ], and occur almost exclusively in two words: *trop* [t r o] and *bon* [b õ]. Both open to [ɔ], with denasalization occurring in the second case, before liaison:

trop heureuse   bon anniversaire
[t r ɔ p (ø) r ø z œ]   [b ɔ n a n i v ɛ r s ɛ r ə]
(too happy)   (happy birthday)

Note that in final *-er* sounding as [e], the *e* retains its closed quality in liaison:

rêver en paix
[r ɛ v e r ɑ̃ p ɛ]
(to dream in peace)

Special Words and Liaison

Donc

Sound the final *c* as [k] only if

1. followed within the line by a vowel-sound:

> Mais où donc est l'amour?
> [mɛzudõkɛlamur]
> (But where then is love?)
>   (*Fiançailles pour rire*, Poulenc-Vilmorin)

> Où donc les vents l'ont-ils chassée?
> [udõ→lɛ→vã→lõ→ti→lʃase]
> (Where then have the winds driven it?)
>   ("Romance," Debussy-Bourget)

2. initial in line, for emphasis:

> Donc, ce sera par un clair jour d'été.
> [dõksœ→sœra→parœ̃→klɛ→rʒu→rdete]
> (So, it will be on a bright summer day.)
>   (*La Bonne Chanson*, Fauré-Verlaine)

3. but *never* when final

> Frappe-moi donc!
> [frapœmwadõ]
> (Strike me then!)
>   (*Carmen*, Bizet)

Soit

Sound the final *t* as [t] only if

1. followed within the line by a vowel-sound:

> Soit lui, soit un autre.
> [swalɥiswatœ̃notrə]
> (Whether it be he or another.)

2. final in line, and alone, for emphasis:

> Soit!
> [swat]
> (So be it!)

Mais

Sound the final *s* in liaison, whether followed by a comma or not, as a general rule:

> mais, en attendant   mais, hélas . . .   Mais il me fuit.
> [mɛzãnatãdã]   [mɛzelɑs]   [mɛzilmœfɥi]
> (but, while waiting)   (but, alas . . .)   (But it eludes me.)

Except when liaison would obscure or weaken the text, especially in direct address:

> Mais,/ô mon bien-aimé, pour mieux sécher mes pleurs
> [m ɛ / o → m õ → b j ɛ̃ → n (e) → m e → / p u → r m j ∅ → s e → ʃ e → m ɛ → p l œ r]
> (But, oh my beloved, to better dry my tears)
>   (*Samson et Dalila*, Saint-Saëns)

Chacun, Quelqu'un, Un (as pronoun), Eux

Do not make liaison on these pronouns:

> Chacun à son goût   Quelqu'un entre.
> [ʃ a k œ̃ a s õ g u]   [k ɛ l k œ̃ ã t r ə]
> (Each to his taste)   (Someone is entering.)

> Plus d'un aurait donné sa vie.
> [p l y → d œ̃ → ɔ → r ɛ → d ɔ → n e → s a → v i → œ]
> (More than one would have given his life.)
>   ("Le Spectre de la Rose," Berlioz-Gautier)

> Devant eux/il chante.
> [d œ v ã t ∅ / i l ʃ ã t ə]
> (Before them he sings.)

Puis

Liaison is generally recommended on this word, whether followed by a comma or not, except between it and the word *on*:

> Puis, il s'épanche.   Puis,/on se sépara.
> [p ɥ i z i l s e p ã ʃ ə]   [p ɥ i õ s œ s e p a r a]
> (Then, it overflows.)   (Then, we separated.)

Yeux

Always make liaison into this word when appropriate:

> les yeux   de gros yeux
> [l e z j ∅]   [d œ g r o z j ∅]
> (the eyes)   (big eyes)

But not into other words beginning with *y*:

> un/yankee
> [œ̃ j ã k i]
> (a Yankee)

Interjections

Avoid liaison whenever possible between an interjection and a preceding or following word:

Tu mens, Ah!   Il meurt, hélas!   Reviens,/ô nuit!
[t y m ɑ̃/ɑ]   [i l m œ r/e l ɑ s]   [r œ v j ɛ̃/o n ɥ i]
(You lie, ah!)   (He is dying, alas!)   (Return, oh night!)

But, a gently sounded consonant may be in liaison before an interjection to separate two similar vowel-sounds:

Je dis, hélas . . .
[ʒ œ d i (z) e l ɑ s]
(I say, alas . . .)

Note parentheses around [z] to indicate lightness of attack.

Toujours

Liaison is made on this word only when it is followed by another word that it modifies or that modifies it. Otherwise the *r* is normally linked up, as in most words in *-rs*, the *s* remaining silent:

Le flot est toujours amer.
[l a → v i → ɛ → t u → ʒ u → r z a → m ɛ r]
(Life is still bitter.)
   (*Le Bestiaire,* Poulenc-Apollinaire)

Et nous étions liés pour toujours ainsi.
[e → n u → z e → t j õ → l i e → p u → r t u → ʒ u → r z ɛ̃ → s i]
(And we were linked forever thus.)
   (*Chansons de Bilitis,* Debussy-Louÿs)

Il y a toujours un silence extraordinaire.
[i → l i a → t u → ʒ u → r œ̃ → s i → l ɑ̃ → s ɛ → k s t r a → ɔ → r d i → n ɛ → r œ]
(There is always an extraordinary silence.)
   (*Pelléas et Mélisande,* Debussy-Maeterlinck)

Numbers, Numerical Words

Avoid liaison before and after the numerical pronouns *un* and *une*:

J'en vois un.   un ou deux   les heures, une à une
[ʒ ɑ̃ v w a œ̃]   [œ̃ u d ø]   [l ɛ z œ r œ/y n a y n ə]
(I see one of them.)   (one or two)   (the hours, one by one)

Avoid liaison into the numbers *huit* (eight) and *onze* (eleven):

    dan$ huit jours   Tu aura$ onze ans demain.
    [d ɑ̃ ɥ i ʒ u r]   [t y ɔ r a → õ → z ɑ̃ → d œ m ɛ̃]
    (in one week)   (You will be eleven tomorrow.)

But, in composite numbers, liaison is required into *huit,* but still not into *onze*:

    quatre-ving$-onze   dix-huit   vingt-huit
    [k a t r œ v ɛ̃ õ z ə]   [d i z ɥ i t]   [v ɛ̃ t ɥ i t]
    (ninety-one)   (eighteen)   (twenty-eight)

Avoid liaison after *cent* (one hundred), except when used as a numerical adjective:

    cen$-un   J'en ai cen$ aussi.   cent ans
    [s ɑ̃ œ]   [ʒ ɑ̃ n e → s ɑ̃ → o s i]   [s ɑ̃ t ɑ̃]
    (one hundred one)   (I have one hundred of them, too.)   (one hundred years)

EXERCISES

Based on this discussion of liaison, and with the help of the translations provided, decide where liaison should occur in the following examples and give the reason why. Phoneticize all words. Then intone each example.

1. Les hauts talons (the high heels)
2. Les autres ont entendu. (The others have heard.)
3. Un an et une semaine (one year and a week)
4. Le vent a changé. (The wind has changed.)
5. Nous avons espéré. (We have hoped.)
6. Dors encore! (Sleep on!)
7. En attendant (while waiting)
8. Il est mort inaperçu. (He died unnoticed.)
9. Filles et garçons (girls and boys)
10. Six ans après (six years later)
11. Après un an (after a year)
12. Une nuit éternelle (an eternal night)
13. Le joyeux et doux printemps arrive. (The joyous and sweet springtime arrives.)
14. Chacun est entré. (Each one has entered.)
15. Toujours heureux, toujours avec toi (always happy, always with you)
16. Il faut aimer, espérer; aimer et espérer toujours! (One must love, hope; love and hope forever!)

for
Tues
3/27

4

How to Phoneticize and Prepare the Text of a Song or Aria

The Phoneticization and Intoning Procedures

1. Reconstruct the poem by copying it line for line, making sure to leave *two* spaces between each line of verse. Remember that as a rule a capital letter in the text, even when within the musical phrase, may indicate a new line of poetry. In this way, line length, rhyme scheme, and overall structure of the poem will be more evident. Skip extra lines between stanzas or verses. If possible, obtain a reliable edition of the poetry of the text and compare this original version with your own.

2. Now underline vowel-sounds, circle semi-consonant sounds, mark elisions and liaisons, and divide words syllabically.

3. Insert the phoneticization directly above the individual line of verse, using the rules and examples from this manual.

4. Directly beneath the line of verse, insert a word-by-word translation, rearranging to the best of your ability the one provided in your edition, the one provided in Pierre Bernac's *The Interpretation of French Song,* or your own. A sample line would appear thus:

[l ɛ ⟶ r b ɛ -----⟶ m ɔ ---⟶ l o ⟶ s ɔ m ɛ ⁱ]

L ' h e r b e   e s t   m o l l e   a u   s o | m m e i l

(The grass   is   soft   for   sleeping)

[s u ⟶ l ɛ ⟶ f r ɛ ---⟶ p œ ⟶ p l i e]

S o u s   l e s   f r a i s   p e u | p l i e r s

(under the   cool   poplar trees)

"Phidylé," H. Duparc-Leconte de Lisle

5. When this process has been completed, copy your phoneticization into your score above the musical line, synchronizing carefully symbols and notes, and insert the word-by-word translation beneath the text:

"Phidylé," **H. Duparc**-Leconte de Lisle

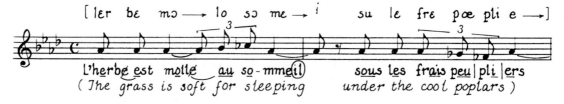

6. Now, using your phoneticized and translated score, intone the phoneticization. Intoning involves singing legato, with a fully supported, well resonated sound on one note, preferably in the upper middle register of the voice. Sit up straight or stand while doing so, giving the intonation all the energy you would give to actual singing. Intone the phoneticized syllables of the text while strictly observing the note-values assigned to each syllable in the exact tempo in which the song or aria is to be eventually sung. The note used for intoning may be changed from phrase to phrase to avoid fatigue or monotony, but not within the phrase itself. If the actual tempo is too fast for accurate vocalization of the sounds at first, it would be wise to start intoning at half the tempo, gradually accelerating it with each repetition of the text until the actual tempo can be realized. The tempo must not fluctuate within any one repetition of the text, but should instead be kept uniform throughout. Not until you can intone the text with ease and fluency in the correct tempo are you ready to attempt the actual singing of the text on the various pitches.

7. Then, sing through the song or aria on any given syllable (*mi, la,* etc.), *not* on the text itself, giving careful attention to the accuracy of pitches and rhythms. Pitch and rhythm must always be learned separately from text and rhythm. Rhythm is the common denominator of the two and is crucial to their synchronization.

8. Next, on the assigned pitches and rhythms of the composition, sing the vowel-sounds of the text, legato, excluding all the consonant-sounds. Make the shift from vowel-sound to vowel-sound clearly and cleanly, but without any interruption of the vocalic flow. At this point in your study, analyze which vowel-sounds will need modification in the high and low registers, and practice them accordingly, paying attention to vocal facility and vocalic intelligibility. Then, line up the vowel-sounds by matching them as closely as possible while retaining their particular qualities. Analyze what they have in common and preserve this in the singing process. Beware of pinching, over-rounding, and exaggerated nasalization. Do not

allow a particular vowel to "stick out" except for expressive reasons, and keep all vowel-sounds *alive* and *resonant* at all times. Make the vowels fit and enhance your voice; vowel-sounds should be to the voice what clothes are to the body.

9. Now, sing the whole phoneticization of the song or aria, vowel-sounds, semi-consonants, and consonant-sounds alike, at a uniform dynamic level, on the given pitches and rhythms. Observe carefully the principle of legato throughout by making the consonants *rapid, late* and *clear,* and by prolonging the vowel-sounds as long as their assigned note-values will permit. In staccato sections, articulate the consonants with precision and lightness, always without shortening the duration of the vowel-sounds. Remember that a vocal staccato is achieved by an energetic but lightweight consonantal articulation, *not* by shortening the vowel-sounds. Elongate the shorter syllables of the score and text to give them sonority and to allow them to participate in the legato. If possible, record your preparation on tape and listen to it critically, noting in your score any improvements to be made. Now you are ready to think about *interpretation.*

The Interpretation of a French Song or Aria Text

Too many stop here in their study of "diction," assuming that once the technical aspects have been mastered, their work in this area is done. It has truly only begun, for correctly pronounced and vocalized words are worthless if they do not express feelings, moods, ideas, and so on. The singer must be able to convey effectively the content of his text to his listeners.

SELECTION OF THE SONG OR ARIA

How many singers choose a composition before carefully considering its text, simply because it "lies well," only to find after further reflection that they (or their voice) cannot accept, interpret, or even understand its text? If a selection seems vocally appropriate (and this should, of course, be the initial consideration since interpretation is impossible if the singer cannot "sing" the song or aria), then the singer should immediately examine the text. A *good* translation must be obtained, not one of those unrelated English paraphrases found beneath and often above the original text in so many scores.

The singer must know the meaning and expressive intent of every word, of every line, and of the overall text he is to sing. Indeed, a singer should develop his literary sensitivity to the level of his vocal ability before considering public performance on any kind of professional level. The complete vocal artist must cultivate and refine this sensitivity to the word, to poetry, and to literature in general. His job is manifold and somewhat more encompassing than that of the instrumentalist. The singer is always working through a text that in some way or another inspired the vocal line and its texture. It is this inseparable relationship of the text and its music that confronts the vocal artist at every moment, be it in opera, oratorio, or art song. Practically without exception, all texts, whether poetry, prose, or the dramatic lines of a libretto, existed in their own right as literature before being set to music.

In evaluating a piece of vocal music, one of the first considerations should be the composer's sense of *prosody*—or his ability to set the text to music with respect to the verbal structure, rhythm, and mood. In art song, where the text and its music are most inextricably linked, it is the composer's reaction to and his subsequent musical realization of the poem that determine the artistic quality of his composition. A composer with a low poetic sensitivity may be quite capable of turning out a "singable" song, and, indeed, a very "musical" one. But the more aware the singer is of the text, the more problematic this song will be to "interpret," due to this discrepancy between the word and the music. This is not to advise complete abstinence from all songs with bad prosody. Most of Berlioz, Bizet, Franck, and even some Fauré could be accused of this shortcoming, not to mention more recent composers such as Milhaud and Boulez, who seem to delight in the obscuring of a text. Rather, an awareness of weak prosody can guide the singer in his resultant interpretation. He can avoid accenting unstressed syllables that fall on strong beats or high notes, concentrate on clarifying what has been obscured by the musical setting, and attempt to preserve the message and mood of a line that has been assigned music unsuited to it. However, when setting a text to music, the composer's awareness of prosody will facilitate the singer's interpretation, because the score and its details will serve as hints rather than obstacles to that interpretation. If only all composers had the literary perception coupled with the musical expertise of Debussy, Ravel, or Poulenc! But, in truth, they all do not, and it is a singer's duty to discriminate between music that illuminates, illustrates, and complements the poetry and music that distracts from, obscures, or even obliterates it.

FLUENT RECITATION OF THE TRANSLATION

The singer must next set about mastering a fluent recitation of the translation, in his mother tongue, of the text. For those who speak French fluently, a recitation of the translation may be unnecessary. This must be thought of as a poetry reading or a dramatic recitation in which the singer reads aloud the translation while mentally following and audibly displaying the musical setting to which the text is married, as it were, taking into consideration pauses, dynamics, tempos, etc. The significance of this achievement can be most appreciated when reading aloud the same text set to different music by different composers. The poems are the same, but they have been set to music by men or women with different personalities and sets of reactions. A performer's reaction to the setting should be equally differentiated, and must be reflected in his readings as well as in his finished performances. Declaim, murmur, tell, whisper, shout, project, but, above all, *communicate* and explain audibly the meaning, moods, and content of the text. Get it into your blood as dramatic literature and it will "get into your voice." If you have chosen well, your voice will be able to take it!

FLUENT RECITATION OF THE ORIGINAL TEXT IN FRENCH

Those singers whose French is fluent can catch up with us here. Now that the meaning, moods, and content of the text are clear, the poem can be recited aloud in French, with its musical setting always in mind, as well as the singer's personal reaction to the poetry. Assuming that all the pronunciation is correct, the objective here is expressive and interpretive recitation of literature in a foreign tongue. This is not always an easy task. Again, avoid parody of any kind. For some reason, non-French people adopt a suggestive, almost lewd tone of voice whenever they utter a word of French. A Viennese doctor once said, "What a sensual language French is! Why, imagine, the word for 'pig' is *cochon*!" One could perhaps argue that French poetry, more than any other, explores and penetrates the subject of sensual experience and that the language itself with its liquid-like legato flow and its rich endowment of voluptuous vowel-sounds, such as the nasals, lends itself most successfully to the description of physical pleasure. Fine! But not all song texts are limited to one subject or mood. Some are narrative and are best delivered as one would read a story to a child. Others are violent and bitter, still others proud, humble, innocent, prayerful, despairing, and so on. *See the text for what it is.* Let it speak *to* you so that it can speak *through* you. Do not allow any lack of real experience to inhibit you in the expression of a text; use your imagination and make others use theirs while listening to you. Be *simple* and *direct* and become the text and its poet. Only then will it be yours. Only then will it be *you,* not someone else.

RESEARCH ON THE TEXT

Always try to study a text separately from its musical setting and in its original form, as it existed before being set to music. If it is verse, it is very interesting and significant to know whether the composer left out any stanzas or changed any of the words. This often sheds new light on the text and upon the composer's appreciation of it. It is also important to determine the original punctuation so often omitted in scores. Or, as the case may be, punctuation may have been added to the original. What appears as whimsical capitalization of unimportant words, may it be stressed again, is usually due to the fact that the first word of each line of verse is traditionally capitalized and that this practice is carried over in the printing of a score.

In the case of opera, it is both helpful and fascinating to trace the libretto back to its original source for clarification of plot, character, and background, as well as to see what was added or omitted by the librettists in their adaptations.

The texts of oratorios may appear dry and irrelevant to the twentieth-century performer estranged from religious literature and history. A little study can make the most obscure oratorio text come to life with the fire that once inspired many a composer and his devout audience.

INTERPRETATION WHILE SINGING

It is here that all previous preparation, however concentrated and thorough it may have been, can be promptly forgotten because of the added and most significant element here: singing. How often it is that a singer can draw an interpretative blank when he starts to sing. The process, or possibly duress, of singing may take over his concentration and, at the same time, stifle any possibility of true interpretation.

The word "interpretation" is dangerously misunderstood and "misinterpreted." Too often, singers (and musicians in general) feel they owe it to themselves artistically to impose their "interpretation" upon what is given. They feel that in this way they "make it their own," placing upon it a weighty, indelible stamp that obscures the outlines beneath. This approach to interpretation can be compared to the cook who spices his food so highly that its natural taste is hidden. One's first duty in interpreting music is to observe *all* that the composer requests in the realization of his creation. Only after sincerely attempting to do so can the singer permit himself the luxury of making the slight adjustments necessary to satisfy both his inspirations and limitations. The fear that such "blind and unimaginative" fidelity might conceal one's own artistic identity is a dangerous admission. Two artists can follow every indication in a score and come out with two very personal statements, just as two fine cooks can follow the same recipe and produce very different results. What counts in both cases is the quality of the ingredients. True artistic individuality refuses to be so easily hidden. But the artist who has the courage and integrity to observe faithfully every detail of a score is a rare one, and is the only one who will penetrate fully into the mystery of the creation before him.

Instead of "dreaming up" an interpretation (or running to a coach for one before trying one himself), the singer must *uncover* the interpretative demands that will be made upon him by the total composition, and consequently allow that these indications guide him in his technical confrontation of the composition. Before singing a given note or phrase *pianissimo* or *fortissimo,* and lacking any explicit indication to do either in the score, it is imperative to see what the text indicates. How often singers boom out vociferously about the silence of a forest, or cheep blithely on about the raging of a torrent! Also, it often helps to determine the "space" of the text and its setting. Is it oratorical (with a lot of space around it), or is it intimate (enclosed in a small space)? Is this a betrayed lover venting his wounded passion on all of nature, or is it a contented one cooing in the ear of his beloved? The same song or aria can demand spaciousness and intimacy, especially in recitatives (see Chapter 6).

To study the *singing* of music before coming to general well-founded conclusions about its interpretative demands is putting the cart before the horse. Vocal study, with public performance in mind, cannot effectively begin until the interpretative itinerary has been mapped out. All the answers are right there on the page, in the score and in the text, and, of course, in the singer's intelligent and responsible reaction to what he sees there.

For most people, interpretation includes "expression," and singing most certainly should be "expressive." But expressive of *what*? is the point here. Expression can be negative as well as positive. It is of great importance to know when and when *not* to "pour it on," what and what *not* to express. Expression is not just pathos-oriented. There is everything to express: joy, sorrow, boredom, enthusiasm, hope, despair, extroversion, introversion, strife and peace—the list is as endless as human feeling and experience. The best and most reliable rule should be simplicity and honesty in one's confrontation of the text and its setting. One would not read a grocery list the same way one would a love poem. Contrivances such as grimaces, false accents, irresponsible *crescendi* and *diminuendi* (what Bernac calls "involuntary nuances"), "cute" or pompous gestures—all are substitutes for real inspiration, and effective, direct communication. Fancy inflections should be sparsely superimposed upon texts and only after due reflection on the part of the singer. Thoughtless embroideries, especially those that are not spontaneous, can often set an understanding audience to embarrassed tittering. Expression must be honest, sincerely felt, and, again, *simple*. It must be effectively projected with healthy and appropriate vocal production and diction. The chain must be unbroken, with no missing links.

"FRENCH STYLE"

Ours is an era of "performance practice" and "style." Under these two puristic (and not so pure) banners musical murder has been committed. Much has been said about the "French style," yet it has never been successfully defined. It seems to be an all-inclusive term that veils the whole repertoire in an aura of impenetrable mystery. Of course there are a few characteristic tendencies in the performance of French vocal music distinguishing it from the Italian, German, and other repertoires (see Bernac, *The Interpretation of French Song,* Chapter 3).

Portamento is used sparingly in French vocal music, especially in the realm of song, but it is certainly used, and at times is requested by the composer ("portando" or "portez la voix"). When *portamento* is used, there is one "stylistic" rule to remember: the syllable upon which the *portamento* takes place must give way to the following one as soon as this syllable's note is reached at the end of the *portamento,* unlike the *portamento* in Italian where the old syllable is extended indefinitely into the note of the new syllable. To be avoided are excessive, pointless ritards, unnecessary sacrificing of the legato, involuntary (or thoughtless) nuances, irresponsible tempo changes, and the like.

But can this not be recommended in the performance of all music? Preconceptions about such a mysterious entity as "French style" might better be dismissed in favor of a purity and simplicity of approach, a clarity and naturalness of diction, and an adherence to the score and to the demands of the text. Add to that a pleasant, well-produced voice, a dash of sensitivity, intelligence, and good taste. Baste these constantly with a little artistry, common sense, and life-giving energy. Something truly beautiful may result.

5

The Application of Diction Techniques to Other Aspects of Singing

Recitative

Let us not announce gloomily that "the art of recitative is dying," but rather lament the neglect into which it has fallen. Some of the most directly communicative and moving vocal music is in the form of recitative. Certainly there is no need to justify it here; recitative is as old as singing itself. Yet how often in performances, both with orchestra and in recital, and in auditions, the "recit" is cut with the excuse that it is "boring." A recitative sets the tone and provides the dramatic spark for the ensuing aria. However, it may truly be dull if its meaning is unknown to the singer and consequently unexpressed, or if performed metrically with little regard for verbal inflection and dramatic change of pace.

Recitative is the closest the singer comes to actual theatrical declamation. A prolonged recitative such as Donna Anna's in Act I of *Don Giovanni* could be compared to a Shakespearean soliloquy or a Racinian *tirade*. In its broadest, most inclusive sense, recitative is the vocal declamation of a text set to music, following inflections, the changing tempo, and the varying moods of speech. With few exceptions, recitative should, however, be *sung* and *delivered* with vocal beauty, crisp diction, and appropriate expressivity. But how often it is merely "spoken," indeed mumbled or rattled off with impatience. Oddly enough, those singers who constantly sing out of time deliver recitative "in rhythm," when the innate meter of any recitative is in the words themselves.

In a sense, any vocal music that is not governed by regular meter and inflexible rhythm may be considered a form of recitative. Of those who may disagree with this statement it is hereby requested that for the moment and for the sake of understanding they suspend their judgment.

The oldest-known recitative styles of "modern" music, those of Gregorian chant and of the earliest Italian opera, still serve as bases for much recitative-style vocal writing today, notably in *Pelléas et Mélisande,* Debussy's lyric drama. The earliest known operas—those of Caccini, Peri and Monteverdi—were written in a style called *monody,* in which a harmonically conceived vocal line followed the stress patterns and natural rhythms of the word. Caccini called it "speaking in music"; Peri perceived it as "imitation of a person speaking in song." Monteverdi provided a perfection of the style in his opera *Orfeo* (1607). The style described above is *recitative.*

The earliest French opera composers of the late seventeenth and early eighteenth centuries, best represented by Lully and Rameau, led a crusade against the overwhelming Italian influence in vocal music all over Europe at the time. They preferred a recitative style known as *récitatif mesuré,* or "metered recitative," which may seem at first to be a slight contradiction in terms. Here an underlying rhythmic structure was subject to frequent changes in time signature and tempo relative to the demands of the text. In fact, at first the French sought to confuse the Italian distinction between meterless recitative and the formal rhythm-based aria by promoting the *récitatif mesuré* style, which in reality was simply an adaptation of the Italian recitative style to the demands and character of the French language. As a matter of fact, the *recitativo secco* prevalent in Mozart and Rossini, with its dry, clipped, chattery delivery, never really caught on in representative French opera of the late eighteenth and early nineteenth centuries. Instead, right from the beginning of French opera the recitative style was flowing, semi-metered, and above all *sung* as opposed to *parlando,* yet was intimately related to the rhythm, inflections, and punctuations of the French language.

In the following examples of *récitatif mesuré,* the stressed syllables have been underlined. Here, primary stress is marked by double underlines; secondary stress by a single underline. Note in the example from Lully's *Thésée* how the syllables of primary and secondary stress generally fall on the strong beats of longer duration. Observe also the typical anapestic rhythms (short-short-long), the most characteristic pattern of French speech rhythm ("est ici," "-tre étonnés," "il ne vous," "de ces lieux," "à la seule victoire il permet de le suivre"). Here, in nine bars of *récitatif mesuré* occur no less than four changes of time signature. An edited version is given ("to be sung") after the original ("as written"), without time signatures but with consistent note-values that the singer can use to break the rhythmic code, so to speak. Also, the recitative is grouped into four sections, according to meaning and expression, with suggested breathing spots. Singers may note that a rest in recitative (as in all music) does not necessarily dictate or allow a breath. The rest after ''Mars'' is perhaps a means of suggesting an emphasis on ''lui-même,'' and the one after ''ici'' no more than a ''punctuating lift,'' but not one of interruption. Fluctuations of tempo in recitative are determined by the text itself. On the third phrase of the recitative a slight *accelerando* is suggested, then a gentle ritard to bring the singer back to the lilting *ritornello* of the aria *Revenez, revenez, Amours, revenez.*

Thésée (**Prologue; 1675), J.-B. Lully**

Thésée (Prologue; 1675), J.-B. Lully

To be sung (indications my own):

Mars lui-même est i - ci, ces-sez d'être é - ton-
Mars himself is here, cease your alarm.

nés. Est-il quel-que dan - ger dont il ne vous dé -
Is there any danger from which he cannot

li - vre? Il chas-se les Fu- reurs de ces lieux for-tu -
save you? He banishes the Furies from these chosen

nés, À la seu-le Vic - toire il per-met de le sui - vre.
sites, To victory alone does he allow you to follow him.

Throughout the execution of this and any other recitative the watchword is *rubato*, or what Caccini so aptly called the "noble neglect of the rhythm." Once the sense of the text is understood and it is appropriately grouped together, the singer's breath will dictate the tempo and word-flow. It is significant that Lully, born an Italian, studied elocution with La Champmeslé, the great French *comédienne* of the Comédie-française. Before setting any text to music, Lully insisted that she declaim it in the grand theatrical manner.

The following example from Rameau contains four changes of time signature within ten bars. Note the similarity to characteristics observed in the example of Lully. Note, too, that the step-wise writing is more graceful and rhythmically varied. Whereas Lullian recitative tends to be triadic, syllabic (one note per syllable), and fast-moving with the rapid click of French utterance, Ramellian recitative is in the true *arioso* style: it is more melodic; some syllables are set to more than one note; and there are occasional leaps, spaces, and appoggiaturas. More than sixty years elapsed between the two composers' active periods in opera, and music itself had undergone a certain evolution. But both Lully and Rameau produced true *récitatif mesuré*, each in his own time, thus demonstrating the durability of this approach to recitative. Another interesting innovation in the Ramellian style as shown here is the changing of the stress, for

"Tristes apprêts," *Castor et Pollux* (1737), **J.-P. Rameau**

As written : (N.B.: Embellishments given here as they appear in the Grovlez edition are erroneous; they should begin with the upper note on the beat.)

Très lent

Non, je ne ver-rai plus que vos clar-tés fu-
No, I shall see from now on only your funereal brilliance.

-nè - bres. Non, non, je ne ver-rai
No, No, I shall see

plus que vos clar-tés fu-nè - - bres.
from now on only your funereal brilliance.

"Tristes apprêts," *Castor et Pollux* (1737), **J.-P. Rameau**

To be sung (indications my own) :

Très lent

accel.

Non, je ne ver-rai plus que vos clar-tés fu-nè - bres.
No, I shall see from now on only your funereal brilliance.

Broadly

Non, non, je ne ver - rai plus que vos clar-
No, No, I shall see from now on only your

move

tes fu-nè - - bres.
funereal brilliance.

dramatic emphasis, on ''Je ne verrai plus.'' Although the presence of the orchestral accompaniment would demand the control of a conductor, the rhythmic flow is resilient and subject to the fluctuations of dramatic declamation.

Gluck, another foreigner on the French operatic scene and a truly international musician, introduced the French to the dramatic *recitativo concitato* style typical of the latter part of the eighteenth century in Europe. In the following example from his French version of *Orphée et Euridice* (1774), all the earmarks of the *récitatif mesuré* of earlier French opera have been incorporated into a style that is turbulent, constantly changing in tempo, volume, and range, but accompanied by an orchestral commentary of harmonic progressions and harmonic rhythm, abrupt chordal interpolations, and enthusiastic *tremoli*.

Orphée et Euridice (Act III; 1774), C. W. R. von Gluck

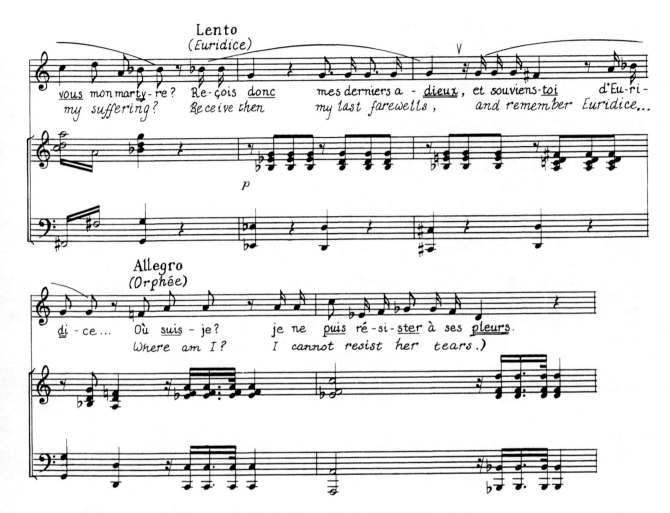

Tempo changes are characteristically indicated in Italian, while the time signature remains generally the same throughout. At times, the recitative takes on a monotonous, chant-like character that adheres to a rhythm less flexible than usual (as in Euridice's lines in the *Lento* section). Groupings and suggested breathing have again been inserted here to aid in the textual flow and dramatic declamation. Remember: a rest does not necessarily indicate a breath! Note the same anapestic formula prevalent throughout, the falling of stressed syllables on longer notes and stronger beats, and the rise and fall of the vocal line in adherence to the dramatic sense and import. As in all French recitative, crispness and clear articulation are *de rigueur,* and *singing,* not speaking, is called for. But indispensable here is a variety of vocal volume and color, something less prevalent in earlier examples. Again, music itself had undergone a profound change in the decades separating Rameau and Gluck. Note that only a century separated Lully from the classical style. With Gluck, the grandiose and pompous recitative style of *opera seria* was established in France, announcing the recitative characteristic of French grand opera in the nineteenth century best represented by Meyerbeer and Berlioz.

Recitative is certainly not confined to opera, nor is it always labeled as recitative. It is essential to be able to detect the presence of recitative, or a quasi-recitative, declaimed style, when it is not obviously presented as such. The famous song ''Absence'' from Berlioz' *Nuits d'été* (c. 1840) must be released from the confines of meter and bar-lines if its total effect is to be made. It is vocal declamation cushioned by orchestral accompaniment that presents little metrical restriction, its periodic melody demanding a recitative-oriented approach. The opening bars of the orchestra predict ''verbatim'' what is to be declaimed a moment later by the voice. The *fermatas* eliminate any pulsation of rhythm and appropriately isolate the lonesome lament of the deserted lover who calls to his beloved in the distance. The second ''reviens'' is prolonged by the first *fermata*, and the sixteenth-note rest that follows is itself marked with a *fermata*. In contrast, the unstressed final *-e* of ''bien-aimée'' is without a *fermata* and should be released long before the diminishing F-sharp major chord in the orchestra. The rests following in the voice part, each one beat marked by *fermatas*, separate this prelude from the ensuing, more rhythmically regular section.

''Absence,'' *Nuits d'été* (1840), **H. Berlioz**-T. Gautier

The vowels must be closely matched to facilitate the execution of this difficult passage. The [œ] of the first syllable of ''reviens'' should be mixed judiciously with the [ɛ̃] of the second syllable. This should not be difficult if nasality per se is kept to a minimum on the high F-sharp. Instead, as discussed previously in the section on [ɛ̃], this nasal vowel should be rich, "tall," and slightly rounded, especially in the upper register. The sound should be one that could travel over the miles to the ears of the beloved. The vowels of "ma bien-aimée ([a ɛ̃(e) e œ]), all of which are frontal, can help guide the voice through this treacherous tessitura if they are uniformly produced and placed. No nasal rasp on "bien," please. The first two syllables of "aimée" may be vocalically harmonized ([(e) m e œ]) *en route* to the final [œ] upon which a short *diminuendo* occurs before release. Over-holding on this final syllable will betray both the prosody and the musical setting (there is *no fermata* on the final F sharp!). The orchestra instead holds its F-sharp major chord past the voice, completing the *diminuendo*. After the *point d'orgue* (grand pause) the song continues on at its leisurely, mournful pace.

"Absence," *Nuits d'été* (1840), **H. Berlioz**-T. Gautier

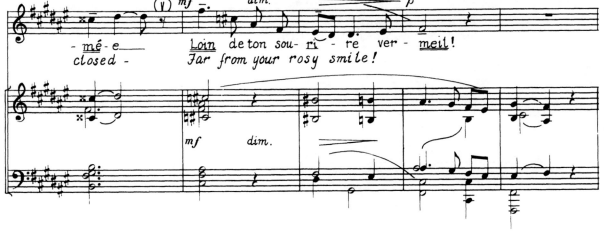

The excerpt from "Absence" illustrates Berlioz' occasional lapses into bad prosody. In the first phrase, "Comme une fleur loin du soleil" (to be grouped together as one in spite of the punctuating rest), the highest and longest notes are not on the most important words or stressed syllables. In this instance the aware singer must improve upon the prosody by a gentle emphasis on and elongation of the G-sharp of "fleur" and the F-sharp of the second syllable of "soleil." The second phrase of the section, consisting of a long arch from "la fleur" all the way to "vermeil," is punctuated by two "breathing rests." But these rests must not stop the flow of sound and motion to the top of the arch on the word "loin." The prosody is good, with the -ri- of "sourire" and the final syllable of "vermeil" receiving the strong beats and the longest note-values. In spite of the presence of a time signature and the curve of the phrases, the vocal writing is not melodically but textually and harmonically conceived. An ebb-and-flow must preside over the declamation here, as if time stood still. The steady movement of the vocal line will then be surrounded by the immobile solitude of the lover.

Berlioz' admiration for Gluck's recitative style can be felt in the following eleven bars of "Absence," in which the tempo quickens and the volume increases as the lover complains of his painful abandonment.

"Absence," *Nuits d'été* (1840), **H. Berlioz**-T. Gautier

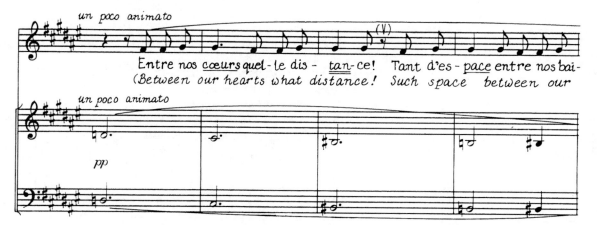

Entre nos cœurs quel-le dis - tan-ce! Tant d'es - pace entre nos bai-
(Between our hearts what distance! Such space between our

In the first phrase of this example, punctuated by a breath after "distance" the voice wavers between two notes before launching into the second phrase (*con agitazione*), gradually expanding into a wailing outburst on the words, "O grands désirs inapaisés." Not until this second phrase is any metric pulse dictated by the accompaniment, which almost immediately subsides to a standstill on the A-sharp[7] chord marked by a *fermata*. At this point, the initial "Reviens, ma bien-aimée" cited above is reiterated, and the song continues on in a similar manner—freely, ever-changing, and in true *declamato* style.

Gounod, a master of recitative in his operas, uses the style with great dramatic effect in "Il était un roi de Thulé" from *Faust*. The plaintive, irrelevant narrative intoned by Marguerite is periodically interrupted by recited outbursts that reveal what is really going on in her mind: her pre-occupation with the young Faust. Then an extended recitative further reveals to us the wonderings and delicate character of the heroine. It is a recitative in the grand manner, constantly fluctuating, with significantly interpolated orchestral commentary.

Faust (Act I; 1859), C. Gounod

All indications in parentheses have been inserted here and are not the composer's. Just the opening phrase ("Un bouquet . . . C'est de Siebel sans doute! Pauvre garçon!") is enough to illustrate the resistance of recitative to strict meter and vocal monotony. Marguerite sees the bouquet (surprise) . . . she decides it must be from the adolescent Siebel who has a cloying crush on her (end of surprise, slight disappointment) . . . she considers tenderly his pointless pursuit (musing compassion). Then she sees the jewel box! She hesitates to open it, then decides it would do no harm, does so, and sees the jewels. Enraptured, she pinches herself to see if she is dreaming. Imagine an actress *saying* these lines. Say them out loud in English and then in French, following the changing states of mind within this simple, sensitive young woman. Then insert the appropriate inflection and timing into your singing of the text, always taking into account the stressed syllables and their longer note-values while resisting a metronomic delivery. Do not scream out the high F-sharp on "Ah!"—it is an "ah" of pleasant surprise, not one of terror. Touch upon it lightly and connect it dramatically to what follows. With a sense of urgency in the declamation, Marguerite discovers the mirror (all in one breath). A line of text repeated *verbatim* is rarely to be uttered in the same tempo and volume. The first "Comment n'être pas coquette" may be sung *forte* and relatively in tempo, but the second is charming if sung more softly and slowly, with a surrendering *portamento* on the octave (get to the first syllable of "n'être" on the low E-natural!). Note that when the formal aria (the "Jewel Song") begins, a tempo marking is given (*Allegretto*) and that the bass of the orchestra pulsates with a decided rhythm. Here, on the last two syllables of "coquette," the singer must sing somewhat in time with the conductor. Her recitative is over and the rhythmic rigidity of the aria has begun.

Although the recitatives in *Carmen* are not Bizet's but Guiraud's, it is useful to discuss here Micaëla's recitative preceding her aria in Act III. Typically, the recitative is provided with no dynamic indications or tempo markings of any kind. How often a supposedly anxious Micaëla ventures forth into the smugglers' den, only to give an impression of utter calm when she sings her recitative. The girl's timidity and fragility, her fearful determination and desire for courage must all be present in these opening bars.

Carmen (Act III; 1873–74), G. Bizet

The first phrase should be sung softly but *agitato,* with a certain dread present in the voice. In one breath and in full voice, as if to convince herself, Micaëla declares her intention to find Don José, and then *declamato,* a little more deliberately and *forte,* she repeats aloud her intention to bring him back to his mother (and in so doing perhaps win him for herself—note that Micaëla may not be so selfless and dull as she may seem to be on the surface). All indications in parentheses have been inserted and are not the composer's. Her ensuing aria, so often discarded as beautiful but dramatically misplaced and uninteresting, might then make more sense in its portrayal of an essentially timid, homespun soul that must assert itself before thieves and a siren-gypsy like Carmen.

In his *Manon,* Massenet revives the *récitatif mesuré* of Rameau, a contemporary of the Abbé Prévost who was the author of the eighteenth century tale upon which Massenet's opera was based. Although the opera *Manon* is undeniably late nineteenth-century, Massenet attempts to imbue it with the flavor of its eighteenth-century origins through the use of dance rhythms, courtly themes, and, importantly, the stylized recitative. Like other French operas of its time, *Manon* constantly vacillates between recitative and aria—two measures in time, then three that are free, followed by four in time, two free, etc. Occasionally what is actually recitative appears disguised as song in strict meter. A complete conversation in *récitatif mesuré* style occurs in the first scene of Act III between the Count and Manon, their verbal exchange bobbing up and down in the rhythm and pacing of conversation over a minuet played and danced to in the next room, a technique already explored by Mozart in his *Don Giovanni.*

In the following excerpt from the Manon-DesGrieux duet in Act V, not one indication has been inserted. They are *all* Massenet's, and, what is more, they work. It seems that from this period on, composers began taking the same pains to include interpretative indications in recitative passages as they had previously in strictly metered sections. Massenet's dramatic sense is marvelous.

Manon (Act V; 1883), J. Massenet

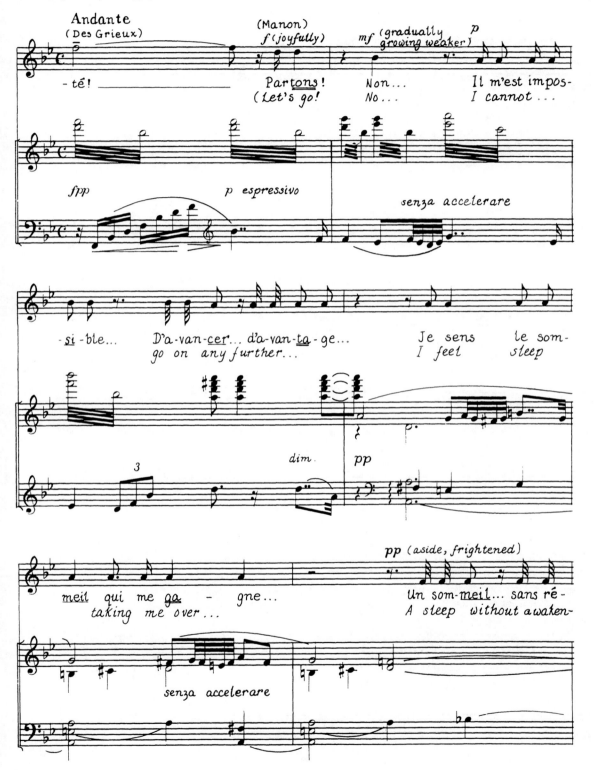

Note the graduation from *forte* to *mezzo forte* to *piano* in Manon's "Partons . . . non . . . il m'est impossible," with the recommendations "joyfully, gradually growing weaker" above the staff. Massenet typically bids the orchestra *not* to accelerate, for he wants the staggered mumblings of the dying Manon to be relatively in time, as he wrote them, since only then will they resemble free declamation. On a monotone Manon declares that sleep is overcoming her. Then, in agonized accents, first *piano,* then *forte,* she says her sleep will be eternal. She becomes short of breath (short outbursts surrounded by gasping rests), is about to expire (*quasi parlando* or half speaking, half singing), when DesGrieux exhorts her to regain her senses and points out the evening star. Massenet indicates stress in the text by inserting a line over the D-natural of "étoile" and a *fermata* plus a stress line over Manon's "Ah!" Another stress with a characteristic *tenuto* is requested on the second syllable of "encore." An observance of such stresses indicated by Massenet himself renders the delivery all the more poignant and expressive. They must *not* be overlooked or ignored. Then, two bars of 9/8 in time (*Andante*) serve as a good example of disguised recitative. Note the characteristic request by Massenet to give equal stress to the first three syllables of "C'est un adieu. . . ." Announcing Debussy and later composers, and aware of the need for stylized, expressive delivery of the recitative, Massenet leaves little room for tinkering around with the execution of his semi-melodic, semi-rhythmic recitative style.

Debussy, rivaled only by Hugo Wolf in the art of setting a text to music, was perhaps, with the possible exceptions of Ravel and Poulenc, the most literary of all French composers to date. In much of his early vocal writing, traces of Gounod and Massenet are easily detected. Debussy utilized Massenet's recitative style in his cantata *L'Enfant prodigue,* as can be seen, for example, in Lia's famous recitative and aria. But, the refinement of his own superlative sense of prosody and speech-melody can be found in his opera *Pelléas et Mélisande,* as well as in the song cycle *Chansons de Bilitis.* In the eighteenth century Jean-Jacques Rousseau wrote that one day a Frenchman would produce a "recitative appropriate to the simplicity and clarity of our language," and that it "should proceed by very small intervals. The voice should neither rise nor descend very much. There should be few sustained notes; no sudden bursts and still less any shrieking; nothing that resembles song; and little inequality in the duration of the value of the notes." If one qualifies "nothing that resembles song" by inserting the word "conventional," this is a perfect description of the vocal writing in the *Chansons de Bilitis,* from which an example is provided here:

"La Chevelure," *Chansons de Bilitis* (1897), **C. Debussy-**P. Louÿs

In the example below from *Pelléas et Mélisande,* note the tightness of the intervallic rise and fall, the regularity with which stressed syllables receive higher pitches and longer note values, the rhythmic variety and its uncanny simplicity, the gradual acceleration of the delivery from *modéré* to *animé* following the increasing urgency of Pelléas' plea to be allowed to travel to his sick friend's bedside. A mere recitation of these words demonstrates Debussy's sensitivity to the innate melodic rise and fall of his language, to its rhythm, stress, and expressive flow.

Pelléas et Mélisande **(Act I; 1892–1903), C. Debussy**

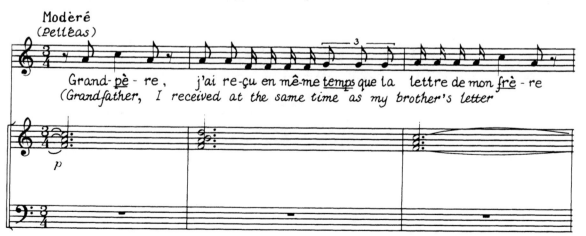

e-lle si je veux, mais qu'il n'y a pas de temps à per-dre.
it does if I want, but that there's no time to lose.)

Arianna (1608), **C. Monteverdi**

Ahi, che non pur ris-pon-di, Ahi, che più d'aspe è

sor-do a-mici la-men-ti. O nem-bi, o tur-bi, o venti sommerge te-lo voi den-

- tr'a quell' on - de cor-re-te orche e ba-le-ne e delle membra immon- de em -

pie-te le vo-ra-gi-ni pro-fon-de   Che par - lo,   ahi,   che va -

p

neg - gio? mi - se-ra   oi - mè   che chieg-gio?   o

Almost three hundred years after Monteverdi's *Arianna*, recitative style
had completed its circle with Debussy's *Pelléas*. In the example given

from Arianna's lament, note how intervallic leaps rarely exceed four steps, how stressed syllables receive longer and higher notes, and—something Debussy himself pointed out in his own recitative style—how expressive silences punctuate the delivery of the text. Even the realization of the accompanying chords sounds ''Debussyan'' in its tonal ambiguity and textually oriented rhythm.

From the examples of recitative written by these two masters, Monteverdi and Debussy, it would seem to be the oldest and least changed style of vocal delivery in existence. Was it but mere coincidence that Debussy called himself ''Claude de France,'' so much like Monteverdi's ''Claudio d'Italia''? The greatest difference between the recitative of the two was in their rhythmic notation and in their use of interpretative indications. Debussy wrote at a time when composers inserted explicit directions to the performer that were simply taken for granted by the early Italian opera masters.

In the twentieth century recitative, along with other vocal styles of preceding centuries, has been steadily perpetuated. One of the greatest composers for the voice of all time, Francis Poulenc, saw fit to write a whole opera in recitative style—*La Voix humaine*. Unlike Debussy, Poulenc used a more melodic and dramatic approach to recitative, with a tighter sense of recitative rhythm, more in the Ramellian tradition of *récitatif mesuré*. Also, his particular brand of ''arioso'' recitative spans a considerably greater vocal range than that of most of his predecessors. In the following excerpt from Act II of the *Dialogues des Carmélites*, Poulenc's recitative style can be easily identified. The evident characteristics seen here are a keen sense of prosody coupled with a willingness to use the extreme registers of the voice, an underlying, often metronomic, rhythm with frequent changes in time signature.

Dialogues des Carmélites (Act II; 1957), F. Poulenc

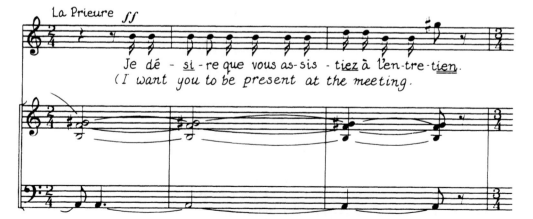

Mère Marie (hésitant)

Si vo tre Révé rence vou-lait bien le per-met-tre...
If your Reverence would kindly permit...

La Prieure

Vous, ma Mère, et non une au - tre!
You, my mother, and not another!)

Tempo agitato ♩ = 120

For Poulenc, the word was all important, as was the human voice. When setting a text to music, he delightfully declared that the union of word and music would be, in his words, a "marriage of love and not one of convenience."

Diction in Coloratura Passages

Coloratura is simply florid writing for the voice. It demands vocal flexibility, and it typically moves step-wise with leaps rarely exceeding a fourth.

Coloratura serves many purposes. First and foremost, it is a means of vocal display—virtuosity, agility, and range. It also ornaments what might otherwise be plain, without charm or drama. Sometimes it conceals a basic lack of musical interest and is an end in itself. Coloratura may create an atmosphere of cheeriness and buoyancy, in which case it is called "lyric coloratura," or it may bring turbulence and even violence to an aria when it is "dramatic" in nature.

Coloratura, from the standpoint of diction, is the exact opposite of recitative. The word is no longer supreme here; vocal production and facility are. First of all, by necessity, some syllables of the text receive more than one note, often several. The question must be asked: What atmosphere is appropriate to the overall meaning and intended impact of the coloratura passage? Indeed, all coloratura worth its dramatic salt has some transcendent, added significance.

The specific word upon which the coloratura falls is usually less important than the dramatic effect created by the coloratura. Furthermore, the text of most coloratura is usually repeated again and again in the course of the aria and is, alas more often than not, of inferior literary quality. At times, coloratura is vocalized on single exclamatory words such as "Ah," "Oh," etc.

But "diction" (ah! there's that word again!) has its place here. It might be appropriate to restate the two purposes of good singing diction cited earlier:

1. to *facilitate* the singing process by a mastery of the sounds to be sung, and
2. to *communicate* the sounds, meanings, and overall message (or intent) of the text in an intelligible, natural, and appropriately expressive way.

Diction must aid the singer intelligently in his execution of the coloratura, not impede him. The singer's acquired awareness of the vowel-sounds of the language and their vocal properties and functions can help him to be a better singer of coloratura. Vocal comfort and vowel modification will be the guiding principles to be followed in all coloratura execution.

This modification must both facilitate the vocal execution of the passage, as well as create the appropriate vocal atmosphere.

In the following excerpt for tenor from *Scylla et Glaucus* by Leclair, the typical characteristics of coloratura are evident: florid, mostly step-wise writing that affords the singer a chance to display agility, breath-control, and range. In this example of lyric coloratura, love is exhorted to enslave men's hearts and to reign over their souls. These are the closing bars of the *air;* the same text has been repeated four times here.

Scylla et Glaucus (1746), **J.-M. Leclair, l'aîné**

The word "règne" upon which the coloratura falls means "reign" and contains the vowel-sound [ɛ]. This is a vowel-sound favorable to the overall atmosphere of such a pleasure-seeking passage of coloratura. It is bright, high, and open. If for one reason or another the singer finds it difficult or unpleasant to sing the whole passage on [ɛ], he must modify the vowel-sound to one that will enable him to:

1. articulate the coloratura with ease and clarity;
2. resonate or place the voice with comfort and carrying power;
3. render the same atmosphere of pleasure and gaiety by maintaining the bright and cheery character of [ɛ]; and
4. approximate as closely as possible the word "règne" without failing to accomplish any of the above.

And in *that* order!

The point may be well-taken: *it is the overall character of the text, not of the individual word, that must be conveyed in a coloratura passage.*

It would not be inappropriate for the singer to open the [ε] to an [a] as he ascends into the upper reaches of the passage. Some singers might prefer the narrower, more focused vowel-sound [e] for the execution of this passage. This vowel modification should be effected gradually, not abruptly. It may remain in the realm of a cross between [ε] and [a] (or [ε] and [e]), or a mixture of the two. To illustrate, it would be far less feasible to use an [ɔ] or a [u] here, for they are darker, rounder, and less "joyous" in nature and would alter and obscure the overall atmosphere. In this case, modification would rob the passage of its flavor. In coloratura, it is the flavor that counts.

At this point, the singer may be reminded that as long as it is done with respect for both the musical phrase and the prosody of the text, syllables and entire words may be repeated to facilitate the execution of coloratura. This is often a good way to (1) replace a troublesome vowel with a more favorable one at a specific point in the passage and (2) to insert an extra breath in a phrase that is too taxing to be done in one. An illustration of how this may be done is shown in the Leclair example above.

Coloratura and "fioritura" (musical embellishment of the vocal line) are not always so easily liberated from the text. Vowel modification and syllabic redistribution may not necessarily be the best or only means of facilitating flexibility. Let us not forget the basic and simplest approach to the consonants and the vowel-sounds as already discussed here in this manual. The consonants can delineate and project flexibility that would otherwise be shapeless and lackluster. Uniformity of vocalic placement will ease and focus production, thus giving the flowery passage of "fioritura," as shown below, resonance and traveling power.

Les Pêcheurs de Perles **(Act I; 1862–63), G. Bizet**

In the above example from Act I of Bizet's *Pêcheurs de Perles*, Léïla chirps away about the clear, star-studded night on a sparkling vocal line in the tradition of Donizetti and Meyerbeer that reached its culmination in *Lakmé* of Delibes. What could be a vocalise is set to a text that, although suffering from occasional lapses into weak prosody, demands due attention. Care should be taken to make the consonants rapid, late, and clear, ever-present and sharply defined like the very stars in the transparent sky. The vowels should be as uniformly placed as possible. Those of the first phrase ("Dans le ciel sans voile, parsemé d'étoiles") are easily matched: [ɑ̃ œ ɛ ɑ̃ a œ / a œ e e a œ]. They are all frontal. But beware of over-rounding the [œ] or over-closing the [e]. The [ɑ̃] should not be somber or "nosey." However, in the following phrase, "Au sein de la nuit/Transparent et pur," the "fioritura" definitely obscures the text by an elongation of the unimportant words "au" and "de" and by the rhythmically weak positions of the key-words "sein" and "nuit." These key words should be most clearly enunciated and given slight stresses in the phrase. It was no doubt for reasons of vocal comfort that Bizet did not place the word "sein" on the high A-natural. But some singers might find the [o] of "au" inhibiting on the rising scale and if so should consider opening it discreetly to an [ɔ] verging on an [ɑ]. There should be no accent on the first syllable of "transparent," here set on the strong beat of the measure. The following rest merely discourages liaison and should not interrupt the vocal flow. Again, the question of the rest and its function come into play here. Ambiguous rests abound in such flowery writing. The eighth rests after "le," *-se-* of "parsemé" and "transparent" should not break the flow of sound as interruptions, but merely punctuate as gentle lifts that lighten the fioritura, making it buoyant and heady. Above all, abrupt staccato on the preceding notes must be avoided at all cost.

Vocal Staccato

On the piano, a staccato is obtained by releasing the key immediately after attack. When there are several staccati in succession, the pianist must make sure there are little spaces between each of the notes.

When in singing, to the contrary, when words are present a staccato is produced by attack rather than by release. Of course, in passages of a coloratura nature that have no text and consequently no consonants, the staccato is effected by the breath and is not the subject of discussion here.

When there *is* a text, it is the crisp attack upon the consonants that will insure the effect of *staccato*. Consonants are always rapid, late, and *clear* in French. In staccato they should be rapid, late, and *crisp*. When Debussy requests a *staccato* delivery of the following passage from his "Green," it is not by releasing the voice between syllables that this will be achieved—there is hardly enough time for that. Rather, the singer must crisply articulate the bouncy consonants over a legato vocalic flow. At first this may seem to be a contradiction, but without a legato there is no voice! (And without voice, there is no sound.) Therefore, in the passage below, the vowels should be sung legato as usual, and over this seamless stream of vocalized sound can be sprinkled neat, clean, crisp consonants. The effect should be one of "chattiness."

"Green," *Ariettes oubliées* (1888), **C. Debussy**-P. Verlaine

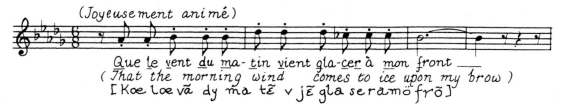

The effect of staccato will be obtained without any reduction or interruption of vocal production and the carrying power of the voice shall be doubly insured by a firm legato and extra-crisp articulation.

Vocalic Harmonization

In the singing of the French vocal repertoire, the practice of vocalic harmonization is utilized both for the sake of linguistic refinement and of ease of production. "Vocalic harmonization" is the rhyming of closely related vowel-sounds in the same or neighboring words. In French singing diction, only *two* vowel-sounds are harmonized with two others: [ɛ] with [e], and [œ] (or [ə]) with [ø].

In vocalic harmonization, it is the *un*stressed, *open* vowel-sound that closes to rhyme with the following *stressed, closed* vowel, not vice versa. Remember, it is the final vowel-sound of a word or word-group that is stressed in French (except for final, unstressed -*e*, -*es*, -*ent*). In the dictionary, the words *baiser* and *cheveux* are phoneticized as follows: [b ɛ z e], [ʃ ə v ø]. But in singing, the first syllable of each word, which is unstressed and open, is closed to rhyme with the final, stressed syllable, rendering [b (e) z e] and [ʃ (ø) v ø]. Because these vocalically harmonized vowels are unstressed and therefore short, they may fail to sound as closed as a stressed closed vowel at the end of the word. For this reason—and as a reminder that they have been transformed, it is a good idea to put their phonetic symbols in parentheses, as shown above.

In the vocalic harmonization of [ɛ] to [(e)], it is mainly the combination -*ai*- (normally [ɛ]) that closes to [(e)] when followed by a stressed [e]: *ai*mer [(e) m e], l*ai*ssez [l (e) s e], ap*ai*sé [a p (e) z e], etc. The only other possibility of such vocalic harmonization is the closing of the [ɛ] in such short words as *les, tes, ces,* and the like, when these are immediately followed by [e] in the following word: le*s* étoiles [l(e)z e t w a l ə], te*s* baisers [t(e) b (e) z e], and so on.

"Lydia" (c. 1865), **G. Fauré**-Leconte de Lisle

Other examples of the vocalic harmonization of [ɛ] to [(e)] are:

"Laissez-la s'apaiser de la bonne tempête" (*Green*, Verlaine), which is originally:

[l ɛ → s e → l a → s a → p ɛ → z e → d œ → l a → b ɔ → n œ → t ã → p ɛ t œ]

when the unstressed -*ai*-'s are vocalically harmonized, becomes:

[l (e) → s e → l a → s a → p (e) → z e → d œ → l a → b ɔ → n œ → t ã → p ɛ t œ]

"Les délices comme un essaim sortent de toi (*Lydia*, Leconte de Lisle), which is originally:

[l ɛ → d e → l i → s œ → k ɔ → m œ̃ → n (e) → s ɛ̃ → s ɔ → r t œ → d œ → t w a]

when the short word *les* is vocalically harmonized, becomes:

[l (e) → d e → l i → s œ → k ɔ → m œ̃ → n (e) → s ɛ̃ → s ɔ → r t œ → d œ → t w a]

When unstressed, short [œ] or [ə] is followed in the same word by stressed [ø], it may be vocalically harmonized as [(ø)]. Here, the second syllable of *dangereuse*, normally short [œ] or [ə], may be rhymed vocalically with the stressed [ø] following it:

"Elle est dangereuse, elle est belle," originally:

[ɛ → l ɛ → d ã → ʒ œ → r ø → z ə / ɛ → l ɛ → b ɛ → l œ]

becomes:

[ɛ → l ɛ → d ã → ʒ (ø) → r ø → z ə / ɛ → l ɛ → b ɛ → l œ]
    (*Carmen*, Bizet Act III)

"J'avais tes cheveux comme un collier noir" (*Chanson de Bilitis*, Debussy), which is originally:

[ʒ a → v ɛ → t ɛ → ʃ œ → v ø → k ɔ → m œ̃ → k ɔ → l j e → n w a r] becomes:

$$[ʒa\rightarrow vɛ\rightarrow tɛ\rightarrow ʃ(ø)\rightarrow vø\rightarrow kɔ\rightarrow mœ̃\rightarrow kɔ\rightarrow lje\rightarrow nwar]$$

These vocalically harmonized syllables must never be accented or overly closed, and at times need only tend toward the closed sound of the following stressed syllable. Again, it is a naturalness that must prevail in the diction in order that it sound authentic and unmannered. Overly zealous closing or a false emphasis of the unstressed syllable will merely result in an obscuring of the text.

6

A Catalogue of French Vocal Repertoire

Abbreviation Key

The following is a comprehensive but by no means exhaustive list of French vocal repertoire.

S   any soprano voice except very high, light
LS   lyric soprano
LLS   light lyric soprano (generally high tessitura and/or need for
               light, floating production, possible flexibility)
CS   coloratura soprano (flexibility and/or coloratura tessitura or
               range)
DS   dramatic soprano (heavier vocal writing and/or rich,
               orchestral accompaniment)
MS   any mezzo-soprano
LMS   lyric mezzo-soprano
DMS   dramatic mezzo-soprano
T   any tenor voice except very high, light
LT   lyric tenor
LLT   light lyric tenor (generally high tessitura and/or need for light,
               floating production, possible flexibility)
DT   dramatic tenor (heavier vocal writing and/or rich, orchestral
               accompaniment)
B   any baritone voice except high, light
HB   high lyric baritone ("lieder" baritone, with working range
               from C below middle-C to A above, from *forte* to
               pianissimo throughout)
DB   dramatic baritone
BB, BS   bass baritone, bass

AV	all voices (may indicate small range avoiding extreme high or low registers and/or possibility of transposition to any comfortable key)
WV(P)	women's voices (preferred)
MV(P)	men's voices (preferred)
excHL	except high, light voices
excLH	except low, heavy voices
OK	original key
WR	wide range (where extremes of both registers may be used)
MR	middle range (confined to staff, but not necessarily for all voices)
HKP	high key preferred (meaning transposed key)
MKP	middle key preferred (meaning transposed key)
Cpp	command of high pianissimo, or floated head voice
flex	flexibility (coloratura) required
DFR	difficult French
dram(at)	dramatic (at times)
sus	sustained, long lines
orch	with orchestral accompaniment also
orchO	with orchestral accompaniment only
cham	with chamber ensemble accompaniment
MBSS	may be sung separately
MBST	must be sung together
STP	sung together preferred

Songs

This compilation of songs with pianistic, chamber, or orchestral collaboration includes recommendations as to vocal suitability as well as indications of various technical demands and occasional linguistic difficulty.

Titles of groups or cycles of songs are italicized. Very often these were not intended to be performed together at all, or were written for different voices, in which case the underlined title is marked MBSS (see Abbreviation Key). On the other hand, some cycles or groups contain songs that can stand alone in performance without the rest of the group, but are more effective as a whole when all are sung together. These are marked STP. Those cycles that must be performed in their entirety and without interruption, for poetic and musical reasons, are indicated by the initials MBST.

The singer should make it a general practice to sing songs in their original keys and include this as a factor in his selection of repertoire. Just because a song is printed in different keys does not condone its being sung in a transposed key. Each vocal tessitura has its own color and power to evoke an atmosphere. The composer usually chooses a certain tessitura for a song because it offers a specific tonal climate and dictates a vocal type and quality appropriate to its text. Also to be considered here is the piano. A transposition can completely alter the tonal aura of an accompaniment and occasionally render its execution unnecessarily difficult and at times almost impossible. Although it is considered a "breach of contract" to transpose an operatic aria, songs are often shifted from key to key without hesitation. This attitude, although vocally accommodating, is artistically unsound, especially in certain areas of the French repertoire where key color and vocal tessitura are crucial to a valid and esthetically satisfying performance. As a general rule, the songs of Debussy and most of those of Ravel and Poulenc suffer serious deformation when transposed. Only in very rare cases is a transposed version preferable for vocal or atmospheric reasons. This will be indicated below with the abbreviations HKP and MKP.

CATALOGUE OF SONGS

All the songs listed below are to be performed with piano except when otherwise indicated.

Composer	Title
Auric, G.	Les Joues en feu (AVexcHL, dram)
	Trois poèmes de Léon-Paul Fargue (MS, B)
	Trois poèmes de Max Jacob (S, MS, B)
	Six poèmes de Paul Eluard (MS, B, dram)
	Huit poèmes de Jean Cocteau (MS, B, BB)
	Alphabet (Sept quatrains de Raymond Radiguet, AVexcLH, MR)
	Trois Caprices (AVexcLH, MR)
	Valse (from *Mouvements du coeur*) (MVexcHL, sus)
Bachelet, A.	Chère nuit (S, T, orch, sus, Cpp)
Barber, S.	*Mélodies passagères* (5 songs, MBSS, HBP, AV)
Bemberg, H.	A toi (AV)
	Il neige (AV)
Berger, J.	*Five Songs on Poems of Mary Stuart* (STP, MS, cham: fl., vla., cello)

COMPOSER	TITLE

Berlioz, H. *Mélodies irlandaises,* Op. 2 (not all listed here, MBSS, orch)
  Chant de bonheur (S, T, dram)
  Elégie (T, dram)
  Adieu, Bessy (T)
  La belle voyageuse (MS, B, orch)
  L'origine de la harpe (S, T)
Le coucher du soleil (S, T, dram)
Le chasseur danois (MVexcHL, orch)
La captive (MS, orch, cham: cello, pno.)
Le jeune pâtre breton (T, HB, orch, cham: horn, pno.)
Zaïde (S, T, orch and/or castanets)
Les Nuits d'été (MBSS, orch)
  Villanelle (LT, LS)
  Le Spectre de la rose (MS, S, WR)
  Sur les lagunes (DS, S, DMS, B)
  Absence (AVexcLH, sus, Cpp)
  Au cimetière (AV, sus, Cpp)
  L'île inconnue (AVexcHL)

Bizet, G. Adieux de l'hôtesse arabe (WV, flex)
Chanson d'avril (AVexcLH)
Ouvre ton coeur (T, S, flex/at)
N'oublions pas (AV)
Douce mer (AV, sus, flex/at, Cpp)
Tarantelle (CS)
Guitare (AV)
Le matin (LS, LLS, LT, flex)
Vieille chanson (LS, LLS, LT, flex)
Rêve de la bien-aimée (WV, dram/at, flex/at)
Vous ne priez pas (WV, dram/at)
Pastorale (AVexcLH, flex)
La chanson du fou (AV)
Absence (AVexcHL, dram/at)
Après l'hiver (AVexcLH, sus)
La coccinelle (MVexcLH)
Chant d'amour (AVexcHL, dram/at)
L'esprit saint (AVexcHL, dram/at, sus)
Sonnet (AV, flex/at)

Boulanger, L. Psaume CXXIX, "Ils m'ont assez opprimé dès ma jeunesse" (B, dram, orch)
Clairières dans le ciel (13 songs, MBSS, S, LS, T, LT, HB, Cpp, dram/at)

Boulanger, N. Cantique (S, T, sus, Cpp)

COMPOSER	TITLE
Boulez, P.	Improvisation No. 1 sur Mallarmé, "Une dentelle s'abolit" (S, WR, cham: harp, vibraphone, piano, celesta, percussion)
	Improvisation No. 2 sur Mallarmé, "Le Vierge, le vivace et le bel aujourd'hui," (S, WR, cham: harp, bells, vibraphone, piano, celesta, percussion)
Britten, B.	*Les Illuminations* (9 songs, STP, S, T, HB, dram, string orch)
Caplet, A.	La croix douloureuse (MS, B)
	La mort des pauvres (MS, B)
	La cloche fêlée (MS, B)
	Prière normande (AVexcHL)
	Nuit d'automne (AVexcHL)
	Deux sonnets (LLS, LT, w/harp)
	Viens, une flûte invisible (AVexcHL, w/fl.)
	En regardant ces belles fleurs (S, T)
	La part à Dieu (AVexcHL)
	Le pain quotidien (S) (15 vocalises)
	Trois fables de La Fontaine (HB, S)
	Le corbeau et le renard
	La cigale et la fourmi
	Le loup et l'agneau
	Le vieux coffret (Quatre poèmes de Rémy de Gourmont) (MBSS, AVexcHL)
	Songe
	Berceuse
	In una selva oscura
	Forêt
	Cinq ballades françaises de Paul Fort (MBSS, AVexcHL)
	Cloche d'aube (Cpp)
	La ronde (MS, B)
	Notre chaumière en Yvelines (WR)
	Songe d'une nuit d'été
	L'adieu en barque (MS, B, BB)
	Le Miroir de Jésus (MS, B, sus, dram/at, w/women's chorus, string orch, harp)
Chabrier, E.	L'île heureuse (HBP, MS, WR, Cpp)
	Ballade des gros dindons (B, MS, BB, MR, Cpp)
	Les cigales (AVexcHL)
	Villanelle des petits canards (AVexcHL)
	Pastorale des cochons roses (B, MS, BB)
	Lied (AVexcHL, MR)
	Romance de l'étoile (AVexcHL, WR, Cpp)
	Chanson de Jeanne (MVexcHL, BB, BS, B)

COMPOSER	TITLE

Charpentier, G.   *Poèmes chantés* (MBSS, selected list here)
    La petite frileuse (LS, LLS)
    Prière (T, HB, S)
    A une fille de Capri (AV)
    Chanson d'automne (AVexcHL, sus)
    La cloche fêlée (AV, sus)
    Parfum exotique (AV, sus)
    Complainte (S, MS, dram/at)
    Les trois sorcières (AVexcLH, flex/at)
    Les chevaux de bois (S, T, HB, dram/at, sus, Cpp)
    Allégorie (S, T, sus)
    La musique (S, T, HB, sus, dram/at)
    Sérénade à Watteau ("Votre âme est un paysage choisi") (AVexcLH, sus, Cpp)

Chausson, E.   Nanny (AVexcHL, dram)
Le charme (AV, MR)
Les papillons (AVexcLH, MR)
Sérénade italienne (AVexcLH, MR)
Hébé (AV, MR)
Le colibri (AV, sus)
La cigale (S, T, dram)
Nocturne (AVexcLH)
Les heures (MS, B)
Cantique à l'épouse (MV, B, BB)
Dans la forêt du charme et de l'enchantement (S, HB, WR)
La caravane (DS, DT)
Chanson perpétuelle (S, DS, DMS, cham: string qt., pno.)
Sérénade (S, T, sus, Cpp)
Serres chaudes (5 songs, MBSS, AV, MR)
Poème de l'amour et de la mer (3 songs, MBSS, orch, WR, S, MS, T, HB)
    La fleur des eaux (sus)
    La mort de l'amour (dram/at)
    Le temps des lilas (AVexcHL, dram, MKP)
La chanson bien douce (AV, MR)
Le chevalier malheur (AV)
L'aveu (AVexcHL, sus)
Amour d'antan (AVexcLH)
Printemps triste (S, T, dram, sus)
Nos souvenirs (AV, MR)
Chansons de Shakespeare (4 songs, MBSS, B, BB, BS)
Les couronnes (AV)
Chanson d'Ophélia (WV, MR)

COMPOSER	TITLE
Dallapiccola, L.	Rencesvals (AVexcHL, DFR)
Debussy, C.	Nuit d'étoiles (AV)
	Beau soir (AVexcLH, HBP, sus, Cpp)
	Fleur des blés (AVexcLH)
	La belle au bois dormant (AV)
	Voici que le printemps (AVexcLH, Cpp)
	Pantomime (CS, LLS, flex)
	Clair de lune [1] (LS, LT, sus, Cpp)
	Pierrot (CS, LLS, flex)
	Apparition (S, WR, Cpp)
	Mandoline (AVexcHL/LH, MR)
	Cinq poèmes de Charles Baudelaire (MBSS, SexcHL, HB, WR, Cpp)
	Le balcon
	Harmonie du soir
	Le jet d'eau (orch)
	Recueillement
	La mort des amants
	Ariettes oubliées (MBSS, LS, LT, WR)
	C'est l'extase (WR, Cpp)
	Il pleure dans mon coeur (Cpp)
	L'ombre des arbres (sus, WR, Cpp)
	Chevaux de bois (MVPexcHL, DFR)
	Green (Cpp, DFR)
	Spleen (S, T, WR, dram/at)
	Romance (AVexcLH, Cpp)
	Les cloches (AV)
	Les angélus (AV)
	La mer est plus belle (MVP, HB, T, Cpp, dram)
	Le son du cor s'afflige (AVexcHL)
	L'échelonnement des haies (AVexcLH, DFR)
	Fêtes galantes I (STP, originally to be sung in order below)
	En sourdine (MR, Cpp)
	Fantoches (LS, LLS, LT, Cpp, DFR)
	Clair de lune [2] (LS, LT, WR, Cpp)
	Proses lyriques (STP, S, T, sus, dram/at, Cpp, DFR)
	De rêve
	De grève
	De fleurs (dram)
	De soir
	Chansons de Bilitis (MBST, MSexcLH, DFR)
	La flûte de Pan

COMPOSER	TITLE

La chevelure (dram/at)
Le tombeau des naïades
Deux Rondels de Charles d'Orléans (STP, AV, MR)
   Le temps a laissié son manteau
   Pour ce que Plaisance est morte
Le Promenoir des deux amants (STP, MS, B)
   Auprès de cette grotte sombre . . .
   Crois mon conseil, chère Climène . . .
   Je tremble en voyant ton visage . . .
Fêtes galantes II (STP, MS, B, BB, BS)
   Les ingénus
   La faune
   Colloque sentimental (DFR)
Trois Ballades de François Villon (STP, MV, HB, WR, orch, DFR)
   Ballade de Villon à s'amie
   Ballade que feict Villon à la requeste de sa mère
   Ballade des femmes de Paris
Trois poèmes de Stéphane Mallarmé (MBST, AVexcLH)
   Soupir
   Placet futile
   Eventail
Noël des enfants qui n'ont plus de maison (MR, SexcHL, MS, B, DFR)

Delage, M.   *Quatre poèmes hindous* (cham: 2fl., string qt., harp, HBP)

Delibes, L.   Les filles de Cadix (CS, LLS)
Chant de l'Almée (CS)
Bonjour, Suzon (MVexcLH)

D'Indy, V.   Lied maritime (AV)
Madrigal dans le style ancien (AV)
Mirage (AV)

Donizetti, G.   Le crépuscule (T)
La dernière nuit d'un novice (DS)
La mère et l'enfant (DS)

Duparc, H.   Chanson triste (LS, LT, Cpp, orch)
Extase (S, T, Cpp, sus)
Sérénade florentine (LS, LLS, LT, LLT, HB, sus)
Le manoir de Rosemonde (B, BB, BS, dram, MKP)
La vague et la cloche (BexcHL, BB, BS, dram)

COMPOSER	TITLE
	Sérénade (AV, MR)
	Testament (B, BB, BS, dram, orch)
	Soupir (AVexcLH, sus, Cpp, MKP)
	Le galop (B, BB, dram, WR)
	Elégie (T, dram/at)
	Lamento (MS, B, BB, sus, dram/at)
	Au pays où se fait la guerre (DMS, DS, WR)
	Phidylé (T, S, orch, sus, dram/at)
	Invitation au voyage (AVexcHL, sus, orch)
	La vie antérieure (AVexcHL, dram, orch, MKP)
Dupont, G.	Mandoline (AVexcLH)
Durey, L.	*Le Bestiaire* (STP, B)
Enesco, G.	*Sept chansons de Clément Marot* (MBSS, B, MS, DFR)
Falla, M. de	*Trois mélodies* (MBSS, S, T, HB)
	Les Colombes
	Chinoiserie (MVP)
	Séguedille (WV)
	Psyché (MS, cham: fl., harp, vln., vla., cello)
Fauré, G.	Le papillon et la fleur (AVexcLH)
	Barcarolle (LS, LT)
	L'aurore (AV, MR, unpub.)
	Mai (AV, MR)
	Dans les ruines d'une abbaye (AV, MR)
	Les matelots (AV)
	Seule! (AV)
	Sérénade toscane (AVexcLH)
	Chanson du pêcheur (B, MS)
	Lydia (AVexcLH, MR)
	Chant d'automne (AVexcHL)
	Rêve d'amour (AV)
	L'absent (AV)
	Aubade (AV)
	Tristesse (AVexcHL, dram/at, DFR)
	Sylvie (MVPexcLH)
	Après un rêve (AVexcHL, sus, dram/at)
	Hymne (AV)
	Au bord de l'eau (AVexcLH, sus, MR)
	La Rançon (AV)

COMPOSER	TITLE

Ici-bas (AV, sus)

Nell (LS, LT, Cpp, sus)

Le Voyageur (AVexcHL, dram)

Automne (DMS, B, BB, BS, dram, sus)

Poème d'un jour (STP, AVexcHL)

   Rencontre (sus)

   Toujours (dram)

   Adieu (Cpp)

Les Berceaux (AVexcHL, dram/at, sus)

Notre amour (LS, LLS, LT, LLT, DFR)

Le Secret (AVexcLH, sus, Cpp)

Chanson d'amour (MVPexcLH)

La fée aux chansons (WVPexcLH, DFR)

Aurore (AVexcLH, Cpp)

Fleur jetée (AVexcHL, dram)

Le pays des rêves (AVexcLH)

Les Roses d'Ispahan (AVexcLH, sus)

Noël (AV)

Nocturne (MS, B)

Les Présents (AVexcLH)

Clair de lune (AVexcLH, MR)

Larmes (AVexcHL, dram, sus)

Au cimetière (AVexcHL, dram, sus)

Spleen (AVexcLH, MR, sus)

La Rose (S, T, sus)

Venise, Cinq mélodies

   Mandoline (AVexcLH, flex)

   En sourdine (AVexcHL, MR, sus)

   Green (AVexcLH, DFR)

   A Clymène (AVexcLH, sus)

   C'est l'extase (AVexcLH, sus, Cpp)

En prière (AV, sus)

La Bonne Chanson (MBSS, HBP, AV excLH, DFR, also cham:
    string qt., pno., not recommended by composer)

   Une sainte en son auréole (sus)

   Puisque l'aube grandit (DFR, WR)

   La lune blanche luit dans les bois (sus, Cpp)

   J'allais par des chemins perfides (DFR)

   J'ai presque peur, en vérité (DFR)

   Avant que tu ne t'en ailles (sus, dram)

   Donc, ce sera par un clair jour d'été (WR)

   N'est-ce pas? (sus)

   L'hiver a cessé (WR, DFR)

Composer	Title
	Le parfum impérissable (AV, MR, sus)
	Arpège (AVexcLH, MR)
	Prison (AVexcHL, dram/at, sus)
	Dans la forêt de septembre (AV, MR)
	La fleur qui va sur l'eau (AV, MR)
	Accompagnement (AV, MR)
	Le plus doux chemin (AV)
	Le ramier (AV)
	Le don silencieux (AVexcHL, MR)
	C'est la paix! (AV, MR)
	Chanson (AV)
	Vocalise (AVexcHL)
	Soir (AV, MKP, sus)
	La Chanson d'Eve (10 songs, MBSS, MS, sus)
	Le Jardin clos (8 songs, MBSS, MS, B, MR)
	Mirages (4 songs, MBSS, MS, B, MR)
	L'horizon chimérique (4 songs, STP, B, sus, Cpp)
Ferrari, G.	Le miroir (AV, MR)
Fourdrain, F.	Carnaval (AVexcHL)
	Chanson norvégienne (WVexcHL)
Françaix, J.	*L'adolescence clémentine* (5 songs, MBST, B)
	Prière du soir (AVexcLH, w/guitare)
	Chanson (LS, LT, w/guitare)
	Huit anecdotes de Chamfort (B)
	Cinq poèmes de Charles d'Orléans (MS, B)
	Trois épigrammes (S, T)
	Scherzo impromptu (from *Mouvements du Coeur* (BB, BS)
Franck, C.	S'il est un charmant gazon (AV)
	Nocturne (AVexcHL)
	La Procession (AVexcHL, orch)
	Le mariage des roses (AV)
	Lied (AV)
	Souvenance (AV)
	Mignonne (AV)
	Aimer (AVexcHL, sus)
	Ninon (AV)
	Les cloches du soir (AV, sus)

COMPOSER	TITLE
Godard, B.	Embarquez-vous! (LT, flex)
	Je ne veux pas d'autres choses (MS, B, sus, Cpp)
	Contemplation (AVexcLH)
	Fleur du vallon (MS, B)
	Chanson du berger (MVexcLH)
	Les adieux du berger (HB, B)
	Qui donc vous a donné vos yeux? (HB, T)
	Fleur d'exil (MV, MR)
	La chanson des prés (AV, MR)
	Chanson arabe (B, BB, BS, flex)
	D'où venez-vous? (AVexcLH)
	Viens! (LT, MS, Cpp)
	Fille à la blonde chevelure (HB, B)
	Te souviens-tu? (MS, dram/at)
	Le banc de pierre (MS, sus, dram/at)
	Guitare (AV, MR)
	Le voyageur (HB, B, Cpp)
Gounod, C.	Sérénade (AVexcLH, flex, vln. obbligato optional)
	L'absent (AVexcLH, sus)
	Au rossignol (AV)
	Chanson du printemps (AVexcLH)
	Chanson de la glu (AV, MVP)
	Mignon (WVexcHL)
	Viens, les gazons sont verts (AVexcLH)
	Où voulez-vous aller? (AVexcLH, flex/at)
	Ma belle amie est morte (MS, B, BB, BS, sus/dram)
	Ce que je suis sans toi (AV)
	Venise (AVexcLH, DFR)
	O ma belle rebelle (AV, MVP)
	Les deux pigeons (AVexcLH)
	Medjé (AVexcHL, MVP)
	Réponse de Medjé (S, MS, dram/at)
	Le Temps des roses (AVexcLH)
	La Vierge d'Athènes (AVexcLH)
	Le vallon (MS, BB, BS, sus)
	Les champs (AV)
	Elle sait! (LT, HB)
	Les cloches (T)
	Blessures (T)
	A Cécile (T)
	Les lilas blancs (AVexcHL)

COMPOSER	TITLE
	Prière du soir (MVP, T, HB)
	Que ta volonté soit faite (AVexcHL, sus, dram/at)
	L'ouvrier (T, HB, S, MS, dram)
	La fleur du foyer (T, S, MS)
	Le pays bienheureux (MS)
	Chanson d'avril (S, T)
	Heureux sera le jour (T, HB)
	Si vous n'ouvrez pas votre fenêtre (AVexcLH)
	A toi, mon coeur (LT, HB)
	Tombez, mes ailes! (WVexcLH)
	L'âme d'un ange (MVexcLH, sus, flex/at)
	Le lever (MV)
	Chanson d'automne (AV, sus)
	Aubade (MV, flex/at)
Hahn, R.	D'une prison (AVexcLH, sus)
	Fêtes galantes (HBP, AVexcHL, WR, Cpp)
	Fumée (AV, Cpp)
	Trois jours de vendange (AV)
	Infidélité (AV)
	Chansons grises (7 songs, MBSS, MS, HB, B, sus, Cpp)
	Chanson d'automne
	Tous deux
	L'allée sans fin . . .
	En sourdine
	L'heure exquise
	Paysage triste
	La bonne chanson
	Etudes latines (10 songs, AV, w/choral accpt./at)
	Les feuilles blessées (11 songs, MR, Cpp)
	Offrande (AVexcHL, sus)
	Paysage (MS, B, sus)
	Quand je fus pris au pavillon (AVexcLH)
	Si mes vers avaient des ailes (AVexcLH)
	Le rossignol des lilas (S, T)
	Mai (MR, AV, sus)
	L'enamourée (AVexcHL, sus, WR)
	La nuit (MS, B, BB, sus)
	Les cygnes (AVexcHL, sus)
	Dernier voeu (HB, MS, sus)
	Nocturne (AVexcLH)
	Je me souviens (AVexcHL/LH, sus)

COMPOSER	TITLE
	La vie est belle (S, T)
	Naïs (S, T)
	La nymphe de la source (AV, MR)
	Sous l'oranger (S, T, flex)
Herberigs, R.	*La Chanson d'Eve* (11 songs, MBSS, S, WR)
Hively, W.	Paysage méditerranéen (S, T)
	Le dit du bergerot (LT, HB)
	Sur les taffetas de bambou (LT, HB, flex)
	Il pleut! il mouille! (S, T, HB, WR)
	Chanson dans un jardin (S, T)
Honegger, A.	*Trois psaumes* (MBSS, HB, MS, dram/at)
	Six poèmes de G. Apollinaire (MBSS)
	A la 'Santé' (MS, BB, BS)
	Clotilde (S, T)
	Automne (MS, C, BB, BS)
	Saltimbanques (AV)
	L'adieu (AV)
	Les cloches (MS, B)
	Six poèmes de Jean Cocteau (HB, MS)
	Trois poèmes de Paul Claudel (HBP, STP)
	Petit cours de morale (5 songs, MBST, AVexcLH)
	Deux chants d'Ariel (LT)
	Quatre chansons pour voix grave (MBSS, MS, C, BB, BS)
	Chanson (B, BB, MS, C, cham: fl. and string trio)
	Trois poèmes des Complaintes et dits de Paul Fort (MS, B)
	Quatre poèmes (1921) (MS, B)
Hüe, G.	*Chansons printanières* (7 songs, MBSS, S, T)
	J'ai pleuré en rêve (T, B, MS, dram)
	A des oiseaux (AV, Cpp)
Ibert, J.	*La Verdure dorée* (4 songs, AV, MR)
	Chansons de Don Quichotte (4 songs, STP, BB, BS, orch)
	Quatre chants (1927) (S, T)
	Deux stèles orientées pour voix et flûte (cham, MVP, HB, T)
	Chanson du rien (AVexcHL, cham: wind quintet or pno.)
	Deux chansons de Melpomène (extraits de *Barbe-bleue,* LLS, CS w/harpsichord)
	Aria (S, T, flex, w/fl. and pno.) (also duo for two voices w/piano)

COMPOSER	TITLE
Jolivet, A.	*Trois complaintes du soldat* (MBST, B, orch)
	Poèmes intimes (5 songs, STP, B, MS, orch)
	Trois chansons de ménestrel (MBSS, MVPexcLH)
	Suite liturgique (8 sections, 2 instrumental, S, T, w/Eng. horn, cello, harp, in Latin)
Jollas, B.	Quatuor II (phonetic syllables, CS, LLS, cham: vln., vla., cello)
Koechlin, C.	Si tu le veux (AVexcLH)
	A toi! (AVexcLH)
	Le thé (AV, MR)
	Chansons de Bilitis (5 songs, MBSS, S, MS, WR, dram/at)
Lalo, E.	Guitare (AVexcLH)
	Oh, quand je dors! (T)
	Amis, vive, vive l'orgie! (T)
	L'esclave (S, MS, sus)
	Souvenir (AV)
	Dieu qui sourit et qui donne (LLS, LT, Cpp)
	L'aube naît (S, T)
	Puisqu'ici-bas toute âme (S, T)
	Ballade à la lune (AVexcHL)
	Aubade (HB)
	Marine (MS, B, sus)
	Humoresque (T, HB, flex/at)
Leguerney, J.	*Vingt poèmes de la Pléiade* (MBSS, AV)
	First Set (S, T)
	Je vous envoie . . .
	Genièvres hérissés . . .
	Je me lamente . . .
	Bel aubépin . . .
	Au sommeil . . .
	Si mille oeillets . . .
	Second Set (B, MS)
	Ah! Bel-Accueil . . .
	A sa maîtresse (Sérénade)
	A son page
	Third Set (MS, B)
	Ma douce jouvence est passée . . .
	Ode anacréontique

COMPOSER	TITLE

Je fuis les pas . . .
La fontaine d'Hélène
Le jour pousse la nuit . . .
Fourth Set (DS)
Invocation
Un voile obscur . . .
Comme un qui s'est perdu . . .
Fifth Set (LS, T)
Chanson triste
A la Fontaine Bellerie
Villanelle
Le Carnaval (Trois poèmes de Saint-Amant, STP, BB, BS, DFR)
La Solitude (4 songs, STP, BB, BS, sus)

Leoncavallo, P.
Madame, avisez-y (LT, LHB)
C'est le renouveau, ma Suzon (LT, LHB)
Si c'est d'aimer (LT, LHB)

Liszt, F.
Oh, quand je dors! (MVP, T, HB, S, Cpp, sus, orch)
Elégie (S, T)
S'il est un charmant gazon (AV, MR)
La tombe et la rose (MS, C, BB, BS)
Le vieux vagabond (BB, BS, dram, sus)
Jeanne d'Arc au bûcher (S, MS, dram)
Comment, disaient'ils (AVexcLH, Cpp)
Enfant, si j'étais roi (T)
Tristesse (J'ai perdu ma force et ma vie) (BB, BS, MS, sus, dram/at)
Il m'aimait tant! (DS, MS, dram/at)

Martin, F.
Trois chants de Noël (STP, HB, MS, cham: fl., pno.)
Quatre sonnets de Cassandre (MBST, B, MS, cham: fl., vla., cello)

Massenet, J.
Poème d'avril (8 songs, MBSS, 2 entirely spoken, AVexcLH, incl. "Que l'heure est donc brève . . .")
Poème d'hiver (4 songs, STP, MS, B, BB)
Poème d'octobre (5 songs, STP, MS, B, BB)
Poème pastoral (6 songs, duo for WVexcLH and LT, flex/at, w/3-voice women's chorus, orch, incl. "Crépuscule")
Poème du souvenir (5 songs, STP, T, sus)
Poème d'un soir (3 songs, STP, MS, B)
Poème d'amour (6 songs, duo for HB/T and S/MS, MBST, incl. "Ouvre tes yeux bleus")

COMPOSER	TITLE

Poème des fleurs (3 songs, WV)
Elégie (AV)
Nuits d'Espagne (AV)
Ninon (T)

Messiaen, O. *Trois mélodies* (STP, S, MS, HB)
Pourquoi?
Le sourire
Le fiancée perdue (dram/at)
Chants de terre et de ciel (6 songs, MBSS, DS)
Poèmes pour mi (9 songs, MBSS, S, MS, T)

Milhaud, D. *Chants populaires hébraïques* (6 songs, MBSS, S, HB, B, MR, dram/at)
Catalogue de fleurs (7 songs, MBST, MS, B)
Chansons de Ronsard (4 songs, MBSS, CS, LLS, LT, orch, DFR)
Poèmes juifs (8 songs, MBSS, AVexcHL)
Trois chansons de troubadour (HB, STP)
Chansons de négresse (3 songs, STP, MS) (string qt.)
Chants de misère (4 songs, B, MS)
Adieu (AV, MR, cantata w/cham: fl., vla., harp)
Cantate de l'enfant et de la mère (recited poems, string qt., and pno. or orch, 3 parts)
Rêves (6 songs, STP, LS, LT, WR, flex/at)
Quatre poèmes de Catulle (T, MBST, flex, Cpp, w/vln. only)
Hymne de Sion (B, dram)
Le Voyage d'été (15 songs, STP, MS, B)
Trois poèmes (MS, B)
Petites légendes (MS, B)
L'amour chante (S, T)
Sept poèmes de la connaissance de l'est (MBSS, B, MS, dram/at)
Quatre poèmes de P. Claudel (STP, B)
Trois poèmes de Lucile de Châteaubriant (MS, B, Cpp)
Trois poèmes de J. Supervielle (3 songs, MBST, MS, C, B, BB)
Deux poèmes d'amour (S, T)
Cinq chansons (MS, B)
Quatre poèmes de Léo Latil (MS, B, STP)
Les soirées de Pétrograd (12 songs, HB, S, MS)
Tristesses (23 songs, suite for B and pno.)
Chansons bas (8 songs, MBST, MS, B, BB, BS)
Deux petits airs (MS, B)
Trois poèmes de Jean Cocteau (MS, B)
Psaume 129 (B, orch or two pnos.)
Poème (MS, B)

COMPOSER	TITLE

Les Quatre Eléments (CS, LT)
Fontaines et sources (LS, T)
Vocalise (CS)
Ballade nocturne (from *Mouvements du Coeur*) (BB, BS)

Moret, E. *Sous le ciel de l'Islam* (12 songs on texts of J. Lahor and A. Renaud, S, T, MS, HB,
     Cpp, with prelude, 3 interludes, and "epilude" for piano) (incl. "Nélumbo")
Sérénade florentine (S)
Sérénade mélancolique (MS, B)
Dans les fleurs (T)
Dans ton coeur dort un clair de lune (MS, B)
Tendresse (AV)
L'orgue de mon âme résonne (T, DS, MS)
Oh! la nuit d'avril (S, T)
Frissons de fleurs (AV)
Rêve (AV)
L'heure inoubliable (MS, B)
A vous, ombre légère (AV)
Heures mortes (AV)
Entends mon âme qui pleure (AV)
Devant le ciel d'été (AV)

Nigg, T. *Mélodies sur des poèmes de P. Eluard* (3 songs, MS, B)

Paladilhe, E. Psyché (AV, sus)

Pierné, G. En barque (AV)
Sérénade (AVexcLH)
Six ballades françaises de Paul Fort (MBSS, MS, B)

Poulenc, F. *Le Bestiaire* (*ou Cortège d'Orphée*) (6 songs, MBST, HB, Cpp, cham: 2 vlns., vla.,
     cello, fl., clar., bsn.)
Cocardes (3 songs, STP, S, LT, Cpp) (cham: vln., tpt., tromb., bass drum, triangle)
Poèmes de Ronsard (5 songs, MS, B)
Chansons gaillardes (8 songs, MBSS, MV, HB, DFR)
Vocalise (AV)
Airs chantés (4 songs, MBSS)
   Air romantique (AVexcHL, MR, DFR)
   Air champêtre (AVexcLH, WR, Cpp)
   Air grave (AVexcHL, dram/at, sus)
   Air vif (AVexcLH, DFR, flex)
Epitaphe (MS, B, BB)
La Dame de Monte Carlo (S) (cham)

COMPOSER	TITLE

Trois poèmes de Louise Lalanne (MBSS, WV, LS, LLS, DFR)
Quatre poèmes de G. Apollinaire (STP, MVP, B, BB, DFR)
Cinq poèmes de Max Jacob (STP, WV, LS, LMS, DFR)
Huit chansons polonaises (AV, in Polish w/Fr. translation)
Cinq poèmes de Paul Eluard (STP, AVexcHL)
A sa guitare (AVexcLH, sus)
Tel jour telle nuit (9 songs, MBST, HBP, MR, available in two keys, DFR, sus, dram/at)
Trois poèmes de Louise de Vilmorin (MBST, WV, LS, LMS, WR, DFR, Cpp)
Deux poèmes de G. Apollinaire (MBSS, AV, DFR)
    Dans le jardin d'Anna
    Allons plus vite
Miroirs brûlants (MBSS)
    Tu vois le feu du soir (HBP, WR, sus)
    Je nommerai ton front (MS, B, dram/at)
Le portrait (AV, MR, DFR)
La grenouillère (AVexcHL, Cpp)
Priez pour paix (AV, MR, sus, available in two keys)
Ce doux petit visage (LS, LT, Cpp)
Bleuet (MVP, T, HB, dram/at, WR)
Fiançailles pour rire (6 songs, MBSS, WV)
    La dame d'André (SexcLH, LMS, MR)
    Dans l'herbe (S, sus, dram/at)
    Il vole (S, WR, DFR)
    Mon cadavre est doux comme un gant (SexcHL, sus)
    Violon (SexcHL, sus)
    Fleurs (SexcLH, sus)
Banalités (5 songs, MBSS, MR)
    Chanson d'Orkenise (MVP, HB)
    Hôtel (MVP, HB, Cpp)
    Fagnes de Wallonie (AVexcHL, DFR)
    Voyage à Paris (AVexcLH, Cpp)
    Sanglots (AVexcLH, sus, Cpp, dram/at)
Chansons villageoises (6 songs, MBSS, MV, B, HB, DFR, orch)
    Chanson du clair tamis (DFR)
    Les gars qui vont à la fête (WR, AVexcHL)
    C'est le joli printemps (Cpp, AVexcLH, HBP)
    Le mendiant (AVexcHL, sus, dram/flex/at)
    Chanson de la fille frivole (DFR, AVexcLH, HBP)
    Le retour du sergent (DFR, WR)
Métamorphoses (3 songs, MBSS, HB, T, MS)
    Reine des mouettes (AVexcLH, DFR)
    C'est ainsi que tu es (AVexcHL, MR)
    Paganini (AVexcLH, DFR)

COMPOSER	TITLE
	Deux poèmes de L. Aragon (MBSS)
	C. (LS, LT, Cpp, sus)
	Fêtes galantes (AVexcHL, MR, Cpp, DFR)
	Montparnasse (AVexcLH, HBP, sus)
	Hyde Park (AV)
	Le Pont (AV, DFR)
	Un poème (AV)
	Paul et Virginie (AV)
	Mais mourir (AV)
	Hymne (MV, BB, BS)
	Trois chansons de Garcia Lorca (STP, AVexcHL)
	Le disparu (MVP, B, BB)
	Main dominée par le coeur (AVexcLH)
	Calligrammes (7 songs, MBST, AVexcHL, HBP)
	Mazurka (BB, BS, sus) (from *Mouvements du Coeur*)
	La Fraîcheur et le feu (7 songs, MBST, MS, B, dram/at, DFR)
	Le Travail du peintre (7 songs, STP, MS, B, dram/at)
	Parisiana (2 songs, AV)
	Rosemonde (AVexcLH, HBP)
	Deux mélodies (1956) (AVexcHL)
	Dernier poème (MVexcHL)
	Une chanson de porcelaine (AVexcHL)
	La courte paille (7 songs, STP, WV, S, LMS)
	Le Bal masqué (suite for B, HB w/cham orch)
	Rapsodie nègre (suite for B, HB w/cham orch)
Rameau, J.-P.	Solo Cantatas (STB)
Ravel, M.	Sainte (AVexcLH, sus)
	Deux épigrammes de Clément Marot (STP, AvexcLH, HBP)
	Manteau de fleurs (AV)
	Shéhérazade (3 songs, STP, WV, orch, DFR)
	Asie (S, MS, dram/at)
	La flûte enchantée (S, LMS)
	L'indifférent (AVexcHL)
	Histoires naturelles (5 songs, STP, MR, AVexcHL/LH, DFR, HBP, LMS)
	Cinq mélodies populaires grecques (STP, MVP [excNo.4], HBP, MS, orch)
	Chants populaires (4 songs in Sp., Fr., Ital., Yiddish, AV, MR)
	Trois poèmes de S. Mallarmé (MBST, MS, B, cham: picc., fl., clar., b.clar., string qt., pno.)
	Deux mélodies hébraïques (AV, MR, dram/at, orch, in Hebr., Yiddish)
	Ronsard à son âme (AVexcLH)

COMPOSER	TITLE
	Chansons madécasses (3 songs, MBST, SexcHL, MS, HB, cham: fl., cello, pno., dram/at, DFR)
	Rêves (AV)
	Don Quichotte à Dulcinée (3 songs, MBST, B, WR, orch)
	Le Noël des jouets (AVexcLH)
	Les grands vents venus d'outre-mer (AV)
	Sur l'herbe (AV)
	Vocalise en forme de habanera (AV)
Rhené-Baton	Idylle morte (MS, B, sus, dram/at)
	Les heures d'été (6 songs, MBSS, HB, MS, dram/at, sus)
	Testament (B, sus, dram/at)
	Pour celles qui restent (7 songs, MBSS, AVexcLH)
	Chansons pour Marycinthe (6 songs, MBSS, B, BB, BS)
	La mort des amants (S, MS, T, sus, dram/at)
	Rêve gris (MS, T, dram, sus)
	Chansons bretonnes (8 songs, MR)
	Chansons douces (12 songs, MBSS, MS, B, sus)
Rivier, J.	*Huit poèmes d'Apollinaire* (STP, AVexcLH)
	Automne (AV)
	Clotilde (AVexcLH, WR, Cpp)
	L'adieu (AV)
	Aubade (AV, WR, dram/at)
	Le départ (AVexcLH, WR, Cpp)
	Linda (AVexcLH, Cpp)
	Saltimbanques (AVexcLH)
	Les cloches (S)
Ropartz, G.	La mer (AV, sus)
	Prière (B, sus, dram/at, orch)
	Berceuse (MS, BB)
	Quatre poèmes (STP, MS, C, BB)
	Veilles du départ (5 songs, STP, MS, C, BB, BS)
	Poème d'adieu (HB, T, sus)
	Chanson d'automne (MS, BB, sus, dram/at)
	En mai (MS, BB, BS, sus)
	Tout le long de la nuit (MS, B, sus)
	Chanson de Bord (MS, B, BB, dram)
	Le temps des saintes (MS, BB, BS, sus)
	Il pleut (B, sus, dram/at, Cpp)
	Près d'un ruisseau (MS, B, sus)
Rorem, N.	*Poèmes pour la paix* (6 songs, AVexcHL, HB, MS, dram/at, string orch)

Composer	Title
Rosenthal, M.	*Chansons de Bleu* (12 songs, AVexcLH)
	Ronsardises (5 songs, AVexcLH)
Roussel, A.	Le jardin mouillé (AVexcHL/LH)
	Flammes (T, DS)
	A un jeune gentilhomme (S, Cpp)
	Amoureux séparés (AVexcLH)
	Réponse d'une épouse sage (S)
	Le bachelier de Salamanque (AVexcHL)
	Sarabande (HB)
	Coeur en péril (T, HB)
	Jazz dans la nuit (S, T, HB, DFR, WR)
	Light (AV)
	L'heure du retour (S, MS)
	Deux poèmes de Ronsard (LS, LT, HB, w/fl. only)
	Deux poèmes chinois (AVexcLH)
	Le départ (AVexcLH)
	Voeu (MS, B)
	Madrigal lyrique (MVexcLH)
	Adieux (MS, S, HB, T, dram/at)
	Invocation (AV)
	Nuit d'automne (AVexcHL/LH)
	Odelette (S, MS)
	La menace (MS, B, orch)
Saint-Saëns, C.	Le bonheur est chose légère (LS, CS, vln. optnl., pno.)
	L'attente (S, MS)
	La cloche (AV)
	Aimons-nous (S, T, sus, dram/at)
	Vocalise (CS)
	Chanson triste (MS, B, BB, BS)
	Danse macabre (B, BB, BS, DFR, orch)
	Air du rossignol (CS)
	Une flûte invisible (AVexcLH, fl., pno.)
	Le pas d'armes du roi Jean (BB, BS, orch)
	La cigale et la fourmi (AV, MR)
	La fiancée du timbalier (orch)
	Primavera (S, T)
	Clair de lune (AV, MR)
	Extase (MS, B)
	Peut-être (S, T)
	Pourquoi rester seulette? (CS)

COMPOSER	TITLE
	Le rossignol (S, T)
	Guitare (AV)
	Guitares et mandolines (S, T, flex)
Satie, E.	*Trois mélodies* (1916) (S, MS, HB, STP)
	La Statue de Bronze (AV exc HL)
	Daphénéo (MR, DFR)
	Le Chapelier (WR, DFR)
	Je te veux (AVexcHL)
	Tendrement (AVexcHL)
	Trois mélodies (1886) (LS, LLS, LT)
	Les Anges
	Elégie
	Sylvie
	La Diva de l'Empire (AVexcHL)
	Ludions (5 songs, MBST, AVexcLH, DFR)
	Trois poèmes d'amour (MS, B, BB, BS)
Sauguet, H.	*La Voyante* (scene for LS and cham orch in 3 parts, DFR)
	Six sonnets de Louise Labé (MBSS, LS, WR, Cpp)
	Cirque (5 songs, LS, T)
	Les pénitents en maillots roses (5 songs, STP, AVexcLH, WR)
	Visions infernales (6 songs, STP, BB, BS)
	Quatre mélodies sur des poèmes de Schiller (MBSS, AVexcLH)
	Mouvements du coeur (extraits) (BB, BS)
	Prélude: Une forêt surgit des flots
	Postlude: Dans les campagnes de Pologne (dram)
Sévérac, de, D.	Le ciel est pardessus le toit (S, T, sus)
	Temps de neige (T, sus)
	Un rêve (MS, sus)
	A l'aube dans la montagne (S, T, dram/at, sus)
	Philis (T)
	Chanson de Jacques (T, sus)
	Chanson de la nuit durable (T, HB, sus)
	Chanson pour le petit cheval (T, HB)
	Les hiboux (S, MS, HB, sus, Cpp)
	Ma poupée chérie (WV)
	Aubade (MV)
	Chant de Noël (AV)
Thomas, A.	Le soir (AVexcLH)

Composer	Title
Vellones, P.	*Cinq épitaphes* (MS, B)
Villa-Lobos, H.	L'oiseau (MS, B)
	Les mères (MS, B)
	Fleur fanée (AV)
Wagner, R.	Les adieux de Marie Stuart (WV, MR)
	Attente (MS, SexcHL)
	Dors, mon enfant (WVexcLH, MR)
	Mignonne (HB, T)
	Tout n'est qu'images fugitives (AVexcHL)
	Les deux grenadiers (B, BB, dram)

Arias

An attempt has been made here to categorize representative arias from the French operatic repertoire according to generally accepted vocal classifications and subdivisions. These lists are intended to serve as a directive guide that will suggest repertoire to the singer, who, in turn, should follow it with relative flexibility. Within any musical environment, great discrepancies exist in operatic classification, not to mention those from country to country or from era to era. For this reason, several arias may be found under different classifications. Because of their greater number and variety, a more detailed breakdown is provided for the soprano, mezzo-soprano, and tenor repertoires. For opposite reasons, the baritone repertoire is listed intact with delineation from within, and the bass-baritone and bass classifications have been grouped together with distinctions made where appropriate.

Composer, opera, and title of recitative (R) and/or aria (A) are provided. In some cases where the term "aria" is inappropriate (e.g., Debussy), excerpts are indicated that might be useful for auditions or performance. An effort has been made to include repertoire from the earliest French opera (Lully) up to the present (Poulenc), but there have by necessity been several omissions.

The abbreviations are the same as those used for the section on the song repertoire.

CATALOGUE OF ARIAS

Coloratura Soprano

For coloratura soprano with maximum flexibility.

COMPOSER	OPERA	TITLE (RECITATIVE AND/OR ARIA)
Adam, A.	*Le Postillon de Longjumeau* Any (for interpolation)	R/A: Je vais donc le revoir Variations on: "Ah, vous dirai-je, maman" (with flute)
Auber, D.	*Le Domino noir*	{ R: Je suis sauvée enfin { A: Ah! quelle nuit!
	La Muette de Portici	{ R: Plaisirs du rang suprême { A: O moment enchanteur!
	Fra Diavolo	{ R: Ne craignez rien, Milord { A: Quel bonheur, je respire
Bizet, G.	*Les Pêcheurs de perles*	{ R: Dieu Brahma (sus) { A: Dans le ciel sans voile
Campra, A.	*Les Festes vénitiennes*	Air de l'Amour: Venez, venez, fières beautés
David, F.	*Le Perle du Brésil*	A: Charmant oiseau
Delibes, L.	*Lakmé*	A: Air des clochettes: Où va la jeune Indoue
Donizetti, G.	*La Fille du Régiment*	{ A: Chacun le sait { R: C'en est donc fait A: Par le rang et par l'opulence (sus)
Gounod, C.	*Mireille*	{ R: Le ciel rayonne, l'oiseau chante! { A: O légère hirondelle { R: Trahir Vincent! { A: Mon coeur ne peut changer
	Philémon et Baucis	{ R: Il a perdu ma trace { A: O riante nature
	Roméo et Juliette	{ R: Non! je ne veux pas t'écouter. . . . { A: Ah, je veux vivre dans ce rêve
Grétry, A.	*Zémire et Azor* *Les deux avares* *Anacréon chez Polycrate*	A: La Fauvette avec ses petits A: Plus de dépit, plus de tristesse (sus/at) A: Eprise d'un feu téméraire (dram/at)

Composer	Opera	Title (Recitative and/or Aria)
Hérold, L.	*Le Pré aux clercs*	A: A la fleur du bel âge A: Jours de mon enfance (WR, dram/at)
Massé, V.	*Les Noces de Jeannette*	A: L'air du rossignol: Au bord du chemin
Massenet, J.	*Werther*	⎰ R: Frère, voyez! ⎱ A: Du gai soleil plein de flamme
	Cendrillon	A: Ah, douce enfant—ah, fugitives chimères
Meyerbeer, G.	*Dinorah*	A: Ombre légère
	Le Prophète	A: Mon coeur s'élance et palpite (sus/at)
	L'Etoile du Nord	⎰ R: C'est bien lui ⎱ A: La, la, la, air chéri (with 2 flutes)
Mondonville, J.	*Titon et l'Aurore*	A: Ariette de l'Aurore: Venez, venez sous ce riant feuillage
Monsigny, P. A.	*Les Aveux indiscrets*	A: Un jeune coeur nous offre l'image du papillon
Offenbach, J.	*Les Contes d'Hoffmann*	A: Air d'Olympia: Les oiseaux dans la charmille
Rameau, J.-P.	*Hippolyte et Aricie*	A: Rossignols amoureux (sus/at)
Ravel, M.	*L'Enfant et les Sortilèges*	A: Air du feu: Arrière! Je réchauffe les bons
Rimsky-Korsakov, N.	*Le Coq d'or*	A: Hymne au soleil (sus/at)
Thomas, A.	*Hamlet*	Scène et air d'Ophélie: Mais quelle est cette belle et jeune demoiselle—A vos jeux, amis
	Mignon	⎰ R: Oui, pour ce soir ⎱ A: Je suis Titania, la blonde A: J'avais fait un plus doux rêve (alternate)

Note: See also, lyric soprano with some coloratura flexibility and range.

Lyric Coloratura

For lyric soprano with some coloratura flexibility and range.

Composer	Opera	Title (Recitative and/or Aria)
Adam, A.	*Le Postillon de Longjumeau*	A: Mon petit mari
	Any (for interpolation)	Variations on: "Ah, vous dirai-je, maman" (w. fl.)
Auber, D.	*Fra Diavolo*	R: Ne craignez rien, Milord A: Quel bonheur, je respire
	La Muette de Portici	R: Plaisirs du rang suprême A: O moment enchanteur
Barthe, A.	*La Fiancée d'Abydos*	A: O nuit, qui me couvre (Cpp, sus)
Bizet, G.	*Les Pêcheurs de perles*	R: O Dieu Brahma (sus) A: Dans le ciel sans voile R: Me voilà seule dans la nuit A: Comme autrefois (sus)
Boieldieu, A.	*La dame blanche*	A: Enfin je vous revois
Chabrier, E.	*Gwendoline*	A: Blonde aux yeux de pervenche (from duet, Act I, Cpp)
Donizetti, G.	*La Fille du Régiment*	A: Chacun le sait A: Il faut partir (sus) R: C'en est donc fait A: Par le rang et par l'opulence (sus)
Gounod, C.	*Mireille*	R: Le ciel rayonne, l'oiseau chante! A: O légère hirondelle R: Trahir Vincent! A: Mon coeur ne peut changer
	Philémon et Baucis	R: Il a perdu ma trace A: O riante nature
	Roméo et Juliette	R: Non! je ne veux pas t'écouter. . . . A: Ah, je veux vivre dans ce rêve R: Depuis hier je cherche en vain A: Que fais-tu, blanche tourterelle (sus)
Grétry, A.	*Les deux avares*	A: Plus de dépit, plus de tristesse
	Anacréon chez Polycrate	A: Eprise d'un feu téméraire

COMPOSER	OPERA	TITLE (RECITATIVE AND/OR ARIA)
Halévy, J.	*La Fée aux roses*	A: En dormant (WR)
Hérold, L.	*Le Pré aux clercs*	A: A la fleur du bel âge
		A: Jours de mon enfance (WR, dram/at)
Massenet, J.	*Esclarmonde*	A: Esprits de l'Air
		A: Ah! Roland—Chaque nuit, cher amant
		A: Oh, Roland, tu m'as trahi—Regarde-les, ces yeux (dram/at)
	Manon	{ R: Suis-je gentille ainsi?
		{ A: Obéissons quand leur voix appelle
		A: Fabliau: Oui, dans les bois et dans la plaine (alternate)
	Thaïs	{ R: Ah, je suis seule
		{ A: Dis-moi que je suis belle (sus, dram/at)
	Cendrillon	A: Enfin, je suis ici
Meyerbeer, G.	*L'Africaine*	A: J'espère, j'espère—Adieu, mon doux rivage (Cpp, sus)
		A: Sur mes genoux, fils du soleil (dram/at)
	Les Huguenots	{ R: Nobles seigneurs, salut!
		{ A: Une dame noble et sage (sus/at)
		A: O beau pays de la Touraine (sus/at)
		{ R: Je suis seule chez moi
		{ A: Parmi les pleurs (sus)
	Robert le diable	A: En vain j'espère—Idole de ma vie
	Le Prophète	A: Mon coeur s'élance et palpite
Offenbach, J.	See Lyric Soprano (with minimum flexibility, top high C)	
Poulenc, F.	*Les Mamelles de Tirésias*	A: Non! monsieur mon mari! (sus/at)
Rameau, J.-P.	*Hippolyte et Aricie*	Rossignols amoureux (sus/at)
		{ R: Où suis-je?
		{ A: Quels doux concerts!
Thomas, A.	*Hamlet*	A: Sa main depuis hier n'a pas touché ma main (sus)
		Scène et air d'Ophélie: Mais quelle est cette belle et jeune demoiselle—A vos jeux, amis!
	Mignon	{ R: Me voilà seule
		{ A: Je connais un pauvre enfant
	Psyché	A: Ah! si j'avais jusqu'à ce soir

Lyric Soprano

For lyric soprano with minimum flexibility, top high C.

Composer	Opera	Title (Recitative and/or Aria)
Auber, D.	*Manon Lescaut*	A: C'est l'histoire amoureuse
Bizet, G.	*Carmen*	R: C'est des contrebandiers le refuge ordinaire A: Je dis que rien ne m'épouvante (dram/at)
	Les Pêcheurs de perles	R: Me voilà seule dans la nuit A: Comme autrefois
	La jolie fille de Perth	A: Je n'en dirai rien
Charpentier, G.	*Louise*	A: Depuis le jour (Cpp, dram/at)
Debussy, C.	*L'Enfant prodigue* (cantata)	R: L'année en vain chasse l'année A: A chaque saison ramenée
	Pelléas et Mélisande	Oh! cette pierre est lourde (Act IV)
Delibes, L.	*Lakmé*	R: Les fleurs me paraissent plus belles A: Pourquoi dans les grands bois A: Sous le ciel tout étoilé
Desmarets, H	*Vénus et Adonis*	Air de Vénus: Qu'un triste éloignement (flex/at)
Destouches, A.	*Les Eléments*	Air d'Emilie: Brillez dans ces beaux lieux (flex/at)
Godard, B.	*Le Tasse*	A: Il m'est doux de revoir la place (dram/at)
Gounod, C.	*Faust*	R: Je voudrais bien savoir A: Il était un roi de Thulé R: O Dieu! que de bijoux! A: Ah! je ris de me voir si belle en ce miroir (flex/at)
	Mireille	A: La Chanson de Magali: La brise est douce et parfumée A: Le jour se lève A: Heureux petit berger R: Voici la vaste plaine A: En marche, en marche
	Philémon et Baucis	A: Ah! si je redevenais belle! A: Philémon m'aimerait encore!
	Le Tribut de Zamora	A: Ce Sarrasin disait (from duet, Act I)

Composer	Opera	Title (Recitative and/or Aria)
Grétry, A.	*Anacréon chez Polycrate*	A: Eprise d'un feu téméraire (flex, dram/at)
Halévy, J.	*La Juive*	A: Il va venir (dram/at)
Hérold, L.	*Le Pré aux clercs*	A: Oui, Marguerite, en qui j'espère (dram/at) A: Souvenir de jeune âge
Lully, J.-B.	*Thésée* *Alceste*	A: Revenez, revenez, amours A: Le héros que j'attends
Massenet, J.	*Manon*	A: Je suis encore tout étourdie { R: Allons, il le faut { A: Adieu, notre petite table A: Voyons, Manon, plus de chimères
	Le Cid	{ R: De cet affreux combat { A: Pleurez, pleurez, mes yeux (dram/at)
	Thaïs	{ R: Ah! je suis seule { A: Dis-moi que je suis belle (dram/at) { R: Je ne veux rien garder { A: L'amour est une vertu rare
	Esclarmonde	{ R: D'une longue torpeur { A: Hélas! en retrouvant la vie (Cpp) A: Roland, tu m'as trahi—Regarde-les, ces yeux (dram/at)
Meyerbeer, G.	*Les Huguenots*	{ R: Nobles seigneurs, salut! { A: Une dame noble et sage (flex/at) { R: Je suis seule chez moi { A: Parmi les pleurs (dram/at, "Falcon")
	Robert le diable	A: Robert, toi que j'aime A: Va! dit-elle
Offenbach, J.	*Les Contes d'Hoffmann* *La Périchole*	A: Elle a fui, la tourterelle (dram/at) A: Tu n'es pas beau, tu n'es pas riche A: La Griserie: Ah! quel dîner que je viens de faire! A: O mon cher amant (La lettre de la Périchole, two keys) A: Ah! que les hommes sont bêtes!
	La vie parisienne *Pomme d'Api*	A: Autrefois plus d'un amant A: J'en prendrai un, deux, trois

COMPOSER	OPERA	TITLE (RECITATIVE AND/OR ARIA)
	Madame l'Archiduc	Couplets de l'Alphabet
	Le Voyage dans la lune	A: Monde charmant
	La Fille du Tambourin Major	Couplets du Petit Français
Poulenc, F.	*La Voix humaine*	No. 55: Je sais bien que je n'ai plus aucune chance à attendre (to No. 58)
		No. 61: Hier soir, j'ai voulu prendre un comprimé pour dormir (to No. 65)
	Les Mamelles de Tirésias	A: Non! monsieur mon mari!
Ravel, M.	*L'heure espagnole*	Scene XVII: Oh! le pitoyable aventure
Saint-Saëns, C.	*Etienne Marcel*	A: O beaux rêves évanouis (Cpp)

Soprano (Dramatic or "Spinto")

Flexibility where indicated.

Composer	Opera	Title (Recitative and/or Aria)
Berlioz, H.	*La Damnation de Faust*	D'amour l'ardente flamme
	Béatrice et Bénédict	A: Je vais le voir (flex)
		⎰R: Dieu, que viens-je d'entendre
		⎱A: Il m'en souvient (flex)
	Les Troyens à Carthage	Monologue de Didon: Ah, je vais mourir
		⎰R: Nous avons vu finir
		⎱A: Chers Tyriens (flex/at)
Catel, C. S.	*Sémiramis*	⎰R: J'avais cru que ces dieux
		⎱A: Sous l'effort d'un bras invisible
Charpentier, G.	*Louise*	A: Depuis le jour (Cpp)
Debussy, C.	*L'Enfant prodigue (cantata)*	⎰R: L'année en vain chasse l'année
		⎱A: A chaque saison ramenée (Cpp)
Dukas, P.	*Ariane et Barbe bleue*	A: O mes clairs diamants
Gluck, C. von	*Alceste*	A: Divinités du Styx
		⎰R: Dérobez-moi vos pleurs
		⎱A: Ah, malgré moi, mon faible coeur
		⎰R: Où suis-je?
		⎱A: Non, ce n'est point un sacrifice!
	Iphigénie en Taurdie	A: O malheureuse Iphigénie
		A: O toi, qui prolongeas mes jours
		⎰R: Non, cet affreux devoir
		⎱A: Je t'implore et je tremble
	Orphée et Euridice	⎰R: Qu'entends-je?
		⎱A: Amour, viens rendre à mon âme (flex)
		A: J'ai perdu mon Euridice
Godard, B.	*Le Tasse*	A: Il m'est doux de revoir la place
Gounod, C.	*Faust*	⎰R: Je voudrais bien savoir
		⎱A: Il était un roi de Thulé
		R: O Dieu! que de bijoux!

COMPOSER	OPERA	TITLE (RECITATIVE AND/OR ARIA)
		A: Ah! je ris de me voir si belle en ce miroir (flex/at) (aria lighter than role)
		A: Il ne revient pas (omitted in performance)
	La Reine de Saba	{ R: Me voilà seule { A: Plus grand dans son obscurité
	Philémon et Baucis	A: Ah! si je redevenais belle!
	Polyeucte	A: A Vesta portez vos offrandes
Grétry, A.	*Anacréon chez Polycrate*	A: Eprise d'un feu téméraire (flex) (Cpp)
Halévy, J.	*La Juive*	A: Il va venir ("Falcon")
Lalo, E.	*Le Roi d'Ys*	{ R: De tous côtés j'aperçois dans la plaine { A: Lorsque je t'ai vu soudain
		A: Vainement j'ai parlé de l'absence
Massé, V.	*Paul et Virginie*	Scène et air: Bruits lointains—Quelle sérénité dans les cieux (flex)
Massenet, J.	*Hérodiade*	A: Charmes des jours passés
		{ R: Celui dont la parole efface toutes peines { A: Il est doux, il est bon
	La Navarraise	{ R: Une dot! et combien? { A: Ah, mariez donc son coeur
	Le Cid	{ R: De cet affreux combat { A: Pleurez, pleurez, mes yeux
		A: Plus de tourments et plus de peine (Cpp)
	Marie Magdeleine	{ R: Aux pieds de l'innocent { A: O bien-aimé
	Esclarmonde	A: Comme il tient ma pensée
		{ R: D'une longue torpeur { A: Hélas! en retrouvant la vie et la pensée
	Sapho	{ R: Ces gens que je connais { A: Pendant un an je fus ta femme
	Thais	{ R: Ah! je suis seule { A: Dis-moi que je suis belle
		{ R: Je ne veux rien garder { A: L'amour est une vertu rare
	Le Roi de Lahore	{ R: J'ai fui la chambre nuptiale { A: De ma douleur que la mort me délivre (sus, dram/at)

Meyerbeer, G.	*L'Africaine*	A: D'ici je vois la mer immense
		A: Sur mes genoux, fils du soleil (flex)
	Les Huguenots	⌠R: Je suis seule chez moi
		⌡A: Parmi les pleurs ("Falcon")
	Robert le diable	A: Robert, toi que j'aime (flex/at)
		A: En vain j'espère—Idole de ma vie (flex, "Falcon")
Offenbach, J.	*Les Contes d'Hoffmann*	A: Elle a fui, la tourterelle
	La Belle Hélène	A: Invocation à Vénus
		A: Amours divins, ardentes flammes!
		A: Couplets: Là! vrai, je ne suis pas coupable
	La Grande-Duchesse de Gérolstein	A: Dites-lui (sus)
		⌠R: Vous aimez le danger
		⌡A: Ah, que j'aime les militaires (DFR)
Poulenc, F.	*La Voix humaine*	No. 55: Je sais bien que je n'ai plus aucune chance à attendre (to No. 58)
		No. 61: Hier soir, j'ai voulu prendre un comprimé pour dormir (to No. 65)
Rameau, J.-P.	*Castor et Pollux*	A: Tristes apprêts, pales flambeaux
	Hippolyte et Aricie	⌠R. Quelle plainte en ces lieux m'appelle?
		⌡A: Qu'ai-je fait! Quels remords!

Lyric Mezzo-soprano

Flexibility and other demands where indicated.

Composer	Opera	Title (Recitative and/or Aria)
Adam, A.	*Si j'étais roi*	A: De vos nobles aïeux (flex, high)
Auber, D.	*Fra Diavolo*	A: Voyez sur cette roche
		{R: Ne craignez rien
		{A: Quel bonheur, je respire (flex, WR)
	Le Domino noir	A: Aragonaise: La belle Inès (flex/at)
Campra, A.	*Iphigénie*	A: Seuls confidents de mes peines secrètes (sus)
Debussy, C.	*Pelléas et Mélisande*	Oh cette pierre est lourde (Act IV)
Donizetti, G.	*La fille du Régiment*	A: Pour une femme de mon nom (flex)
Gounod, C.	*Faust*	A: Faites-lui mes aveux
	Mireille	A: Le jour se lève (sus, Cpp)
	Roméo et Juliette	{R: Depuis hier je cherche en vain
		{A: Que fais-tu, blanche tourterelle (sus, flex, high)
Lully, J.-B.	*Amadis*	A: Amour, que veux-tu de moi? (sus/at)
Massé, V.	*Galathée*	A: Sa couleur est blonde (flex)
		A: Air de la lyre: Fleur parfumée (flex, high)
	Paul et Virginie	A: Dans le bois à ma voix tout s'éveille (flex)
		A: Parmi les lianes (Chanson du tigre) (flex, dram/at)
Massenet, J.	*Don Quichotte*	A: Alza!—Quand la femme a vingt ans (flex)
	Don César de Bazan	A: Dors, ami
	Le Roi de Lahore	{R: Repose, ô belle amoureuse
		{A: Ferme tes yeux, ô belle maîtresse (sus, flex, dram/at)
Meyerbeer, G.	*Les Huguenots*	{R: Nobles seigneurs, salut!
		{A: Une dame noble et sage (sus, flex, available in two keys: B flat and G major)
		A: Non, non, vous n'avez jamais, je gage (flex, interpolated)

Composer	Opera	Title (Recitative and/or Aria)
Offenbach, J.	*Le Périchole*	A: Tu n'es pas beau, tu n'es pas riche
		A: O mon cher amant (Lettre de la Périchole)
		A: Ah! que les hommes sont bêtes!
		A: La Griserie: Ah! quel dîner que je viens de faire
	La Grande-Duchesse de Gérolstein	A: Dites-lui (sus)
		⎰ R: Vous aimez le danger
		⎱ A: Ah, que j'aime les militaires (flex, DFR)
	Chanson de Fortunio	A: Chanson de Fortunio
Saint-Saëns, C.	*Ascanio*	A: La Chanson de Scozzone
Thomas, A.	*Mignon*	A: Connais-tu le pays (sus)
		⎰ R: Me voilà seule
		⎱ A: Je connais un pauvre enfant (flex, high)
		⎰ R: C'est moi, j'ai tout brisé
		⎱ A: Me voici dans son boudoir (DFR)

Mezzo-soprano

Dramatic and other demands where indicated.

COMPOSER	OPERA	TITLE (RECITATIVE AND/OR ARIA)
Berlioz, H.	*Les Troyens à Carthage*	Monologue de Didon: Ah, je vais mourir (sus, dram)
	Béatrice et Bénédict	R: Dieu, que viens-je d'entendre? A: Il m'en souvient (flex, sus)
	La Damnation de Faust	A: D'amour l'ardente flamme (sus, dram/at)
Bizet, G.	*Carmen*	A: Habanera: L'amour est un oiseau rebelle (sus)
		A: Séguedille: Près des remparts de Séville (DFR/at)
		R: Carreau! Pique! A: En vain pour éviter (sus)
	Djamileh	A: Sans doute l'heure est prochaine (sus)
Charpentier, M. A.	*Médée*	R: Que d'horreurs! A: Ne les épargnons pas (sus, dram/at)
		A: Quel prix de mon amour (sus)
Debussy, C.	*Pelléas et Mélisande*	Voici ce qu'il écrit à son frère Pelléas (Act I)
Gluck, C. von	*Alceste*	A: Divinités du Styx (dram)
	Orphée et Euridice	R: Qu'entends-je? A: Amour, viens rendre à mon âme (flex)
		A: J'ai perdu mon Euridice (sus)
Gounod, C.	*Cinq-Mars*	R: Par quel trouble profond A: Nuit resplendissante (sus)
	Sapho	R: Où suis-je? A: O ma lyre immortelle (sus, dram/at)
		Ode: Héro sur la tour—Viens dans les bras (WR, flex, dram)
Halévy, J.	*Charles VI*	A: Humble fille des champs (sus, dram/at, low)
	La Reine de Chypre	A: Le gondolier dans sa pauvre nacelle (scena; sus, dram/at)
Hérold, L.	*Le Pré aux clercs*	A: Jours de mon enfance (flex, high)
Lalo, E.	*Le Roi d'Ys*	R: De tous côtés j'aperçois dans la plaine A: Lorsque je t'ai vu soudain (dram)

COMPOSER	OPERA	TITLE (RECITATIVE AND/OR ARIA)
Massé, V.	*Paul et Virginie*	A: Parmi les lianes (Chanson du tigre) (dram/at)
Massenet, J.	*Don César de Bazan*	A: Dors, ami (sus, flex/at)
	Hérodiade	A: Hérode! ne me refuse pas!
		⎧R: Celui dont la parole efface toutes peines ⎨ ⎩A: Il est doux, il est bon (dram, high/at)
	Le Roi de Lahore	⎧R: Repose, ô belle amoureuse ⎨ ⎩A: Ferme tes yeux, ô belle maîtresse (sus, dram/at, flex, WR)
	Don Quichotte	A: Alza!—Quand la femme a vingt ans (flex)
	Le Cid	⎧R: De cet affreux combat ⎨ ⎩A: Pleurez, pleurez, mes yeux (original version)
	Werther	A: Werther, qui m'aurait dit la place (sus, dram/at)
		A: Va! laisse couler mes larmes (sus, dram/at)
Meyerbeer, G.	*Le Prophète*	A: Ah! mon fils (sus, dram/at)
		A: Donnez, donnez (dram/at)
		⎧R: Qui je suis? moi! ⎨ ⎩A: Je suis hélas, la pauvre femme (flex, dram/at)
		⎧R: O Prêtres du Baal ⎨ ⎩A: O toi qui m'abandonne (flex, dram, WR)
Offenbach, J.	*La Grande-Duchesse de Gérolstein*	A: Dites-lui (sus)
		⎧R: Vous aimez le danger ⎨ ⎩A: Ah, que j'aime les militaires (DFR)
	La Belle Hélène	A: Invocation à Vénus
		A: Amours divins, ardentes flammes!
		A: Couplets: Là, vrai, je ne suis pas coupable
Rameau, J.-P.	*Dardanus*	A: O jour affreux! (sus)
	Hippolyte et Aricie	A: O disgrâce cruelle (sus)
Saint-Saëns, C.	*Samson et Dalila*	⎧R: Samson, recherchant ma présence ⎨ ⎩A: Amour, viens aider à ma flamme (sus, dram, flex/at)
		A: Mon coeur s'ouvre à ta voix (sus, dram/at)
		A: Printemps qui commence (sus)
Tchaikovsky, P.	*Pique-Dame (Queen of Spades)*	A: O, jeunes filles! (originally in Russian; sus dram/at)
	Jeanne d'Arc	⎧R: Oui, Dieu le veut ⎨ ⎩A: Adieu, forêts (originally in Russian; sus, dram)

COMPOSER	OPERA	TITLE (RECITATIVE AND/OR ARIA)
Thomas, A.	*Hamlet*	R: Toi partir!
		A: Dans son regard plus sombre (sus, flex, dram/at)
	Mignon	A: Connais-tu le pays (sus)
	Psyché	R: Salut! Divinités des champs
		A: O nymphes! en ces lieux (sus, flex/at)
		R: Non, ne la suivons pas
		A: Sommeil, ami des dieux (sus)

Light Lyric Tenor

Flexibility, range, and other demands where indicated.

COMPOSER	OPERA	TITLE (RECITATIVE AND/OR ARIA)
Auber, D.	*La Muette de Portici*	A: Du pauvre seul ami fidèle (high, Cpp)
	Fra Diavolo	A: Agnès la jouvencelle (flex)
		{ R: J'ai revu nos amis
		{ A: Je vois marcher sous nos bannières (scene; flex)
		A: Pour toujours, disait-elle (sus)
Berlioz, H.	*Les Troyens à Carthage*	Air du poète:
		{ R: A l'ordre de la Reine, j'obéis
		{ A: O blonde Cérès (flex)
	Béatrice et Bénédict	A: Ah! je vais l'aimer (dram/at)
Bizet, G.	*Les Pêcheurs de perles*	{ R: A cette voix
		{ A: Je crois entendre encore (high, sus, Cpp)
	Djamileh	A: J'aime l'amour
Boieldieu, A.	*La dame blanche*	A: Viens, gentille dame (flex, WR)
Bourgeois, L. T.	*Les Amours déguisés*	A: Paisible nuit, suspendez votre cours (sus, flex/at)
Bouvard et Bertin	*Cassandre*	A: Ruisseau dont le bruit charmant (sus, flex/at)
Campra, A.	*Les Festes vénitiennes*	A: Naissez, brillantes fleurs (flex)
Donizetti, G.	*La Fille du Régiment*	A: Ah, mes amis, quel jour de fête! (Pour mon âme, quel destin) (high)
		A: Pour me rapprocher de Marie (sus)
Gluck, C. von	*Armide*	A: Plus j'observe ces lieux (sus)
		A: Ah! si la liberté doit m'être ravie
Godard, B.	*Jocelyn*	{ R: Cachés dans cet asile
		{ A: Oh, ne t'éveille pas encor (Cpp, sus)
Gounod, C.	*Polyeucte*	A: Nymphes attentives (sus, Cpp)
	Sapho	A: O jours heureux (sus, high)
	Roméo et Juliette	{ R: L'amour! l'amour!
		{ A: Ah, lève-toi, soleil (sus, Cpp)

COMPOSER	OPERA	TITLE (RECITATIVE AND/OR ARIA)
Grétry, A.	*Le Jugement de Midas*	A: Certain coucou, certain hibou (flex)
	Zémire et Azor	A: Du moment qu'on aime (flex)
Hérold, L.	*Le Pré aux clercs*	A: O ma tendre amie (flex, high)
Lalo, E.	*Le Roi d'Ys*	A: Vainement, ma bien-aimée (Cpp)
Leclair, J.	*Scylla et Glaucus*	A: Chantez, chantez l'amour (flex, Cpp)
Lully, J.-B.	*Armide*	A: Plus j'observe ces lieux (sus)
	Le Sicilien	A: Pauvres amants, quelle erreur (sus, flex)
	Amadis	A: Bois épais
Massenet, J.	*Manon*	R: Instant charmant A: En fermant les yeux (sus, Cpp)
	Le Jongleur de Notre-Dame	R: Mais, renoncer A: Liberté! c'est elle
Meyerbeer, G.	*Les Huguenots*	R: Ah! quel spectacle enchanteur A: Plus blanche que la blanche hermine (viola d'amore obbligato, flex, Cpp)
	Robert le diable	A: Où me cacher—O ma mère, ombre si tendre (interpolated; sus, flex, Cpp)
Offenbach, J.	*Les Contes d'Hoffmann*	A: Jour et nuit je me mets en quatre
	La vie parisienne	A: En adossant mon uniforme
	Madame l'Archiduc	A: Un p'tit bonhomme' pas plus haut qu'ça
	La Fille du Tambour Major	A: Tout en tirant mon aiguille
	La Belle Hélène	A: Et tout d'abord, ô vile multitude (high)
		A: Le Jugement de Pâris: Au mont Ida (high, "bouffe")
Rameau, J.-P.	*Les Fêtes d'Hébé*	A: Tu veux avoir la préférence (sus, flex)
	Castor et Pollux	A: Séjour de l'éternelle paix (sus)
Rousseau, J.-J.	*Le Devin du village*	A: Je vais revoir ma charmante maîtresse (sus, flex, Cpp)
Thomas, A.	*Mignon*	A: Elle ne croyait pas (sus)
		A: Adieu, Mignon! (sus)
		A: Oui, je veux par le monde (flex/at)

Note: See also Tenor.

Tenor

Dramatic demands, flexibility, and range where indicated.

COMPOSER	OPERA	TITLE (RECITATIVE AND/OR ARIA)
Adam, A.	*Si j'étais roi*	A: Elle est princesse (sus, dram/at)
		A: J'ignore son nom (sus)
	Le Postillon de Longjumeau	A: Mes amis, écoutez l'histoire (sus)
		A.: Romance du Postillon (flex, high)
Auber, D.	*La Muette de Portici*	A: O toi, jeune victime (flex, dram/at, high)
		⎧R: Spectacle affreux
		⎩A: O Dieu, toi qui m'as destiné—Du pauvre seul ami fidèle (flex, sus, high)
Berlioz, H.	*La Damnation de Faust*	A: Merci, doux crépuscule (Cpp)
		A: Nature immense (sus)
	Béatrice et Bénédict	A: Ah! je vais l'aimer (flex/at)
	Les Troyens à Carthage	⎧R: Inutiles regrets
		⎩A: Ah! quand viendra l'instant (dram, WR)
Bizet, G.	*Carmen*	A: La fleur que tu m'avais jetée (Cpp, sus, dram/at)
	La jolie fille de Perth	A: A la voix d'un amant fidèle (sus, flex/at)
	Les Pêcheurs de perles	⎧R: A cette voix
		⎩A: Je crois entendre en core (sus, Cpp, high)
Boieldieu, A.	*La dame blanche*	A: Viens, gentille dame (flex)
Bruneau, A.	*L'Attaque du moulin*	⎧R: Le jour tombe
		⎩A: Adieu, forêt profonde (sus)
Bourgeois, L. T.	*Les amours déguisés*	A: Paisible nuit, suspendez votre cours (sus, flex)
Charpentier, G.	*Louise*	A: Dans la cité lointaine (sus)
	Julien	A: Hélas! ai-je compris?
Cherubini, M. L.	*Les Abencérages*	A: Suspendez à ces murs (sus)
Dalayrac, N.	*Gulistan*	A: Cent esclaves ornaient ce superbe festin (sus, flex, high)
Debussy, C.	*L'Enfant prodigue (cantata)*	⎧R: Ces airs joyeux
		⎩A: O temps à jamais effacé (sus)

Composer	Opera	Title (Recitative and/or Aria)
	Pelléas et Mélisande	On dirait que ta voix a passé sur la mer au printemps (WR, Cpp, sus, ''baryton-martin'')
Delibes, L.	*Lakmé*	A: Fantaisie aux divins mensonges (sus, Cpp)
		A: Lakmé, dans la forêt profonde (sus)
Donizetti, G.	*La Fille du Régiment*	A: Pour me rapprocher de Marie
		A: Ah, mes amis, quel jour de fête— Pour mon âme, quel destin (high)
Gluck, C. von	*Alceste*	R: O moment délicieux
		A: Bannis la cruauté et les alarmes (flex)
		R: Vivre sans toi
		A: Alceste, au nom des dieux (sus)
	Armide	A: Plus j'observe ces lieux (sus)
		R: Enfin il est dans ma puissance
		A: Ah, quelle cruauté de lui ravir le jour
		A: Ah, si la liberté me doit être ravie
		A: Le perfide Renaud me fuit (dram/at)
	Iphigénie en Tauride	R: Quel langage accablant
		A: Unis dès la plus tendre enfance (sus)
Godard, B.	*Jocelyn*	R: Cachés dans cet asile
		A: Ah! ne t'éveille pas encor (Cpp, sus)
Gounod, C.	*Faust*	R: Quel trouble inconnu me pénètre
		A: Salut! demeure chaste et pure (sus, high)
	La Reine de Saba	R: Faiblesse de la race humaine
		A: Inspirez-moi (sus, dram/at)
		A: Comme la naissante aurore (usually cut)
	Mireille	A: Anges du paradis (sus)
	Polyeucte	A: Source délicieuse (sus, dram/at)
	Roméo et Juliette	R: L'amour! l'amour!
		A: Ah, lève-toi, soleil (sus, Cpp)
Halévy, J.	*La Juive*	A: Rachel, quand du Seigneur (dram/at)
Hérold, L.	*Le Pré aux clercs*	A: O ma tendre amie (flex)
Massenet, J.	*Hérodiade*	R: Ne pouvant réprimer
		A: Adieu donc, vains objets (sus, dram/at)
	Le Cid	R: Ah! tout est bien fini
		A: O souverain, ô juge, ô père (sus, dram/at)

Composer	Opera	Title (Recitative and/or Aria)
	Manon	R: Instant charmant A: En fermant les yeux (sus, Cpp)
		R: Je suis seul enfin A: Ah! fuyez, douce image (dram/at)
	Werther	R: Un autre est son époux A: J'aurais sur ma poitrine (sus)
		R: Oui! ce qu'elle m'ordonne A: Lorsque l'enfant revient d'un voyage (sus)
		R: Je ne sais si je veille A: O nature pleine de grâce (sus)
		R: Traduire! Ah! bien souvent mon rêve A: Pourquoi me réveiller (sus, dram/at)
	Le Roi de Lahore	R: Voix qui me remplissez A: O Sita bien-aimée! (sus, dram/at)
Méhul, E.	*Joseph*	R: Vainement, Pharaon A: Champs paternels
Messager, A	*Fortunio*	A: Chanson de Fortunio (sus) A: La maison grise (sus)
Meyerbeer, G.	*L'Africaine*	R: Pays merveilleux A: O paradis (sus, dram/at)
	Les Huguenots	R: Aux armes, mes amis! A: A la lueur de leurs torches funèbres (sus, dram/at, high)
		R: Ah! quel spectacle enchanteur A: Plus blanche que la blanche hermine (flex, Cpp, viola d'amore obbligato)
	Robert le diable	A: Où me cacher—ô ma mère, ombre si tendre (sus, flex, Cpp, interpolated)
Offenbach, J.	*Les Contes d'Hoffman*	R: Allons! courage et confiance A: Ah, vivre deux
Saint-Saëns, C.	*Samson et Dalila*	Entrée de Samson: L'as-tu donc oublié? (Act I; sus, dram/at)
Thomas, A.	*Hamlet* *Mignon*	A: Pour mon pays (sus) A: Elle ne croyait pas (sus) A: Adieu, Mignon! (sus) A: Oui, je veux par le monde (flex/at)

Baritone

See indication for dramatic demands, range, and flexibility.

COMPOSER	OPERA	TITLE (RECITATIVE AND/OR ARIA)
Adam, A.	*Si j'étais roi*	A: Dans le sommeil (sus, high)
Berlioz, H.	*La Damnation de Faust*	A: Une puce gentille A: Voici des roses (sus)
Bizet, G.	*Les Pêcheurs de perles*	R: L'orage s'est calmé A: O Nadir, tendre ami (sus)
	Carmen	A: Votre toast (dram/at)
Campra, A.	*Les Festes vénitiennes*	A: Rassurez votre coeur timide (flex)
Charpentier, G.	*Louise*	R: Les pauvres gens A: Voir naître un enfant (sus, dram/at)
Dauvergne, A.	*Les Troqueurs*	R: J'ai cru faire un bon coup A: Sa nonchalance serait mon tourment (flex/at)
Debussy, C.	*L'Enfant prodigue* (cantata) *Pelléas et Mélisande*	A: Faites silence! Ecoutez tous! (sus) Une grande innocence (Act IV; dram/at) On dirait que ta voix a passé sur la mer au printemps (WR, Cpp, sus, ''baryton-martin'')
Gluck, C. von	*Alceste*	R: Au pouvoir de la mort A: C'est en vain, que l'enfer R: Tes destins sont remplis A: Déjà la mort s'apprête
Gounod, C.	*Faust*	A: Avant de quitter ces lieux (sus, OK, E flat; often transposed to D flat)
	Mireille *Roméo et Juliette*	A: Si les filles d'Arles (flex/at) A: Mab, la reine des mensonges (flex/at)
Grétry, A.	*Anacréon chez Polycrate* *Richard Coeur de Lion*	A: O fortune ennemie! (sus) A: O Richard, ô mon roi (flex, dram)
Lully, J.-B.	*Amadis*	A: Dans un piège fatal (sus)

COMPOSER	OPERA	TITLE (RECITATIVE AND/OR ARIA)
Massenet, J.	_Hérodiade_	R: Elle a fui le palais A: Salomé, Salomé (sus, dram/at)
		R: Ce breuvage pourrait me donner un tel rêve A: Vision fugitive (sus, dram/at)
	Le Jongleur de Notre Dame	A: Légende de la Sauge (sus)
	Manon	A: Regardez-moi bien dans les yeux (sus/at, Cpp) A: Choisir! Et pourquoi! (flex, sus/at)
	Werther	R: Elle m'aime, elle pense à moi A: Quelle prière de reconnaissance (sus)
		A: Au bonheur dont mon âme est pleine (sus)
	Le Roi de Lahore	R: Aux troupes du Sultan A: Promesse de mon avenir (sus, high)
	Thaïs	A: En vain j'ai flagellé ma chair (sus, dram/at) A: Voilà donc la terrible cité (dram, sus)
Méhul, E.	_Stratonice_	R: Sur le sort de son fils A: O des amants déïté tutélaire (sus)
Meyerbeer, G.	_L'Africaine_	A: Adamastor, roi des vagues profondes (flex) A: Fille des rois (sus, dram/at)
	Le Pardon de Ploërmel	A: Ah, mon remords te venge (sus, dram/at, high)
Mondonville, J.	_Titon et l'Aurore_	A: Sur les pâles humains (flex)
Montéclair, M. de	_Jephté_	A: Quel funeste appareil! (sus)
Offenbach, J.	_Les Contes d'Hoffmann_	A: Scintille, diamant (sus, WR)
	La Grande Duchesse de Gérolstein	A: Piff, paff, pouff
	La Périchole	A: Couplets de l'Incognito A: Conduisez-le, bons courtisans (Ronde des Maris Ré)
Philidor, A. D.	_Ernelinde_	A: Né dans un camp parmi les armes (sus, flex/at)
Rameau, J.-P.	_Castor et Pollux_	A: Nature, amour, qui partagez mon coeur (sus)
Ravel, M.	_L'Enfant et les Sortilèges_	A: Ding, ding, ding, ding
Rossini, G.	_Le Siège de Corinthe_	R: Qu'à ma voix la victoire s'arrête A: La gloire et la fortune (flex)
	Guillaume Tell	A: Sois immobile (sus)

Composer	Opera	Title (Recitative and/or Aria)
Saint-Saëns, C.	*Henri VIII*	A: Qui donc commande quand il aime (dram, sus)
Thomas, A.	*Hamlet*	A: Comme une pâle fleur (sus, dram/at)
		A: O vin, dissipe ma tristesse (flex/at)
		⎰R: J'ai pu frapper le misérable
		⎱A: Etre ou ne pas être (dram)

Bass-baritone (BB)

Bass (BS)

For both voices unless specified BB or BS; flexibility and other demands
where indicated.

Composer	Opera	Title (Recitative and/or Aria)
Adam, A.	*Le Chalet*	R: Arrêtons-nous ici A: Vallons de l'Helvétie (flex; BB)
Berlioz, H.	*La Damnation de Faust*	A: Certain rat, dans une cuisine (flex/at; BS) A: Une puce gentille (flex/at; BB) A: Voici des roses (sus; BB)
Bizet, G.	*La jolie fille de Perth*	A: Quand la flamme de l'amour (flex/at)
David, F.	*Herculanum*	A: Je crois au Dieu (sus)
Debussy, C.	*Pelléas et Mélisande*	Je n'en dis rien (Act I) Attention, il faut parler à voix basse, maintenant (Act V)
Delibes, L.	*Lakmé*	A: Lakmé, ton doux regard se voile (sus)
Gluck, C. von	*Iphigénie en Tauride*	R: Le ciel, par d'éclatants miracles A: De noirs pressentiments (dram; BB)
	Alceste	R: Tes destins sont remplis! A: Déjà la mort s'apprête (high; BB)
Gounod, C.	*Faust*	A: Vous qui faites l'endormie (flex, WR) A: Le veau d'or (flex/at, DFR) A: O nuit, étends sur eux ton ombre (sus) A: Souviens-toi du passé
	La Reine de Saba	R: Oui, depuis quatre jours A: Sous les pieds d'une femme (sus, flex; BS; available in two keys, E and F major)
	Philémon et Baucis	A: Au bruit des lourds marteaux d'airain (flex) A: Que les songes heureux (sus, low; BS)
	Roméo et Juliette	A: Buvez donc ce breuvage—C'est là qu'après un jour (sus; BS) A: Allons! jeunes gens!
Halévy, J.	*La Juive*	A: Si la rigueur (sus; BS) A: Vous qui du Dieu vivant (sus; BS)

Composer	Opera	Title (Recitative and/or Aria)
Lully, J.-B.	*Alceste*	A: Il faut passer tôt ou tard (WR)
	Thésée	A: Que rien ne trouble ici Vénus (sus, flex)
Massenet, J.	*Hérodiade*	A: Astres étincellants (dram, sus)
	Manon	R: Les grands mots que voilà
		A: Epouse quelque brave fille (sus, high)
	Don Quichotte	A: Seigneur, reçois mon âme (BB)
Meyerbeer, G.	*Le Pardon de Ploërmel*	R: En chasse!
		A: Le jour est levé (flex)
	Le Prophète	A: Aussi nombreux que les étoiles (flex)
	Robert le diable	R: Voici donc les débris
		A: Nonnes qui reposez (dram)
		A: Je t'ai trompé (dram/at)
	Les Huguenots	A: Piff, paff (flex)
	L'Etoile du Nord	R: Pour fuir son souvenir
		A: O jours heureux (flex)
Offenbach, J.	*Les Contes d'Hoffmann*	A: Scintille, diamant (transposed key, D major BB)
Rameau, J.-P.	*Hippolyte et Aricie*	R: Ah! qu'on daigne du moins
		A: Puisque Pluton est inflexible
	Dardanus	R: Voici les tristes lieux
		A: Monstre affreux (sus; BS)
		R: Tout l'avenir est présent à mes yeux
		A: Suspends ta brillante carrière, soleil (BS)
Rossini, G.	*Robert Bruce*	R: Le roi sommeille . . .
		A: Que ton âme si noble (flex; BB)
Thomas, A.	*Hamlet*	R: C'est en vain
		A: Je t'implore, ô mon frère (sus, dram/at, WR; BS)
	Mignon	A: De son coeur j'ai calmé la fièvre
	Le Caïd	A: Air du Tambourin Major (flex)

Appendix

Index of Vowel-letters, Single and in Combination

This index to vowel-letters is intended to serve as a handy reference to the fifteen French vowel-sounds and their spellings, as well as a convenient means of review.

Before making use of this index a few things should be explained:

1. All the vowel-letters, including *y*, are listed either singly (*a*, *e*, *i*, *o*, *u*, *y*) or in combination (e.g., *ai*, *au*, *aie*, *eau*, etc.) in alphabetical order.

2. Then, according to whether the letter or letters are in initial, medial, or final positions, their phonetic equivalents (with exceptions and references) are provided, followed by examples.

3. The phonetic equivalents given indicate all the possibilities that a single vowel-letter or vowel-letter combination can have. But, a single listed vowel-letter is followed by phonetic equivalents only for that letter when alone in the syllable and not when in combination with any other vowel-letter and not when appearing next to any other vowel-letter in the same word, whether in the same syllable or not. Also, any combination must be looked up under its first letter. Thus, combination *aie* will appear in the *a* section, but not in the *i* or *e* sections.

4. All single letters and combinations are listed first without and then with accent-marks and/or diaeresis, in the order ´, `, ˆ, ¨. Thus, *â* will be listed after *a*, *aï* after *aî*, and so on.

5. Occasionally, a combination will appear here that was not mentioned

previously in the study of the individual vowel-sounds because it was simply too rare or unimportant to merit the space until now.

6. Foreign words are frequently used as examples or are referred to as exceptions to remind the English-speaking singer of the French pronunciation of non-French words that do appear in the French repertoire and which must appropriately receive their French pronunciation.

7. When more than one phonetic equivalent is given side-by-side ([ja], [ja]), this is usually due to the varying effect of the following consonant- or vowel-letter in the word(s) in question, or to some other similar factor already treated in previous sections. In this case, a reference is usually given; if not, reference may be made directly to the section on the vowel-sounds in question.

8. Finally, as concerns the three semi-consonant sounds, musical notation could transform any [ɥ] into [y], any [w] into [u] and any [j] into [i] if the letter or letters that normally result in a semi-consonant sound receive a separate note.

LETTER(S)	WHEN	IS	EXAMPLES
a	initial or medial	[a]	il a, april, balcon, chat
	except:		
	• when nasal (remember the rule)	[ã]	an, dans
	• when followed by silent, final -s	[ɑ]	pas, lilas
	except in verb endings	[a]	tu as, tu iras
	• in some isolated words, and in some suffixes (see [ɑ])	[ɑ]	sable, sabre, paille, cadavre, ah, espace, damner, jadis, hélas!, las!
	• followed by -ss-	[ɑ]	passer, classe
	except in a few words	[a]	bassin, chasser
	final	[a]	gala, açoka
à	in any position	[a]	à, là-bas, voilà
â	in any position	[ɑ]	âme, château
	except in verb endings -âmes, or -âtes	[a]	nous donnâmes
aa	in a few words	[a a]	Galaad
âa	in a few words	[ɑ]	Grâal

Letter(s)	When	Is	Examples
æ	initial	[e]	<u>æ</u>gypan
	medial	[ɛ]	M<u>æ</u>terlinck
	except		
	• when nasal	[ɑ̃]	C<u>ae</u>n
aé	in any position	[a e]	<u>aé</u>rien
aë	in any position	[a ɛ]	Az<u>aë</u>l
	except when nasal	[ɑ̃]	Saint-S<u>aë</u>ns
ai	in any position	[ɛ]	<u>ai</u>le, f<u>ai</u>re, m<u>ai</u>s, m<u>ai</u>
	except:		
	• in words beginning *fais-* (from *faire*)	[œ]	nous f<u>ai</u>sons, f<u>ai</u>sable
	• when nasal	[ɛ̃]	p<u>ai</u>n, f<u>ai</u>m
	• when followed by *-ll-* or final *-l* (check dictionary for [a] or [ɑ])	[a j] [aⁱ] [ɑ j]	trav<u>ai</u>ller, bét<u>ai</u>l p<u>ai</u>lle, c<u>ai</u>lle
	• when final in verb forms	[e]	j'<u>ai</u>, je ser<u>ai</u>
	• in some isolated words and derivatives	[e]	g<u>ai</u>, qu<u>ai</u>, <u>ai</u>gu, <u>ai</u>guille
	• in vocalic harmonization followed by [e]	[(e)]	<u>ai</u>mer, l<u>ai</u>sser
	• in a few words when followed by [z] plus a closed vowel-sound	[(e)]	pl<u>ai</u>sir, m<u>ai</u>son
âi	medial before *-ll-*	[ɑ j]	b<u>âi</u>ller
aî	in any position	[ɛ]	m<u>aî</u>tre
	except in vocalic harmonization	[(e)]	ench<u>aî</u>ner
aï	in any position	[a i]	h<u>aï</u>r, n<u>aï</u>f
aïa	rare	[a j a]	n<u>aï</u>ade
aie	medial or final	[ɛ]	b<u>aie</u>, tu ess<u>aie</u>s, ils ét<u>aie</u>nt
aïe	medial	[a j ɛ̃] *or* [a j ɛ]	p<u>aï</u>en p<u>aï</u>enne
	final	[aⁱ]	<u>aïe</u>!
aïo	medial (rare)	[a j ɔ]	b<u>aïo</u>nnette
aïeu	initial or medial (see pp. 41, 44)	[a j œ] *or* [a j ø]	<u>aïeu</u>l <u>aïeu</u>x

LETTER(S)	WHEN	IS	EXAMPLES
ao	initial or medial (see pp. 35, 36)	[a ɔ] *or* [a o] *or* [a]	aorte chaos paonner
	except when nasal	[ã] *or* [a õ]	paon pharaon
	final	[a o]	cacao
aou, aoû	in any position	[u]	saoul, août
	except in name *Raoul, caoutchouc*	[a u]	Raoul, caoutchouc
aoua	in word *aoua!*	[a w a]	aoua!
au	in any position *except*	[o]	au, automne, cause, faux
	• when followed by *r*	[ɔ]	aurore, laurier
	• in two isolated words	[ɔ]	mauvais(e), Paul
ay	medial	[ɛ i]	pays, paysage
	final	[ɛ]	Souzay
aya	in all positions	[ɛ j a] *or* [ɛ j ã]	il paya ayant, payant
	except in *bayadère, maya*	[a j a]	bayadère, maya
aye	initial	[(e) j e]	ayez
	medial	[(e) j e] *or* [ɛ] *or* [a j ɛ]	payer ty payes Lafayette
	final	[ɛ]	Laye
	except in *abbaye*	[ɛ i]	abbaye
ayie	medial	[ɛ i j e]	vous essayiez
ayio	initial	[a j o]	Ayio Costanndino
	medial	[ɛ i j õ]	nous payions
ayo	initial	[ɛ j õ]	ayons
	medial	[ɛ j õ], [ɛ j ɔ] *or* [a j ɔ]	rayon, rayonner mayonnaise

LETTER(S)	WHEN	IS	EXAMPLES
e	initial and followed by a silent <u>consonant</u>	[e]	e̱t, e̱h
	except when nasal	[ɑ̃]	e̱n
	initial and followed by a double consonant	[ɛ]	e̱lle, e̱rrer
	except:		
	• in *eff-*, *ess-*	[(e)]	e̱ffet, e̱ssor
	• in *enn-*, *emm-*	[ɑ̃]	e̱nnui, e̱mmener
	• in *ennemi*	[ɛ]	e̱nnemi
	initial and followed by two or more different consonants	[ɛ]	e̱st, e̱scale, e̱sclave
	except when nasal	[ɑ̃]	e̱ntier, e̱mporter
	medial and followed by single, final <u>consonant</u>	[ɛ]	ce̱s, ne̱t
			fe̱r, ave̱c
	except when followed by silent *-d*, *-ds*, *-r*, *-z*, and in isolated words	[e]	pie̱d, je̱ m'assie̱ds, alle̱r, ne̱z, cle̱f
	<u>final in syllable and not followed by double consonant</u>	[œ]	de̱voir, re̱ve̱nir, enve̱lopper, pre̱mier
	except in vocalic harmonization when followed by [ø]	[(ø)]	che̱veux, ne̱veu
	medial and followed by double consonant	[ɛ]	be̱lle, faible̱sse
	except:		
	in *dess-*	[(e)]	de̱ssein
		or	
		[œ]	de̱ssus, de̱ssous
	in *ress-*	[œ]	re̱ssembler, re̱ssentir
		or	
		[e]	re̱ssuciter
	medial and followed by two or more different consonants	[ɛ]	re̱ster, offe̱rts
	except:		
	• in *desc-*	[(e)]	de̱scendre
	• when nasal	[ɑ̃]	se̱ntir, re̱mplir
	<u>final</u> (see pp. 46-53)	[œ]	le̱, lune̱
		or	
		[ə]	
	except in some foreign words and expressions (usually Latin)	[e]	De̱ Profundis, Ave̱
é	in any position	[e]	é̱té, pé̱rir
		or	
		[(e)]	dussé̱-je

LETTER(S)	WHEN	IS	EXAMPLES
è	in any position, usually medial	[ɛ]	m<u>è</u>re, fi<u>è</u>vre
ê	in any position	[ɛ]	vous <u>ê</u>tes, fen<u>ê</u>tre
ë	medial	[ɛ]	No<u>ë</u>l, Aza<u>ë</u>l
	final in -guë	silent ([y])	cigu<u>ë</u>
éa	medial	[e a]	b<u>éa</u>titude
	except when nasal	[e ã]	g<u>éa</u>nt
eai	medial or final	[ɛ]	g<u>eai</u>(s)
eau	in any position	[o]	<u>eau</u>, b<u>eau</u>té
éau	medial or final	[e o]	fl<u>éau</u>(x)
ée	medial	[e ɛ]	d<u>ée</u>sse
	final (see pp. 46-53)	[e], [e œ] *or* [e ə]	f<u>ée</u>
ei	medial	[ɛ]	r<u>ei</u>ne, ab<u>ei</u>lle
	except:		
	• when nasal	[ɛ̃]	pl<u>ei</u>n
	• in final -eil (see p. 65)	[ɛⁱ] *or* [ɛj]	sol<u>ei</u>l couchant / somm<u>ei</u>l éternel
éi	medial or final	[e i]	ob<u>éi</u>r, ob<u>éi</u>
eï	medial	[(e) i]	L<u>eï</u>lah
eo	medial, after *g*	[ɔ]	G<u>eo</u>rges
		[õ]	mang<u>eo</u>ns
	in word *Deo*	[(e) o]	D<u>eo</u>
éo	initial or medial	[e ɔ]	<u>éo</u>lien
	except when nasal	[e õ]	L<u>éo</u>n
	final	[e o]	Th<u>éo</u>
eô	medial, after *g*	[o]	g<u>eô</u>le
eoi	medial	[w a]	s'ass<u>eoi</u>r
eu	initial or medial, and followed by a silent consonant	[ø]	d<u>eu</u>x, <u>eu</u>x, bl<u>eu</u>s, ém<u>eu</u>t
	except:		
	• in any form of the verb *avoir*	[y]	il <u>eu</u>t, j'ai <u>eu</u>
	• when nasal	[œ̃]	à j<u>eu</u>n

LETTER(S)	WHEN	IS	EXAMPLES
	initial or medial, and followed by a pronounced consonant	[œ]	fleur, jeune
	except:		
	• in any form of the verb *avoir* and in *gageure*	[y]	ils eurent, gageure
	• when followed by final *-se*, *-ser*, *-te*, *-tre*	[ø]	curieuse, creuser, meute, neutre
	• in vocalic harmonization, followed by [ø]	[(ø)]	heureux
	final	[ø]	feu, jeu
eû	initial and in form of verb *avoir*	[y]	il eût
	medial, in word *jeûner*	[ø]	jeûner
eue	medial or final in form of verb *avoir*	[y]	celles qu'il a eues
eui	medial and in *-euil* or in *-euill-*, (see p. 65)	[œ^{i}]	deuil
		or	
		[œj]	ce deuil‿est sans raison feuille
ey	in any position	[ɛ]	Leguerney
eya	medial (usually nasal)	[ɛjɑ̃]	s'asseyant
eyai	medial	[ɛjɛ]	je m'asseyais
eyaie	medial	[ɛjɛ]	ils s'asseyaient
eye	medial	[(e)je]	grasseyer
	final	[ɛi]	que je m'asseye
eyie	medial	[ɛije]	vous vous asseyiez
eyio	medial	[ɛijõ]	nous nous asseyions
eyo	medial	[ɛjõ]	nous nous asseyons
i	in any position	[i]	il, lilas, cri
	except when nasal	[ɛ̃]	vin, limpide
î	in any position	[i]	île, ci-gît
ia, ïa	initial	[jɑ̃]	ïambique
	medial (see p. 65)	[ja]	piano, diamant
	except when preceded by a consonant plus *l* or *r*, or in forms of *rire*	[ia]	criard
		or	
		[iɑ̃]	oubliant, riant
	final	[ia]	Lia

LETTER(S)	WHEN	IS	EXAMPLES
iae	in name *Messiaen*	[jɑ̃]	Messiaen
	in words of Latin origin	[ie]	Misericordiae
iai	medial (see p. 65)	[jɛ]	niais, liaison
	final	[je]	j'étudiai
	except when preceded by a consonant plus *l* or *r*	[ie]	je priai
		[iɛ]	je priais
ie	medial and stressed	[jɛ]	hier, pierre
		or	
		[je]	pieds, premier
	except:		
	• when nasal	[jɛ̃]	bien, il vient
	• when preceded by a consonant plus *l* or *r*	[ie]	prier, oublier
		or	
		[iɑ̃]	client
		or	
		[i]	tu cries, j'oublierai
	• in final *-ient* of third person plural verb forms	[i]	ils rient
	final	[i]	cérémonie
	(see pp. 46-53)	*or*	
		[iœ] [iə]	vie
ié	medial or final (see p. 65)	[je]	piété, amitié
	except when preceded by a consonant plus *l* or *r*	[ie]	j'ai prié
iè	medial (see p. 65)	[jɛ]	bière
	except when preceded by a consonant plus *l* or *r*	[iɛ]	prière
ieu	medial, and followed by a silent consonant or *-se* (see p. 65)	[jø]	pieux, délicieux
		or	
		[iø]	curieuse, DesGrieux
	except when followed by pronounced consonant other than final *-se* or *-te*	[jœ]	rieur
		or	
		[iœ]	prieur
	final	[jø]	dieu
iio	medial	[ijõ]	nous étudiions
io	initial (see p. 65)	[jɔ]	ionisation
	except when nasal	[jõ]	ion
	medial (see p. 65)	[jɔ]	fioriture, violon

LETTER(S)	WHEN	IS	EXAMPLES
	except:		
	• when nasal	[j õ]	émot<u>io</u>n
	• when preceded by consonant plus *l* or *r*	[i ɔ]	tri<u>o</u>let
	• when both of the above apply	[i õ]	oubl<u>io</u>ns
	final	[i o]	tri<u>o</u>
iou	initial	[j u]	<u>iou</u>ler
o	initial and medial	[ɔ]	<u>o</u>r, r<u>o</u>be
	except:		
	• when nasal	[õ]	b<u>o</u>n
	• when followed by [z]	[o]	r<u>o</u>se, supp<u>o</u>ser
	• when followed by *-tion*	[o]	ém<u>o</u>tion
	• in some exceptional words	[o]	<u>o</u>deur, <u>o</u>bus, f<u>o</u>sse, gn<u>o</u>me, gr<u>o</u>sse, v<u>o</u>mir
	final	[o]	Romé<u>o</u>
ô	in any position	[o]	<u>ô</u>ter, h<u>ô</u>tel
	except in *hôpital*	[ɔ]	h<u>ô</u>pital
oa	initial	[o a]	<u>oa</u>sis
	medial	[ɔ]	t<u>oa</u>st
	final	[ɔ a]	b<u>oa</u>
œ	initial or medial	[e]	<u>Œ</u>dipe, Ph<u>œ</u>be
	except in *moelle*	[w a]	m<u>oe</u>lle
oé	medial or final	[ɔ e]	g<u>oé</u>mon, hisse h<u>oé</u>
oè	medial	[ɔ ɛ]	p<u>oè</u>te
oê	medial	[w a]	p<u>oê</u>le
oë	medial	[ɔ ɛ]	N<u>oë</u>l
œi	initial or medial, followed by *-l* or *-ll-*	[œⁱ]	<u>œi</u>l
		[œj]	<u>œi</u>llet
œu	initial or medial	[œ]	<u>œu</u>vre, (b)<u>œu</u>f
	except when followed by silent final consonant(s)	[ɸ]	n<u>œu</u>d, des (b)<u>œu</u>fs
oi	in any position (see [a], [ɑ])	[w a]	<u>oi</u>seau, dev<u>oi</u>r
	(see pp. 32-34)	*or*	
		[w ɑ]	cr<u>oi</u>re, b<u>oi</u>s
	except when nasal	[w ɛ̃]	p<u>oi</u>nt
oie	in any position, usually final	[w a]	<u>oie</u>, j'empl<u>oie</u>
	except in name *Boieldieu*	[ɔ j ɛ]	B<u>oie</u>ldieu

LETTER(S)	WHEN	IS	EXAMPLES
oo	medial	[u]	b<u>oo</u>m
		[ɔ ɔ]	z<u>oo</u>logie
	final	[ɔ o]	z<u>oo</u>
ou	in any position	[u]	<u>ou</u>, r<u>ou</u>c<u>ou</u>ler
où	in any position	[u]	<u>où</u>
oû	medial	[u]	g<u>oû</u>ter
oua	initial or medial (see p. 66)	[w a]	<u>oua</u>te, g<u>oua</u>che
	except when preceded by a conso-nant plus *l* or *r*	[u a] *or* [u ɑ̃]	cl<u>oua</u>(nt)
ouai	initial	[w ɛ]	<u>ouai</u>s!
	medial (see p. 66)	[w ɛ]	je l<u>ouai</u>s
	except when preceded by a conso-nant plus *l* or *r*	[u ɛ]	il cl<u>ouai</u>t
	final	[u e]	je j<u>ouai</u>
oue	initial or medial (see p. 66)	[w ɛ] *or* [w e] [u e]	<u>oue</u>st, m<u>oue</u>tte l<u>oue</u>r
	except when preceded by a conso-nant plus *l* or *r*	[u e] [u ɛ]	cl<u>oue</u>r, pr<u>oue</u>sse
	final	[u (œ)]	j<u>oue</u>
oué	medial	[u e] [w e]	j<u>oué</u>s
	final	[u e] [w e]	n<u>oué</u>
oui	in any position (see p. 66)	[w i]	<u>oui</u>, j<u>oui</u>r
	except:		
	• when nasal	[w ɛ̃]	béd<u>oui</u>n
	• when preceded by a consonant plus *l* or *r*	[u i]	ébl<u>oui</u>r
	• when followed by -*ll*-, -*l*	[u j]	gren<u>oui</u>lle, An<u>oui</u>lh
ouie	final (see p. 66)	[w i (œ)]	enf<u>ouie</u>
oy	in archaic spellings	[w a]	R<u>oy</u>, f<u>oy</u>
oya	initial or medial	[w a j a]	r<u>oya</u>l, v<u>oya</u>ge
	except when nasal	[w a j ɑ̃]	<u>oya</u>nt
	final	[w a j a] *or* [ɔ j a]	il empl<u>oya</u> G<u>oya</u>

LETTER(S)	WHEN	IS	EXAMPLES
oye	initial or medial	[w a j e]	foyer
		or	
		[w a (œ)]	tu employes
	except when nasal	[w a j ɛ̃]	moyen
oyou	in any position	[w a j u]	voyou
u, û	in any position	[y]	unique, tu, dû, murmurer
	except:		
	• when nasal	[œ̃]	un, parfum
	• in final *-um* or *-ub* in words of	[ɔ]	maximum, rhum, minimum, album
		or	
	foreign origin	[œ]	club, pub
	• in words of Latin origin	[u]	De Profundis
ua	medial (see p. 64)	[ɥ a]	suave
	except:		
	• when nasal	[ɥ ɑ̃]	Juan-les-Pins
	• after *g* or *q*	[a]	quatorze
		or	
		[w a]	aquarelle, quatuor, alguazil
		or	
		[ɑ̃]	quand
	final	[y a]	il tua
uai	medial (see p. 64)	[ɥ ɛ]	sanctuaire
	except after *g* or *q*	[ɛ]	laquais
	final (see p. 64)	[y e] [ɥ e]	je tuai
ue	medial (see p. 64)	[ɥ ɛ]	muet
		or	
		[y e]	remuer
	except:		
	• when preceded by a consonant plus *l* or *r*, or in final *-uer*	[y ɛ]	cruel
		or	
		[y e]	tuer
	• after *g* or *q* (see [œ], [e] [ɛ])	[œ]	querelle, séguedille
		or	
		[ɛ]	guerre, quelle
		or	
		[e]	narguer, remarquer
		or	
	• when nasal	[ɑ̃]	séquence
uë	final (after *g* and *q*)	[y]	ciguë

LETTER(S)	WHEN	IS	EXAMPLES
ué	final (see p. 64)	[y e], [ɥ e]	t<u>ué</u>
uè	medial (see p. 64)	[ɥ ɛ]	dés<u>uè</u>te
uée	final (see p. 64)	[y e], [ɥ e]	n<u>uée</u>
uei	medial, before -ll-, -l (see p. 65)	[œj]	c<u>uei</u>llir
		[œⁱ]	org<u>uei</u>l
ueu	medial (see [œ], [o]) (see p. 64)	[ɥ œ] *or* [ɥ ø]	s<u>ueu</u>r lux<u>ueu</u>x
	except when preceded by *g* or *q* (see [œ], [ø])	[ø] *or* [œ]	g<u>ueu</u>x lang<u>ueu</u>r
ueue	medial or final, after *q*	[ø]	q<u>ueue</u>
ui	medial or final (see p. 64)	[ɥ i]	l<u>ui</u>re, l<u>ui</u>
	except:		
	• when nasal	[ɥ ɛ̃]	j<u>ui</u>n
	• after *g* or *q*	[i] *or* [ɛ̃]	g<u>ui</u>de, q<u>ui</u> g<u>ui</u>ndé, séq<u>ui</u>n
uie	medial	[i e]	banq<u>uie</u>r
	final (see p. 64)	[ɥ i (œ)] *or* [ɥ i ə]	pl<u>uie</u>
uo	medial and after *q*	[ɔ]	q<u>uo</u>tidien
	medial in a few other words	[ɥ ɔ]	quat<u>uo</u>r
	final	[y o]	d<u>uo</u>
uoi	medial or final and after *q*	[w a]	q<u>uoi</u>que, q<u>uoi</u>
uya	medial or final	[ɥ i j a]	f<u>uya</u>rd, il ess<u>uya</u>
	except:		
	• when nasal	[ɥ i j ɑ̃]	f<u>uya</u>nt
	• when preceded by a consonant plus *l* or *r*	[y j ɑ̃]	br<u>uya</u>nt
uyau	final	[ɥ i j o]	t<u>uyau</u>
uye	medial or final	[ɥ i j e] [ɥ i (œ)]	app<u>uye</u>r elles s'ess<u>uye</u>nt
y	in any position	[i]	il <u>y</u> a, l<u>y</u>re, dand<u>y</u>
	except when nasal	[ɛ̃]	th<u>y</u>m, s<u>y</u>ncope

Letter(s)	When	Is	Examples
ya	in any position	[j a]	yak
	except when nasal	[j ɑ̃]	Yankee
yaou	in word *yaourt*	[j a u]	yaourt
ye	in a few foreign words	[j ɛ]	yen
yeu	initial or medial and followed by silent consonant or -*se*	[j ø]	yeux, balayeuse
	except when followed by pronounced consonant	[j œ]	balayeur
yo	in word *yodler*	[j ɔ]	yodler
you	in any position	[j u]	yougoslave

Index of Consonant-letters, Single and in Combination

Below, the consonants are listed alphabetically, singly, doubly and in combination. Under each is described its phonetic function in initial, medial and final positions, when single and when double, as well as its phonetic function in combination with other consonant-letters. All combinations are listed alphabetically under the first consonant-letter of the combination. Thus, to find out how letter *c* sounds in combination *sc*, it would be necessary to look under *sc*, and not under *c*. Under each single letter listing, however, significant phonetic changes are given when this letter is in combination with another consonant-letter.

LETTER(S)	WHEN	IS	EXAMPLES
b, bb	in any position	[b]	<u>b</u>as, a<u>bb</u>esse, clu<u>b</u>, sno<u>b</u>, pu<u>b</u>
	except:		
	• before *s* and *t*	[p]	a<u>b</u>sent, o<u>b</u>tenir
	• when final after nasal vowel	silent	plom<s>b</s>
bl-	initial or medial	[b l]	<u>bl</u>eu, ta<u>bl</u>eau
-bn-	medial	[b n]	a<u>bn</u>égation
br-	initial or medial	[b r]	<u>br</u>un, a<u>br</u>iter
bs	final	silent	Dou<s>bs</s>, plom<s>bs</s>
		or	
		[b]	clu<u>b</u><s>s</s>
-bst-	medial	[p s t]	a<u>bst</u>enir, o<u>bst</u>acle
-bstr-	medial	[p s t r]	a<u>bstr</u>ait
-bt-	medial	[p t]	o<u>bt</u>enir
-bv-	medial	[b v]	o<u>bv</u>enir
c	initial or medial, and followed by *a*, *o*, *u*, or consonant (see *ch*)	[k]	<u>c</u>arré, <u>c</u>orps, la<u>c</u>une, na<u>c</u>ré
	except in two words	[g]	se<u>c</u>ond, ane<u>c</u>dote
	initial or medial, and followed by *e*, *i*, or *y*	[s]	<u>c</u>e<u>c</u>i, fa<u>c</u>ile, <u>c</u>ygne
	final in most words, often monosyllabic	[k]	la<u>c</u>, se<u>c</u>, chi<u>c</u>, par<u>c</u>, bou<u>c</u>, be<u>c</u>, cli<u>c</u>!, cla<u>c</u>!, tru<u>c</u>, sa<u>c</u>, fli<u>c</u>, traffi<u>c</u>, fri<u>c</u>, décli<u>c</u>, tra<u>c</u>
	and in most proper nouns	[k]	Poulen<u>c</u>, Berna<u>c</u>, Dupar<u>c</u>
	in a few less common words	silent	escro<s>c</s>, por<s>c</s>, taba<s>c</s>, caoutchou<s>c</s>, estoma<s>c</s>

LETTER(S)	WHEN	IS	EXAMPLES
ç	initial or medial, before *a*, *o*, or *u*	[s]	ça, reçu, français, façon
cc	medial and before *a*, *o*, *u*, or consonant	[k]	accablé, accord, accuser, accroc
	medial and before *e* and *i*	[k s]	accent, accident
-cch-	medial	[k]	Bacchus
-cd-	medial	[g d]	anecdote
ch	in any position, in most words	[ʃ]	chose, cacher, biche, chercher
	in any position, in most words of Italian or Greek origin	[k]	choeur, Christ, chrétien, orchestre
-ck	final	[k]	bifteck
cl	initial or medial	[k l]	climat, débâcle
cn-	medial	[k n]	acné
-cq-	medial	[k]	grecque, acquérir
cs	medial	[k s]	tocsin
	final	[k]	lac$
	or		
	silent	escro¢$
ct	medial, in most words	[k t]	octobre
	medial and followed by *-ion*	[k s]	action
	final	[k t]	correct, direct
	silent	respe¢$, aspe¢$, instin¢$, exa¢$ *or* exact [k t]
-ctr-	medial	[k t r]	octroyer
-cts	final	[k t]	direct$
	or		
	silent	aspe¢$$
d, dd	initial or medial	[d]	dent, idée, addition
	final, usually	silent	pied, froid
	except in some rare words, mostly foreign in origin	[d]	sud, Le Cid, Alfred, Yniold
	and in liaison	[t]	quand il pleut
-dj-	medial	[d ʒ]	adjoint
-dm-	medial	[d m]	admettre
dr	initial or medial	[d r]	droit, foudroyer

LETTER(S)	WHEN	IS	EXAMPLES
-ds	final	silent	pied$\cancel{s}$, je m'assied$\cancel{s}$
-dv-	medial	[d v]	a<u>dv</u>enir
f, ff	initial or medial	[f]	<u>f</u>in, a<u>ff</u>ection
	final, usually	[f]	oeu<u>f</u>, neu<u>f</u>, i<u>f</u>, soi<u>f</u>, che<u>f</u>
	except:		
	• in some isolated words	silent	cle$\cancel{f}$, cer$\cancel{f}$, ner$\cancel{f}$, che$\cancel{f}$-d'oeuvre
	• in liaison	[v]	neu<u>f</u> ‿heures
-ffl-	medial	[f l]	a<u>ffl</u>iger
-ffr-	medial	[f r]	e<u>ffr</u>oyable
fl	initial or medial	[f l]	<u>fl</u>uide, gi<u>fl</u>er
fr	initial or medial	[f r]	<u>fr</u>ont, bala<u>fr</u>e
-fs	final	[f]	if$\cancel{s}$, veu<u>f</u>$\cancel{s}$
		or	
		silent	cle$\cancel{fs}$, oeu$\cancel{fs}$, boeu$\cancel{fs}$
g	initial or medial, and before *a*, *o*, *u*, or consonant	[g]	é<u>g</u>al, a<u>g</u>onie, ba<u>g</u>ue, <u>g</u>ros
	initial or medial and before *e*, *i*, or *y*	[ʒ]	<u>g</u>émir, a<u>g</u>ile, E<u>g</u>yptienne
	final, usually	silent	san$\cancel{g}$, lon$\cancel{g}$
	except:		
	• in a few words of foreign origin	[g]	gro<u>g</u>
	• in liaison	[k]	san<u>g</u> ‿impur
gg-	medial and before *e*	[g ʒ]	su<u>gg</u>estion
	medial and before a consonant	[g]	a<u>gg</u>raver
gh	initial or medial	[g]	<u>gh</u>etto, Eng<u>h</u>ien
-gn-	medial, usually	[ɲ]	di<u>gn</u>e, a<u>gn</u>eau
	except in a few words	[g n]	sta<u>gn</u>ant, <u>gn</u>ome, Ma<u>gn</u>ificat, inco<u>gn</u>ito
gr	initial and medial	[g r]	<u>gr</u>and, ai<u>gr</u>e
-gs	final, in a few words	[g]	gro<u>g</u>$\cancel{s}$, le<u>g</u>$\cancel{s}$
	except after a nasal vowel	silent	lon$\cancel{gs}$, poin$\cancel{gs}$
-gt	final	silent	doi$\cancel{gt}$
h	in any position	silent	l'$\cancel{h}$omme, $\cancel{h}$éros, Ispa$\cancel{h}$an, At$\cancel{h}$anaël
	except in some words of strong emotion or in some foreign words	[h]	<u>h</u>aïr, la <u>h</u>onte, la <u>h</u>aine, Na<u>h</u>andove
j	in any position	[ʒ]	<u>j</u>e, ré<u>j</u>ouir, Ta<u>j</u> Mahal

Letter(s)	When	Is	Examples
k	in any position	[k]	kermesse, açoka, yak
l	initial or medial	[l]	la, culte, lilas
	final	[l]	ciel, il, parasol, sol, bal, tilleul, fatal, avril, cil, fil ("thread"), péril, vol, poil, col, viril
	except in a few words	silent	genti/, sourci/, cu/, saou/, persi/, grési/, fusi/
	in final -*ail*, -*eil*, or -*euil:*		
	• when followed by vowel-sound	[j]	Ce deuil est . . .
	• when followed consonant-sound or final in line	[ʲ]	soleil couchant, corail léger
-lb-	medial	[l b]	album, albâtre
lc	medial and final	[l k]	alcool, talc
ld	medial and final	[l d]	baldaquin, Yniold
-lg-	medial	[l g]	algue
-lh-	medial	[j]	gentilhomme
-lm-	medial	[l m]	Saint-Elme
-ll-	medial, after any letter but *i*	[l]	hallier, belle
	medial, and after *i*	[j]	fille, abeille, travailler, feuillage
	except:		
	• in initial *ill*-	[l l]	illusion
	• in isolated words	[l]	ville, mille, tranquille, pupille, Séville
-ln-	medial	[l n]	kelnerine
		or	
		[n]	Meau/nes
-lp-	medial	[l p]	Alpes
-lpt-	medial	[l t]	sculpter
-ls-	medial	[l s]	malsain
		or	
		[l z]	Alsace
	final	[l]	bal/, tilleul/, fil/ ("thread[s]")
		or	
		silent	genti//, pou//
		or	
		[s]	fi/s ("son," "sons")
-lt-	medial	[l t]	altier, basaltique

LETTER(S)	WHEN	IS	EXAMPLES
-lz-	medial	[l z]	A<u>lz</u>a!
m	initial or medial, and before a vowel-letter	[m]	<u>m</u>ais, ad<u>m</u>ettre, hu<u>m</u>ilité, â<u>m</u>e
	final	silent	fai<s>m</s>, parfu<s>m</s>, thy<s>m</s>
	except in a few words of foreign origin	[m]	minimu<u>m</u>, maximu<u>m</u>, rhu<u>m</u>, Jérusale<u>m</u>, albu<u>m</u>, boo<u>m</u>
mb	medial	[b]	ni<s>m</s><u>b</u>e, ba<s>m</s><u>b</u>ou
-mb(s)	final	silent	plo<s>mb(s)</s>
-ml-	medial	[m l]	Ha<u>ml</u>et
-mm-	medial	[m]	fe<u>mm</u>e, so<u>mm</u>e
	except in initial *imm-*	[m m]	i<u>mm</u>ense
-mn-	medial	[n]	auto<s>m</s><u>n</u>e, da<s>m</s><u>n</u>er
	except in a few words	[m n]	o<u>mn</u>ipotent, a<u>mn</u>istie, o<u>mn</u>ibus, a<u>mn</u>ésie
-mp-	medial	[p]	i<s>m</s><u>p</u>ortant, e<s>m</s><u>p</u>êtrer
-mp(s)	final	silent	cha<s>mp</s>, te<s>mps</s>
-mpr-	medial	[p r]	e<s>m</s><u>pr</u>unter
-mpt-	medial	[t]	pro<s>mp</s><u>t</u>e
	or	[p t]	so<s>m</s><u>pt</u>ueux
-mpts	final	silent	pro<s>mpts</s>
ms	medial	[s]	Sa<s>m</s><u>s</u>on
	final	silent	parfu<s>ms</s>
n	initial or medial and before a vowel-letter	[n]	<u>n</u>uage, fi<u>n</u>esse, rei<u>n</u>e, u<u>n</u>ique, ca<u>n</u>ot, i<u>n</u>utile
	final	silent	bo<s>n</s>, plei<s>n</s>, u<s>n</s>
	except in some words of foreign origin	[n]	Beethove<u>n</u>, ame<u>n</u>, Carme<u>n</u>, Schwertlei<u>n</u>

-nc-	medial:
	  before *e, i, y*
	  before *a, o, u*
		[s]
		[k]
			scie<s>n</s><u>c</u>e, Na<s>n</s><u>c</u>y
			e<s>n</s><u>c</u>ore

-nc(s)	final	silent	ba<s>nc(s)</s>
-nch-	medial	[ʃ]	ha<s>n</s><u>ch</u>e

Letter(s)	When	Is	Examples
-ncl-	medial	[k l]	incliné
-ncr-	medial	[k r]	encre
-nct-	medial	[k t]	sanctuaire
-nct(s)	final	silent	instincts
-nd-	medial	[d]	bandeau
-nd(s)	final	silent	fond(s)
-ndr-	medial	[d r]	fondrière
-nf-	medial	[f]	enfin
-ng-	medial and followed by *a*, *o*, or *u*	[g]	langue, fringant, tango
	medial and followed by *e*, *i*, or *y*	[ʒ]	mangeons, angine, Longy
-ng(s)	medial	[ã s]	Angsoka
	final	silent	poings
-ngt-	medial	[t]	longtemps, vingtième
-ngt(s)	final	silent	quatre-vingts, quatre-vingt-dix
	except in word *vingt* before another number from 21 to 29	[t]	vingt-quatre
-nh-	medial	[n]	bonheur, inhumain
-nn-	medial	[n]	donner, année
	except in initial *inn*	[n n]	innombrable
-nq-	medial	[k]	cinquante
	final	[k]	cinq
	except when followed by a consonant	silent	cinq cents
-nr-	medial	[r]	enrouer
-ns-	medial, and followed by vowel-sound	[s]	danser
	except in *trans-*	[z]	transatlantique
	final	silent	liens
	except in some foreign names	[s]	Rubens
-nst-	medial	[s t]	instant
-nt-	medial	[t]	entier, pente
	final	silent	content
-ntr-	medial	[t r]	entrer

LETTER(S)	WHEN	IS	EXAMPLES
-nts	final	silent	dents
-nv-	medial	[v]	envoi
-nx-	medial	[k s]	anxieux
-nz-	medial	[z]	enzyme
p	initial or medial	[p]	pas, opéra
	final	silent	loup, coup, trop, beaucoup
	except, rarely	[p]	cap, julep
ph	initial or medial	[f]	phi!, séraphin
-phr-	medial	[f r]	Aphrodite
pl-	initial	[p l]	plaire
pn-	initial	[p n]	pneu
-pp(-)	medial or final	[p]	appeler, Lipp
pr	initial or medial	[p r]	pré, âpre
ps	initial	[p s]	Psyché
	final	silent	coups
-pt(-)	medial	[p t]	crypte
	final, and in word *sept* and derivatives	[t]	sept, septième
q	in any position	[k]	que, coquet, cinq, coq
	except in word *cinq* when followed by consonant	silent	cinq cents
-qs	final	[k]	coqs
r	initial or medial	[r]	ruse, parure
	except in words of strong emotion	[r r]	brûle!, affreux
	final	[r]	cher, pour, hier, amour, sur, mourir, mer, fier, ("proud"), Esther, hiver, Jupiter, Auber, cuiller, par
	except in most words of more than one syllable ending in *-er* or *-ier*	silent	porter, familier, métier, cocher
-rb-	medial	[r b]	herbe
-rbr-	medial	[r b r]	arbre
rc	medial and followed by *a*, *o*, or *u*	[r k]	barcarolle, Hercule
	medial and followed by *e*, *i*, or *y*	[r s]	parce que, Narcisse
	final	[r k]	arc, Duparc

LETTER(S)	WHEN	IS	EXAMPLES
-rch-	medial	[r ʃ]; [r k]	marcher; orchestre
-rcs	final	[r k]	parcs
-rct-	medial	[r k t]	arctique
rd	medial	[r d]	ardent
rd(s)	final	[r]	nord, milord, bords
-rf(s)	final	[r]	nerf(s), cerf(s)
-rg-	medial before *u*; before *e, i, y*	[r g]; [r ʒ]	orgue; orgie
rh-, -rrh-	initial or medial	[r]	rhapsodie, catarrhe
-rr-	medial	[r]	serrer, pierre
	except:		
	• in initial *irr-*	[r r]	irrémédiable
	• in words of strong emotion	[r r]	terrible, horrible
	• in the present conditional tense of some verb forms	[r r]	je mourrais
-rs(-)	medial and sometimes final	[r s]	personne, version, Mars
	final usually	[r]	vers, je pars, tu sors
		or silent	premiers, gars
rt	medial	[r t]	perte, apporter
	final	[r]	art, sort
-rts	final	[r]	forts
-rv-	medial	[r v]	parvenir
s	initial	[s]	silence, santé, Salomé, Saint-Saëns
	medial, and between two vowel-letters	[z]	rose, désert, baiser, iriser
	except in a few compound words	[s]	vraisemblable, susurrer
	medial, and preceded or followed by a consonant-letter	[s]	jasmin, verser
	except in *trans-* and derivatives, and a few words	[z]	transatlantique, Alsace
	final	silent	les gens, sans, plus, tous les os (pl.), las ("weary"), repos, paradis
	except:		
	•in liaison	[z]	sans amour
	•in several words	[s]	lys, sens ("sense"), mœurs, ours, cassis, prospectus, angélus, bis, Hélas, Las! ("alas"), os (sing.), jadis, tous (pron.), fils ("son," "sons"), sus, oasis, mars, biceps

LETTER(S)	WHEN	IS	EXAMPLES
	• in several proper nouns (see pp. 214–215) But silent in *Jésus, Dumas, Lucas, Judas, Paris* (city), *Cinq-Mars*	[s]	Thaïs, Reims, Rubens, Méphistophélès, Pâris (*man's name*), Bilitis, Saint-Saëns, Cérès, Amadis, Baucis, Barabbas, Bacchus, Cadmus, Crésus, Damis, Tircis, Daphnis, Damas, Eros, Juan Gris, Hermès, Lassus, Médicis, Fidès, Mercédès, Mars, Moralès, Willis, De Profundis, Moréas, Tirésias, Vénus, Walpurgis, Ys, Zeus
sc	initial or medial, and before *a, o,* or *u* initial or medial, and before *e* or *i*	[s k] [s]	scandale, scolaire, sculpter, escale scène, conscience, ascenseur
sch	in any position *except* in a few words	[ʃ] [s k]	schisme, haschich scherzo, schizophrénie
-scl-	medial	[s k l]	esclave
sh	in any position	[ʃ]	shah, haschish
sm	in any position	[s m]	smoking, jasmin
sn	initial medial	[s n] [n]	snob Asnières
sp	in any position	[s p]	sport, espérer
-sq-	initial and medial	[s k]	square, puisque
-ss-	medial	[s]	passer, dessert
st	in any position except in *est* (*être*), *Jésus-Christ*	[s t] silent	style, est ("east"), ouest, question est ("is"), Jésus-Christ
-sthm-	medial	[s m]	asthme, isthme
t	initial	[t]	tâche, tour
	medial	[t]	bâtir, détail, coton, cité
	in final *-tié, -tier(s), -tière, -tième* and sometimes *-tie, -tien, -tienne, -tient*	[t]	amitié, entier, volontiers, cimetière, huitième, sotie, chrétien, entretien, antienne, il soutient
	in final *-tion, -tience, -tiel* and sometimes *-tie, -tien(ne), -tient*	[s]	nation, patience, vénitien, haïtienne, essentiel, aristocratie, patient
	final	silent	et, effet, rat, il finit, canot, Albert, Hamlet, Capulet, Mozart

LETTER(S)	WHEN	IS	EXAMPLES
	except in the following words (note that in numeral *huit* is silent when followed by consonant)	[t]	but, brut, dot, tact, l'est ("east"), l'ouest, sept, huit, fait ("fact"), correct, direct, chut!, zut!, soit!, toast, Ernest, Christ (but not in Jésus-Christ), Tybalt
th	in any position	[t]	théâtre, luth, gothique
-thl-	medial	[t l]	athlète
-tl-	medial	[t l]	Atlas
-tm-	medial	[t m]	atmosphère
tr	initial or medial	[t r]	trois, atroce
ts	initial	[t s]	tsar
	final	silent	je mets
	except in plural of word ending in [t]	[t]	buts
-tt-	medial	[t]	attaquer, sottise
v	in any position	[v]	voeu, avenue
-vr-	medial	[v r]	avril
w	in words of Germanic origin	[v]	Wagner, Wallonie
	in words of English origin	[w]	week-end, whisky
	except in the following	[v]	Watteau, wagon
x	initial or medial	[k s]	xylophone, extrême, fixe
	except:		
	• in initial *ex-* followed by vowel-letter or *h*	[g z]	exil, example, exhaler
	• in isolated words	[g z]	Xerxès, [g z ɛ r s ɛ s], Xavier
	• in *-xième*	[z]	sixième
	• in *soixante,* and in second *x* of *Xerxès*	[s]	soixante, Xerxès
	final	silent	voix, faux, deux
	except:		
	• in liaison	[z]	deux amis
	• in numbers 6 and 10 (silent when followed by consonant)	[s]	dix, six
		silent	dix livres, six tableaux
	(but [z] in liaison)	[z]	dix ans, six enfants
	• in isolated words	[k s]	Béatrix, sphinx, index

LETTER(S)	WHEN	IS	EXAMPLES
z	initial or medial	[z]	zèle, Azaël
	final	silent	ne~~z~~, alle~~z~~
	except in some words and many proper nouns	[z] *or*	Boule~~z~~, Berlio~~z~~, ga~~z~~
		[s]	Biarrit~~z~~

Pronunciation of Proper Nouns Pertaining to the Repertoire

Abencérages [a b ɛ̃ s e r a ʒ (ə)]
Achéron [a k e r õ]
Adonis [a d ɔ n i s]
Aix [ɛ k s]
Albert [a l b ɛ r]
Alsace [a l z a s]
Amsterdam [a m s t ɛ r d a m]
Anouilh [a n u j]
Antéchrist [ɑ̃ t e k r i s t]
Apollinaire [a p ɔ l i n ɛ r (ə)]
Atlas [a t l ɑ s]
Auric [ɔ r i k]

Bacchante [b a k ɑ̃ t (ə)]
Bacchus [b a k y s]
Baucis [b o s i s]
Baudelaire [b o d (ə) l ɛ r (ə)]
Béatrix [b e a t r i k s]
Bemberg [b ɛ̃ b ɛ r]
Bensérade [b ɛ̃ s e r a d (ə)]
Berlioz [b ɛ r l j o z]
Bernac [b ɛ r n a k]
Bestiaire [b ɛ s t j ɛ r (ə)]
Bilitis [b i l i t i s]
Bizet [b i z ɛ]
Boieldieu [b ɔ j ɛ l d j ø]
Boulanger [b u l ɑ̃ ʒ e]
Boulez [b u l ɛ z]
Bourget [b u r ʒ ɛ]
Britannicus [b r i t a n i k y s]
Brummel [b r y m ɛ l]
Brutus [b r y t y s]

Cadix [k a d i k s]
Cadmus [k a d m y s]
Caïn [k a ɛ̃]
Camille [k a m i j]
Caplet [k a p l ɛ]
Carmen [k a r m ɛ n]
Cenci [t ʃ ɛ n t ʃ i] [s ɛ̃ s i]
Cérès [s e r ɛ s]
Ceylan [s ɛ l ɑ̃]
Chabrier [ʃ a b r i e]
Charlotte [ʃ a r l ɔ t]
Charon [k a r õ]
Charybde [k a r i b d (ə)]
Chausson [ʃ o s õ]
Chloé [k l ɔ e]
Christ [k r i s t]
Cinq-Mars [s ɛ̃ m a r]
Charpentier [ʃ a r p ɑ̃ t j e]
Claudel [k l o d ɛ l]
Claudius [k l o d j y s]
Connecticut [k ɔ n ɛ k t i k y t]
Cornouailles [k ɔ r n w a j (ə)]
Couperin [k u p ə r ɛ̃]
Courte Paille [k u r t ə p a j (ə)]
Crespin [k r ɛ s p ɛ̃]
Crésus [k r e z y s]

Damas [d a m ɑ s]
Damis [d a m i s]
Dancaïre [d ɑ̃ k a i r (ə)]
Daphnis [d a f n i s]
De Brétigny [d ə b r e t i ɲ i]

Debussy [d ə b y s i]
Degas [d ə g ɑ]
Delibes [d ə l i b (ə)]
De Profundis
  [d e p r ɔ f u n d i s]
Desnos [d ɛ s n o s] [d ɛ s n ɔ s]
Djinns [d ʒ i n]
Don José [d õ ʒ o z e]
Don Juan [d õ ʒ ɥ ɑ̃]
Don Quichotte [d õ k i ʃ ɔ t (ə)]
Dufay [d y f ɛ]
Dukas [d y k ɑ] [d y k ɑ s]
Dulcinée [d y l s i n e]
Dumas [d y m ɑ]
Duparc [d y p a r k]

Eiffel [ɛ f ɛ l]
Elisabeth [e l i z a b ɛ t]
Eluard [e l ɥ a r]
Endor [ɑ̃ d ɔ r]
Erinnyes [e r i n i]
Ernest [ɛ r n ɛ s t]
Eros [e r o s] [e r ɔ s]
Escamillo [ɛ s k a m i j o]
Eulalie [ø l a l i]
Eurydice [ø r i d i s (ə)]

Fauré [f ɔ r e]
Faust [f o s t]
Franck [f r ɑ̃ k]
Frasquita [f r a s k i t a]

Galaad [galaad]
García-Lorca [garsjalɔrka]
Gautier [gotje]
Gérolstein [ʒerɔlstajn]
  [ʒerɔlstɛn]
Gil Blas [ʒilblɑs]
Gounod [guno]
Graal [grɑl]
Gris (Juan) [gris]

Hahn [ɑn]
Hamlet [amlɛ]
Hébé [ebe]
Hermès [ɛrmɛs]
Hoffmann [ɔfman]
Honegger [ɔnɛgɛr]
Hüe [y]
Hugo [ygo]

Ibert [ibɛr]
Iphigénie [ifiʒeni]
Isaac [izaak]
Iseut [izø]
Ispahan [ispaɑ̃]
Israël [israɛl]

Jacob [ʒakɔb]
Janequin [ʒan(ə)kɛ̃]
Janus [ʒanys]
Jason [ʒazõ]
Jean [ʒɑ̃]
Jeanne d'Arc [ʒan(ə)dark]
Jeanneton [ʒan(ə)tõ]
Jéhovah [ʒeɔva]
Jésus [ʒezy]
Jésus-Christ [ʒezykri]
Judas [ʒydɑ]
Juliette [ʒyljɛt]

Klee [kle]
Klopstock [klɔpstɔk]
Koechlin [kɛʃlɛ̃]
Lahor [laɔr]
Lassus [lɑsys]
Laura [laura]
Laure [lɔr(ə)]

Lesbos [lɛsbos] [lɛsbɔs]
Lillas Pastia [lilaspastja]
Louÿs [lwis]

Mab [mab]
Macbeth [makbɛt]
Maeterlinck [mɛtɛrlɛ̃k]
Magnificat [magnifikat]
Marcellus [marsɛlys]
Marguerite [margœrit(ə)]
Médicis [medisis]
Mercédès [mɛrsedɛs]
Messiaen [m(e)sjɑ̃]
Micaëla [mikaɛla]
Michel [miʃɛl]
Michel-Ange [mikɛlɑ̃ʒ(ə)]
Milhaud [mijo]
Mireille [mirɛj(ə)]
Moralès [mɔralɛs]
Moréas [mɔreɑs]
Mossoul [mɔsul]

Offenbach [ɔfɛnbak]
Olympia [ɔlɛ̃pja]

Paladilhe [paladij(ə)]
Pelléas [p(e)lleɑs]
Paris (city) [pari]
Pâris (man's name) [pɑris]
Pâris (antiq.) [pɑris]
Périchole [perikɔl(ə)]
Perth [pɛrt]
Pétrarque [petrark(ə)]
Phaéton [faetõ]
Phoebé [febe]
Pollux [pɔlyks]
Poulenc [pulɛ̃k]
Prunier [prynje]
Psyché [psiʃe]
Pulcinella [pultʃinɛlla]

Roméo [rɔmeo]
Ronsard [rõsar]
Rothschild [rɔtʃild]

Sabaoth [sabaɔt]
Sainte-Menehould
  [sɛ̃təmənəu]
Saint-Esprit [sɛ̃tɛspri]
Saint-Saëns [sɛ̃sɑ̃s]
Salomé [salɔme]
Samson [sɑ̃sõ]
Sancho [sɑ̃ʃo], [santso]
Shéhérazade [ʃeerazad(ə)]
Shakespeare [ʃɛkspir(ə)]
Shylock [ʃailɔk]
Siam [sjam]
Siebel [sjebɛl]
Sindbad [sindbad]
Sophie [sɔfi]
Styx [stiks]
Syrinx [sirɛ̃ks]

Thaïs [tais]
Tirésias [tirezjɑs]
Tircis [tirsis]
Tybalt [tibalt]

Valentin [valɑ̃tɛ̃]
VanLerberghe [vɑ̃lɛrbɛrg(ə)]
Ventadour [vɑ̃tadur]
Vénus [venys]
Verhaeren [vɛrarɛn]
Verlaine [vɛrlɛn(ə)]
Versailles [vɛrsɑj(ə)]
Vilmorin [vilmɔrɛ̃]
Villon [vijõ]

Wallonie [valɔni]
Walpurgis [valpyrʒis]
Watteau [vato]
Werther [vɛrtɛr]
Willis [vilis]

Xavier [gzavje]
Xerxès [gzɛrsɛs]

Yniold [injɔld]
Ys [is]

Zeus [dzøs]

Bibliography

Adler, K. *Phonetics and Diction in Singing*. Minneapolis: University of Minnesota Press, 1965.

Bernac, P. *The Interpretation of French Song*. New York: Praeger, 1970; New York: Norton/Gollancz, 1978 (paper).

Colorni, E. *Singers' Italian: A Manual of Diction and Phonetics*. New York: G. Schirmer, 1970.

Ernst and Levy. *Le français*. Book II, Third Edition. New York: Holt, Rinehart and Winston, 1964.

Ewert, A. *The French Language*. London: Faber and Faber, 1933.

Fouché, P. *Traité de Prononciation française*. Paris: Librairie C. Klincksieck, 1959.

Grammont, M. *La Prononciation française, Traité pratique*. Paris: Delagrave, 1963.

Grant, E. *French Poetry of the Nineteenth Century*. New York: Macmillan, 1932.

Kagen, S. *On Studying Singing*. New York: Dover, 1950.

Mansion's Shorter French and English Dictionary. New York: Holt, Rinehart and Winston, 1940.

Martinon, P. *Comment on prononce le français*. Paris: Larousse, 1913.

Nitze, W., and Wilkins, E. *A Handbook of French Phonetics*. New York: Henry Holt and Co., 1954.

Noske, F. *French Song from Berlioz to Duparc*. 2d Edition. New York: Dover, 1970.

Nouveau Petit Larousse. Paris: Librairie Larousse, 1968.

Peyrollaz, M., and Bara de Tovar, M.-L. *Manuel de Phonétique et de diction françaises*. Paris: Larousse, 1954.

Suberville, J. *Histoire et théorie de la versification française*. Paris: Editions de ''l'Ecole,'' no date.

Vienne, Lucie de. *Nouveau Traité de Diction française*. Paris: Editions de la Presse Moderne, 1966.

Warnant, L. *Dictionnaire de la prononciation française*. Belgium: Edition J. Duculot, S. A., Gembloux, 1968.

217

Answer Key

Pages 32–33 ([i], [e], [ɛ], [a])

1. Intoning (oral)
2. [i] [i] [a] [ɛ]
   [e] [ɛ] [e] [i]
   [e]
   [i] [e]
   [i] [i] [ɛ] [ɛ]
   [i] [e] [ɛ] [ɛ]
   [ɛ] [(e)] [(e)] [e]
   [e] [a] [ɛ]
   [i] [a] [e] [e] [ɛ]
   [i] [i]
   [(e)] [e] [(e)]
   [w a] [e] [ɛ]
   [ɛ] [e] [ɛ] [a]
   [(e)] [e] [ɛ] [a] [i]
   [i] [i] [a] [w a] [a] [i]
   [i] [i]

Pages 37–38 ([ɑ], [ɔ], [o], [u])

1. Intoning (oral)
2. [ɔ] [ɛ] [a] [ɛ] [i] [a]
   [ɛ] [ɛ] [ɔ] [a] [i] [a]
   [ɛ] [e] [ɛ] [u] [a] [w a] [e] [ɔ] [ɔ]
   [ɛ] [ɔ] [ɛ] [ɔ] [ɛ] [e] [(e)] [e] [a] [ɔ] [ɔ]
   [a] [ɛ] [e] [i] [ɛ] [a] [ɛ]
   [u] [i] [a] [ɛ] [w a] [ɛ] [a] [ɛ]
   [ɛ] [u] [u] [u] [ɛ]

[ɔ] [i] [i]
[e] [ɑ] [i] [e] [ɛ] [ɛ]
[a] [ɛ] [o] [i] [w a] [ɛ]
[a] [o] [i] [i] [e] [i]
[a] [ɛ] [ɛ]

Pages 53–54 ([y], [ø], [œ])

1. Intoning (oral)
2. [i] [œ] [œ] [œ]
   [ɔ] [i] [ø] [y] [a] [i] [œ]
   [ɛ] [ɛ] [ɛ] [œ] [œ]
   [i] [e] [ɛ] [œ] [œ]
   [o] [i] [u] [œ] [a] [i ə]
   [a] [ɛ] [e] [y] [ɛ] [w a]
   [u] [œ] [i] [i ə]
   [o] [œ] [i] [œ] [a] [i ə]
   [i] [œ] [œ] [(e)]
   [œ] [œ] [i] [e] [œ] [œ]
   [w a] [y] [œ] [a] [i]
   [œ] [œ] [ɛ] [(e)]
   [ɛ] [a] [i] [œ] [ɛ] [ə]
   [œ] [œ] [a] [w a] [u] [w a]
   [a] [u] [e] [ɛ] [œ]
   [œ] [a] [œ] [ɛ] [œ]

Pages 60–61 ([ɑ̃], [õ], [ɛ̃], [œ̃])

1. Intoning (oral)

219

2. a. [ɛ̃ãaɑ̃uaɛ̃œɛɛœ]

   [uuɔœøœœã]

   [ɛ̃aõãaɑ̃ɛ̃ɛ̃œɛ̃œɛœ]

   b. [ãɛ̃ueie(e)eõœaɛœ]

   [ãɛ̃yɛœa]

   [œaœɛaɛ̃]

   [ɛaœõɛ̃ɛœ]

   [eœãiõa]

   c. [œøiœ]

   [ãœɛœ]

   [iãiœ]

   [õãɑ̃ɔ]

   d. [œãiɛ̃ œaouaɛãœaœœuœwaõaɛœãɛɛɛi

   eãɛɛœœ aoœiaɛuuiiɛõeˀyii aɛyœã(ø)ø

   ãã waõœãeaɛ̃œ aɛ̃ɛyyœ iœuɛa ɛɛœœœ

   iaɔœaaiɛɛiœɛœœœœœaaaɛɛœɛ̃aœõœɛœa

   œɛœɛœ iœaɑuyɛ̃i]

Pages 66–67

1. Intoning (oral)
2. [ãjɛ̃aa(e)õuɛœ]

   [ãɔõiayɛwa]

   [uɛøuiõaɛœ]

   [uœjiœyɛowa]

   [uojeeœãɛɛœ]

   [œõwaoaɛ̃ãe]

   [uiõeuɛɛɛœie]

   [œɛ̃ãɛœyaɛœ]

   [ɛœwaɛaãei]

   [ewaoaiãõɛœ]

   [iɛɛoœɔyi]

   [ojɛ̃õyœãœuœ]

   [uaeœooau]

   [eiwaœawaiuœuu]

   [wɛ̃jɛ̃wɛ̃eaãouœ]

   [œõɥiœaɛ̃ae]

   [eœɛ̃oiwaɛuœ]

   [aiãõãwaãe]

   [ɥieuu(ø)øuɛœ]

   [ãajeãaãowa]

   [œœõaɔãɛɛœɛwa]

Page 79

1. [lɔrskosɔlɛˀkuʃã]

   [lɛrivjɛrœsõrozə]

[ekœtjedœfrisõkursyrlɛʃãdœble]

[œ̃kõsɛˀdɛtr(ø)røsãblœsɔrtirdɛʃozə]

[emõtevɛrlœkœtruble]

[œ̃kõsɛˀdœ gutelœʃarmœ dɛtromõdə]

[sœpãdãkõnɛʒœnekœlœswarɛbo]

[karnunuzãnalõ]

[kɔmœsãvasɛtõdœ]

[ɛl/alamɛr]

[nu/otõbo]

Page 95

1. les/hauts talons [lɛotalõ]

   (Liaison prohibited by aspirate *h*.)
2. Les autres ont entendu. [lɛzotrœzõtãtãdy]

   (Liaison is made between (a) article and pronoun,
   (b) plural subject and verb form, (c) composite verb
   forms.)
3. Un an/et/une semaine. [œ̃nãeynœsœmɛnə]

   (Liaison is made between an article and the noun it
   modifies. Liaison is never made on either a singular
   noun or after the conjunction *et*.)
4. Le vent/a changé. [lœvãaʃãʒe]

   (Liaison is never made on a noun in the singular.)
5. Nous avons espéré. [nuzavõzɛspere]

   (Liaison is made between pronouns and their verb
   forms and between composite verb forms.)
6. Dors encore! [dɔrãkɔrə]

   (Liaison is not made on words ending in *-rs*, except
   in noun pluralizations. Instead, the *r* is normally
   linked with the following vowel-sound.)
7. En attendant [ãnatãdã]

   (Liaison is made between prepositions and their par-
   ticipial objects.)
8. Il est mort inaperçu. [ilɛmɔrinapɛrsy]

   (Liaison is not made on words ending in *-rt*. Instead,
   the *r* is normally linked with the following vowel-
   sound.)
9. Filles et garçons [fijœzegarsõ]

   (Liaison must be made on nouns in the plural and before the word *et*.)
10. six ans/après [sizãaprɛ]

    (Liaison is made between numerical adjectives and
    the nouns they modify. Liaison is *not* made between
    syntactically unrelated words.)
11. après un an [aprɛzœ̃nã]

    (Liaison is made between a preposition and the word

or words it governs. Liaison is made between an article and the word it modifies.)

12. une nuit/éternelle [y n œ n ɥ i e t ɛ r n ɛ l ə]
(Liaison is not made on a noun in the singular.)

13. Le joyeux‿et doux printemps/arrive.
[l œ ʒ w a j ø z e d u p r ɛ̃ t ɑ̃ a r i v ə]
(Liaison is made between an adjective and before the conjunction *et*. Liaison is not made on a noun in the singular.)

14. Chacun/est entré. [ʃ a k œ̃ ɛ t ɑ̃ t r e]
(Liaison is never made on the word *chacun*. Liaison must be made in composite verb forms.)

15. toujours‿heureux, toujours̸ avec toi
[t u ʒ u r z (ø) r ø t u ʒ u r a v ɛ k t w a]
(Liaison is made on the word *toujours* when it is syntactically related to the word following it, and is not made otherwise.)

16. Il faut‿aimer,/espérer; aimer‿et/espérer toujours!
[i l f o t (e) m e ɛ s p e r e (e) m e r e ɛ s p e r e t u ʒ u r]
(Liaison is made between composite verb forms. Liaison is not made in enumerations. Liaison is made between a first conjugation infinitive and before the conjunction *et*, but never from it to another word.